WATCH ME FLY

Also by Myrlie Evers-Williams

For Us, the Living
(as Myrlie B. Evers, with William Peters)

WATCH ME FLY

What I learned on the way to becoming
the woman I was meant to be ❧

Myrlie Evers-Williams

with Melinda Blau

LITTLE, BROWN AND COMPANY

Boston   New York   London

FIRST EDITION

"Getting Ready to Unfold" by Mona Lake Jones, from *The Color of Culture II*, Impact Communications, © 1996.

Photographs on pages 3 and 191, David Rae Morris; photograph on page 273, People Weekly © John Storey; all other photographs from the private collection of Myrlie Evers-Williams.

LIBRARY OF CONGRESS CATALOGING-IN-PUBLICATION DATA
Evers-Williams, Myrlie.
    Watch me fly : what I learned on the way to becoming the woman
I was meant to be / Myrlie Evers-Williams with Melinda Blau. —
1st ed.
        p.   cm.
        ISBN 0-316-25520-3
        1. Evers-Williams, Myrlie. 2. Afro-American women — Mississippi —
Biography. 3. Afro-American women — Conduct of life. 4. Women —
United States — Conduct of life. 5. Single mothers — United States —
Psychology. 6. Child rearing — United States.   I. Blau, Melinda.
II. Title.
E185.97.E95A3   1999
323'.092 — dc21
[B]   98-43357

10 9 8 7 6 5 4 3 2 1

MV-NY

Printed in the United States of America

In memory of Walter Edward Williams
My rock of Gibraltar
My balm in Gilead
The wind beneath my wings

℞ MEW

CONTENTS

A LIGHT THAT SHINES THROUGH

*Dear God, thank you for making my spirit a
light that shines through. And let me never
forget to praise you for my blessings.*

℞ *Anonymous prayer*

This book is a risk. Until now I have reserved my private face for family and very close friends. But throughout my life I've taken chances, and dared to take steps when my own fears nearly paralyzed me, even when others tried to thwart me. Indeed, if I ever reach a point where I'm satisfied with the status quo or fail to listen to what my heart and mind tell me, I might as well cease to be.

Let me say at the outset that this book is not about the civil rights movement, it is not about the NAACP, and it is not about my late husband Medgar Evers. Rather, it is about me — a woman who shares common ground with other women. It is about self-discovery, about the many roads I've traveled and the roadblocks I've faced in my life — how I've gone around them, run over them, blasted through them, and soared above them. As I tell my grandchildren, "It's only through these tests that we become stronger human beings. One must persevere — just persevere."

This is not a book specifically about race, either, although race is an ever-present element in our lives. The very words one uses as a means of self-identification speak volumes. I was born "Colored," and living in Mississippi, I was often called "nigger." To help people pronounce "Negro," which then denoted respect, we often pointed to our knees and slowly enunciated, *"knee-grow,"* as the proper term for one with a dark complexion. Marching through history — mine and America's — I was called "Black" (as in beautiful) and, later, "African-American." I use these words interchangeably throughout this text, not as a political statement but as a reflection of the changes in my life. (I use "White" throughout, both because it always has been acceptable and because it is less cumbersome than either of the current politically correct terms, "Caucasian" or "European American.")

What is important to me is that I know who I am. I am proud of my African heritage, but born in this country, I am also American. I am a woman. I am twice a widow. I am a mother. I am a manager and a mover. I am an activist. I am a human being with strengths and weaknesses, working daily to improve myself. I've spent precious time reflecting on the events of my life, the people I've known, the decisions I've made that have brought me to this point. The place I have reached is not where I expected the path to lead. But here I am, suddenly an elder of my community, pondering the many lessons of my life. I can recall moments of joy and moments of abject despair, some days when I struggled to put one weary foot before the other, some when I felt as if I were flying on the wings of victory.

One of my objectives in *Watch Me Fly* is to dismantle many of the myths that have come to define me in the public eye. I tell stories I've never told, and I talk about feelings and facts that I've rarely revealed. Perhaps some readers will protest that I am too frank, revealing matters that are too personal, but let the truth now be known: I was *not* always the quiet, long-suffering little woman behind the great man. I was *not* the always hopeful, always strong single mother. I was *not* always nice and forgiving, compliant and ladylike. This is the Myrlie who speaks for herself as herself.

This book is an effort to understand how I've experienced my life, how I've made sense out of unpredictable events and found surprises in the outcomes of my choices. It is about my childhood and my children, my mentors and my marriages, my work and my womanhood. It is not an autobiography or a memoir in the traditional sense; I don't deal with my life in a strictly linear manner. Rather, I think of this book as an *instructive autobiography*. You won't find any how-to formulas or step-by-step rules for happiness here, but an account of my life that takes its shape from themes that are universal — despair and hope, struggle and survival, fear and freedom. Throughout, I try to share what I've learned from the exhilarating moments, the challenges, *and* the hard knocks of my life.

Whenever I am about to give a talk, I say a prayer and ask God to let my spirit be a light that shines through. I have done so with *Watch Me Fly* as well. By revealing myself and sharing my stories, I hope that you are encouraged to confront with resolve and confidence your own struggles, and to revel in your triumphs. I hope that, in the end, you are inspired to be the best, the boldest, and the proudest you can be.

Getting Ready to Unfold

Stand back and watch me.
I'm getting ready to unfold!

I've decided to let my spirit go free
I'm ready to become the woman I was meant to be

I've either been somebody's daughter, mother, or wife
And now it's time for me to take charge of my life

I've been pondering all this time trying to decide just who I am
At first I thought it depended on whether I had a man

Then I had the notion that simply just because
Others had more seniority, they could decide who I was

I played all the roles that were expected, and I seldom asked why
I had my wings closed up, but now I'm ready to fly.

I've been awakened, and I finally see the light
I'm about to make some changes and set a few things right

With my new attitude and the knowledge I possess
I may create a whole world order and clean up all this mess!

Stand back and watch me.
                    I'm getting ready to unfold!

                                        ℛ Mona Lake Jones

THE GHOSTS OF
MYRLIE EVERS

February 5, 1994: Addressing the press after the guilty verdict in the trial of Byron De La Beckwith.

Just like a tree that's planted by the water,
I shall not be moved.

                      ☙ Negro Spiritual

T he verdict's in," said a caller from the district attorney's office. "Get here now, or Judge Hilburn is going to start without you." The fate of the man who had murdered my first husband, Medgar Evers, hung in the balance and, more than that, my own salvation.

For thirty years, my focus had not wavered. Like a tree deeply rooted on the banks of a rushing river, *I had not moved.* While raising my children, going to school, working my way through the halls of power, even falling in love again, I had stayed the battle. And finally, on a bleak February morning, in an imposing white granite building in Jackson, Mississippi, those many years of faith, perseverance, and prayer were about to coalesce into a single moment and a few words uttered by a court clerk.

It was a Saturday morning, February 5, 1994, just past ten. When the phone rang, Darrell, my oldest, then forty, was already dressed. My daughter, Reena, a year Darrell's junior, was in the shower. Their younger brother, Van, thirty-four and a professional photographer, was far away in Los Angeles, finishing the last day of an important project at his studio. He was due in Jackson that evening, having assumed he'd at least be in time for the verdict, which we'd anticipated would not be handed down until Monday morning.

When the unexpected call came, I was sitting on the bed, wearing a robe, my hair in rollers, contemplating a weekend of anxious waiting. I had just talked to Walter, my husband of eighteen years. A retired longshoreman and union organizer, he was a gem of a man who willingly lived with Medgar's continuing presence and had staunchly encouraged my quest for justice. The television in our hotel room was tuned to CNN; events were happening in the rest of the world. But my universe was very small that day; the only news I cared about would come from the Hinds County Courthouse.

This was the third and final time the state of Mississippi tried to prove what everyone suspected: On June 12, 1963, Byron De La Beckwith VI, hiding in the bushes of a vacant lot across the street from our house, pulled a trigger and drained the life out of Medgar. In doing so, he forever deprived my children and me of the man we loved — our protector, our guide. He also robbed the world of a courageous and caring man who dared, when few other Negroes stepped forth, to challenge the segregationist way of life.

In membership and fund-raising literature, the NAACP called my husband their "man in Mississippi." In fact, he was *the voice* of civil rights in our state. He investigated murders and lynchings, planned voter registration drives, organized boycotts, and fought to gain access for our people and representation where there was none. Because of such efforts, many die-hard segregationists believed Medgar's voice had to be silenced. Byron De La Beckwith took it upon himself to see that it was.

Twice before, the evidence against Beckwith had been heard, but each trial ended with a hung jury. Both times, twelve men — all of them White — could not agree on a verdict, and Beckwith was set free. Twice before, in the case of Medgar's murder, and in countless other instances as well, Mississippi had sent a message to the world that it was all right to kill a Black man. In my view, Byron De La Beckwith wasn't the only one on trial. So was Mississippi. ₽

Both sides had finished presenting their evidence on the previous Thursday evening; then it was up to the jury. Three Whites, nine Blacks, six men, six women — a far cry from the 1964 juries — had heard six days of testimony. "We expect a quick guilty verdict," I was told by both District Attorney Ed Peters, who conducted much of the cross-examination and the closing summation, and Bobby DeLaughter, the assistant district attorney who had prepared the case and acted as second chair during the trial.

"They don't have a case," Ed reassured me, referring to Beckwith's court-appointed defense attorneys, Jim Kitchens and Merrida "Buddy" Coxwell. But he also warned, "Anything less than a quick verdict means the case is about race."

What in Mississippi isn't about race? I wondered to myself.

By Friday night, with the twelve men and women still cloistered in the Hinds County Courthouse, we all were decidedly less optimistic. Conventional wisdom has it that the longer a jury stays out, the better it is for the defendant. Darrell, Reena, and I returned to the Holiday Inn with a heavy heart. There were two queen-size beds in our room — Darrell took one bed, Reena and I the other. But I couldn't sleep. I looked first at one child and then at the other, and in my eyes they were not adults anymore but simply my babies, who had been through hell. I heard their soft breathing as they slept, and I thought about Medgar. When he would come home late, as he often did, we would look in on our children and listen to them breathe: our big boy, Darrell, who loved racing down our street, pedaling his bicycle madly to keep up with Medgar's long, loping strides; adorable, bright-eyed Reena, who had her daddy wrapped around her little finger; and our baby, Van, on whom we both doted. We'd go into our room and talk quietly about the three of them, his work, our dreams. Later he'd go take a last look at each child and then come back to bed, whispering how thankful he was for them and how much he wanted to protect them. Now, as I listened to their breathing, a hard rain beat at the windows, and I felt oddly at peace. At least I had given it my all — I had gone the last mile. And no matter what happened, Medgar's and my babies were going to be okay.

After a sleepless night, the unexpected phone call from the DA's office put me into overdrive. I all but pulled my hair out, trying to get those Velcro rollers untangled. "Reena, are you out of the shower yet? Where are my shoes? Hurry!"

Our mad scramble was punctuated by desperate phone calls from the courthouse, each caller reminding me of Judge Breland Hilburn's renowned impatience. "If that man dares to convene court without us," I exclaimed at one point, "all hell is going to break loose!"

The deputy sheriff who had been our constant companion during the trial rushed us out of our room, past the hotel's security checkpoint and into the elevator. The Holiday Inn was only three minutes from the courthouse, but there was no time to lose. We literally ran through the lobby to his car, which was waiting at the curb. As we careened out of the hotel driveway, tires screeched, and the three of us were flung to the right. It felt as if we were riding on two wheels. The police radio crackled with static. "Come in, come in. . . . Where are you?" a voice asked. "Get here . . . get here *now!*"

Moments later we were hustling into the courthouse through a heavily guarded basement door. Our personal battalion of police escorts whisked us into an elevator to the second floor, past a horde of reporters and camera crews, and we made a breathless entrance into the dark, mahogany-paneled courtroom. It was packed to capacity; word had gotten out that the verdict was about to be handed down, and people were still trying to squeeze their way in. Throughout the trial, extensive security precautions had been taken — searches, checklists, scanners. Today, especially, the Hinds County Sheriff's Department was taking no chances with the spectators. We three took the same seats we had occupied every day, reliving the tragedy that defined our family's life.

The jurors were led in. Judge Hilburn, a stern-looking, bearded man who resembled Ulysses S. Grant, admonished the crowd that there would be no outbursts after the verdict was announced. He asked the jurors to line up in front of the bench and face him. Behind them, several armed court officers stood, scanning the courtroom, ready for the slightest disruption.

"Have you reached a verdict?" Judge Hilburn asked.

"We have, Your Honor," replied the jury foreman, an elderly African-American minister, who handed the judge a sheet of paper on which the verdict was written. Hilburn spent what felt like interminable seconds taking in the information and then gave the paper to his clerk, Barbara Dunn, to read. I squeezed Reena's and Darrell's hands, and held my breath.

I glanced over at Beckwith, who sat with his attorneys at the defense table, on the opposite side of the courtroom. Behind them were Beckwith's wife, Thelma; their son, Byron De La Beckwith VII; and their grandson, Byron VIII. In their jacket lapels, the three Beckwith men were wearing identical Confederate flag pins. Behind the family were supporters — the high and low ranks of Mississippi's White supremacists. More than a few Ku Klux Klan luminaries were scattered among them.

I dared not let my eyes linger on that hateful man or his cronies, fearing the old urge to destroy him would surface. I dared not contemplate the warnings that so many people had voiced over the years: Nothing's going to come of your efforts; no jury in Mississippi will ever convict Beckwith. Everyone agreed that times had changed, but not *that* much. I dared not imagine what I'd feel if they were right.

But then, as Barbara Dunn's voice resonated through the courtroom, one simple sentence proved them wrong: "The jury finds the defendant, Byron De La Beckwith, guilty as charged."

There were gasps from the crowd. Beckwith himself didn't react, but Thelma screamed: "He's not guilty. And y'all know he's not. The Jews did it!" And then a roar of relief and redemption began to build in the back of the courtroom. It traveled the length of the hallway and down the stairs, steadily gaining momentum and volume as it spread throughout the lobby and, finally, rolled out the front doors, where Whites and Blacks alike stood waiting to see if justice could prevail in Mississippi. Ed Bryson, a TV reporter I had come to know in the years preceding the trial, told me later that it was as if "a scream had come up from the bowels of the building." Inside and out, the crowds exploded in ecstatic amens, with people yelling, "Yes!" clapping hands, hugging one another in disbelief. Even the members of the press who were relegated to the balcony — once the only place we "Coloreds" were allowed to sit — cried and cheered, giving up any pretense of impartiality.

At that moment, healing finally felt possible, for my soul and the soul of Mississippi.

I sat between Darrell and Reena, and tears of release poured from my eyes. My whole body was shaking; I went hot and I went cold. I wished Van could have been there, and of course my precious Walter, whom the DA's office had advised to stay home in Oregon; they deemed it best that the jury not be reminded of my remarriage. I reflected not only on the trial, on Medgar's death, and on Beckwith, who had been allowed to walk free while my children and I lived in fear, but also on my own life and the turns it had taken in the many years since the murder. I had battled mightily to preserve Medgar's memory and, at the same time, to be seen as myself, as Myrlie — as a *woman* and not simply as "the widow of."

I had been haunted and driven by demons for so long — to be the perfect child, the perfect wife, the perfect and always brave mourner. But suddenly I could see this collective set of demons fly out of me like a fluorescent fireball. My ghosts were purged from the very inside of my being. Hatred was finally released, too — the hatred I had thought was gone but that always managed to creep back in; hatred that made me determined to avenge Medgar's death. What irony that in 1967, when I wrote *For Us, the Living* with William Peters, the opening sentence read: "Somewhere in Mississippi lives the man who murdered my husband." Now I knew exactly where that man was and would be — behind bars — and I could finally put that long chapter of my life to rest.

I held on to my children, embracing them, crying with them. As Medgar's assassin was led out, finally, to jail, the booing from Beckwith's minions was drowned out by triumphant bravos from our camp. Meanwhile, the children and I, along with DeLaughter, Ed Peters, and several court officers, pushed through the crowd of well-wishers and curiosity-seekers and hastened upstairs to the DA's office, which had become our second home during the trial. A woman who had been writing about the trial edged her way into the elevator with us and audaciously tried to elicit my reaction. One of the officers promptly asked her to leave. This was a private and sacred moment for all of us who had waged the long, arduous battle for justice; no interlopers would be allowed to intrude.

My first phone call was to Walt, who was in tears. "You've done it," he said proudly the moment he heard my voice. I was disappointed that a friend had already called to inform him of the verdict. My next call was to Van, who was equally overcome with emotion — relief that it was over, regret that he wasn't with us. While I spoke with vari-

was announced, I read in the *Clarion-Ledger*, Jackson's largest newspaper, that, due in part to my efforts to bring justice to our family, "Mississippi is free at last." That same year, I encouraged a citizens' group to fund a statue that was erected in Medgar's memory, and a post office was also dedicated in his name. The year after that, I was elected chairman of the NAACP, the very organization Medgar sought to preserve. Almost none of those accomplishments were things that I, Myrlie Louise Beasley, from Vicksburg, Mississippi, was raised to do.

1

At age 3, with my mother, Mildred.

ONCE UPON A TIME WHEN I WAS COLORED

Learning from the past

Mama, Aunt Myrlie, and I (age 12).

It takes a village to raise a child.

› *African Proverb*

Those Saturday afternoons when I walked from my grandmother's house on Magnolia Street to my aunt's home on Farmer Street — a two-mile hike, over unpaved roads, around potholes large enough for a small child to fit in, down a hill, and across the railroad tracks — I always paused at the neighborhood juke joint. Getting as close as I dared, I crouched in front of the stores across the street and craned my neck to get a peek into the ramshackle building. I was an inquisitive nine-year-old, listening to wartime rhythm and blues. Inside was a world backlit by the neon of a jukebox, where men still in work clothes pressed their bodies against women who wore low-cut dresses, stiletto heels, and black fishnet stockings with seams up the back, their hair oiled and coiled into tight little rat-lick curls.

Fights frequently broke out, usually between two women over a man. I'd stand there mesmerized by the sights and sounds of those beautiful, full-bodied, ruby-lipped women in big hoop earrings, getting down and dirty, screaming and pulling each other's hair. This was all part of a world I wasn't supposed to know — it was the only swearing, the only hard drinking, and the only violence I ever saw as a child.

My paternal grandmother, Annie McCain Beasley — the indomitable woman I called Mama — tried to schedule my walk so that I'd go past the juke joint before the revelers got off work. Mama timed my passage, and along the way our neighbors — other God-fearing women who kept almost as tight a rein on their own girls — saw me and said to one another loud enough for me to hear, "There goes Mrs. Beasley's granddaughter," or "There's Mrs. Polk's niece." Some called out, "Hello, Myrlie the Second" (my aunt was Myrlie the First), or "Hey there, Baby Sister." But I knew it was more than friendliness; they too were keeping a watchful eye.

I was raised in a village and by a village, long before that idea became a fashionable bromide. I was deeply loved and fiercely protected, taught to achieve and made strong enough to withstand the racial insults and danger that awaited me. As a child, I was never comfortable with the degree of proprietorship that my grandmother, my aunt, and the larger community exercised toward me, but that's the way things were. Today, though, I know just how blessed I was to have been so cherished and protected.

Indeed, I don't look back in anger or indignation at the constraints of my childhood. I could be embittered that the elders in their sheltering had a limited view of how far I could go in life. And I could be resentful about their rules or feel "misunderstood," as do some adults, who complain that their parents were too rigid or laissez-faire, smothering or unloving, or otherwise damaging to their future selves. In contemporary psychological parlance, my family might be labeled dysfunctional, too. But there comes a time in everyone's life when we must put away the lens of childhood and re-view our roots through adult eyes. To understand where we came from is to make visible the invisible forces that drive us. Only then can we hope to appreciate and accept ourselves, not only as individuals but as members of a society. *

When I was a few months old, Annie McCain Beasley — Mama — took charge of my life and became the driving force of my childhood. "I can at least save my granddaughter," she simply decided one spring day in 1933, as she rose from a straight-backed rocking chair in her kitchen. She marched down the front steps, across the dirt road that was Magnolia Street, and into the house where her new daughter-in-law, sixteen-year-old Mildred Washington Beasley — my mother — lived. Mildred was impoverished, unable to work, and burdened with an infant she scarcely knew how to care for. Married in name only to Annie's son, Jim, who had made it clear that he had no intention of living with Mildred or helping her raise their child, she had a roof over her head but little else — scarcely any food and no hope for a future.

"I'm taking the baby," Annie Beasley announced to my mother — whom I would later call M'dear. Annie then grabbed a blanket from a chair, bundled me up, and took me across the street to her house. And that was simply that. Whatever M'dear had was due to the kindness of neighbors and friends. She was frightened, had my best interest at heart, and knew only too well her mother-in-law's determination. Therefore, when Mama decided I would be *her* baby, my mother didn't argue. She didn't dare.

Nobody crossed Annie McCain Beasley. Stern, slight, ivory-skinned, she was, on both her mother's and father's side, the grand-daughter of a White plantation owner and a slave. She was a schoolteacher who had attended two years of college at Hampton Institute in Virginia, a rare achievement for a woman only two gener-ations removed from slavery. She was twice divorced and had raised two children. She owned her own home and was considered, in the rigid hierarchy of her peers, a pillar of the community. Annie was a devoted "mother" of the church; she appreciated classical music and art; she kept her long, straight, ash-blond hair in a prim chignon, dressed in muted tones and tasteful clothes, and wore hats and white gloves — in short, she was part of the upper echelon of Vicksburg's Negro society.

Her daughter, Myrlie Louise — my aunt — was a young version of herself, a schoolteacher, hardworking and serious, who happily adopted her mother's values and her sense of propriety. Annie's son, James Van Dyke, whom everyone called Jim, was wild and irrespon-sible, more like his father, Annie's first husband, Ennis Beasley, who abandoned the family when the children were quite young. Annie was particularly worried when Jim began flirting with Alice Washing-ton's beautiful, honey-brown adopted daughter, who lived across the street and was a year short of finishing high school.

Jim was nine years Mildred's senior when he led her down the garden path. Pregnant and unwed, she was marked for life, because in those days a woman was either saint or sinner; there was nothing in between. Ironically, history was repeating itself. Sixteen years earlier,

Mildred had been abandoned by *her* unwed mother, left in a basket on Alice Washington's doorstep. Alice, who had always wanted children, raised the baby as her own. And now her adopted daughter was doubly shamed: born out of wedlock, and bearing a child out of wedlock. Alice disowned her, but unlike most parents of her day, she gave Mildred a roof over her head, allowing her to stay in the house on Magnolia Street while Alice, a maid and a cook, went to live with the Robinsons, the White family for whom she worked.

Annie Beasley resolved that no grandchild of hers was going to be illegitimate. At her insistence Jim and Mildred, her belly bulging for all the world to see, were married on Groundhog Day of 1933. Beyond marriage, my father offered Mildred nothing. He simply saved me from being branded a bastard child and that just barely, for I was born a mere month later, on St. Patrick's Day.

As a very young child, I'd overhear Mama and her friends gossiping about my mother's "bad blood." I didn't understand what they meant, but whenever I had a bloody nose (which I often did), or when I scraped my knee from running too fast and falling (which I often did), I checked to see if maybe my blood was the wrong color. Maybe *I* had bad blood too. ⧫

I spent the first ten years of my life in Mama's modest, one-story white-washed house, which sat on a steep hill, its front part resting on stilts, its back on rich brown soil. The roomy triangular crawl space under the front of the house — high enough for an adult to stand upright — served as a storage area for old furniture and garden tools and, for me, a secret playhouse. On the rear wall, Mama had built shelves almost down to the dirt, and on them she kept a summer's worth of canned fruits and vegetables, which sustained us through the long winter.

Surrounding the house was a large yard, one side reserved for washing and hanging clothes, the other for visiting. Part of the back was fenced off, a coop for our cackling, egg-laying hens. Behind that was a sizable garden, where we grew corn, tomatoes, string beans, butter beans, snap peas, green peas, crowder peas, potatoes, mustard greens, collards, cabbage, and black-eyed peas. In the summer and fall I helped with the hot, laborious work of harvesting our prodigious crops. We raised more than enough to feed ourselves, so we sold the excess or gave it away to those less fortunate.

We took great pride in that property; it was *ours*. At dusk, Mama swept and raked the brown earth in the yard into intricate patterns that, when I look back now, I realize had a Japanese feeling — a custom in many poor Black neighborhoods in the South, where few had lawns. We dared not walk on the designs until the next morning, a test that proved to be one of my early exercises in restraint. On summer evenings after dinner, the children played in the street and the adults visited, complimented, and (silently) compared. The competition among women my grandmother's age was fierce in many areas — their homes, their children, their cooking, their Sunday clothes, and especially their gardens.

In our little neighborhood it was understood that it was our responsibility to make whatever we had beautiful. I wish more people nowadays would subscribe to this idea. A poor neighborhood doesn't also have to be poor in community spirit; it's always possible to somehow transform your own environment into a place to be proud of. Pick up the trash, cut the grass, plant flowers.

We also had lots of fruit trees in the garden, including apricot, peach, pear, and plum. In the summer, I would become ill after eating half-ripe plums. My most special warm-weather spot, though, was the vee of a massive fig tree, which bore my favorite fruit — sunkissed, sugar-sweet confections. I'd carefully position my wiry body in the branches, my back turned to the house, and just sit quietly. I was a shy, timid child, but I hesitate to say I went there to *think*. I was certainly not encouraged to have thoughts of my own, but having pored through photos in magazines and encyclopedias, I could sit there and dream of what it might be like to live in other places.

I remember our small house as clean and cozy, with a pitched tin roof that amplified every sound; raindrops were like soft, steady drumbeats that lulled me to sleep at night. The largest of the five rooms, which doubled as a living room and bedroom, had several wood rockers and straight chairs, a footstool, and a bed for guests, covered with a huge, fluffy feather mattress. The adjoining dining area had a long oak table with massive round legs that ended in tripods of claw feet. In the winter, the big potbelly stove in the living room was the centerpiece of the house. Mama and her friends gathered round it, rocking and talking, sometimes quilting. I often climbed under the oak table, pretending I was invisible as I listened to the adult chatter. With my dolls and their tiny dresses and furniture, I playacted the grown-up lives I saw around me.

One of the two small bedrooms in the house was reserved for my father, who was rarely there. I slept with Mama in the other room, which also had a large feather bed. Our running water came from a cold-water pump just outside the kitchen door. Our only heat was from the potbelly stove and from a long, black wood-burning stove in the kitchen, which looked very much like the expensive designer stoves of today. It had two ovens below and a warming oven on top; lids over the six burners served as hot plates. During a typical winter's day, the kitchen was warmed by steaming, flavorful pots of food — chicken and dumplings; black-eyed peas and fatback simmering with chopped onions and cloves of garlic; succotash; vegetables from the garden; and occasionally a beef stew. A pan of "crackling" cornbread, a variety laced with crisply fried fatback, almost always sat atop the stove. A special Sunday meal was prepared on Saturday evenings; Sunday, the Lord's day, was the only day Mama didn't cook.

Magnolia Street turned muddy in summer and treacherously slippery during the icy Mississippi winters. On rare occasions the city would grudgingly send a truck of gravel to reinforce the unpaved surface, but that didn't make the going much safer. Then again, no one on our street owned a car. The only vehicle that came our way regularly was a big, open-bed truck filled with all kinds of fish. We'd hear the truck chugging up the hill, the driver shouting, "Fresh fish, come get your fish. Catfish! . . . Buffalo! . . . Gaaaaaspergoo!" As an adult, I learned that the word was actually "gaspergou," a large freshwater fish, but then I had no idea what it was — I just enjoyed the way the word rolled off the old man's tongue. The women came out of their houses clutching loose change and crumpled dollar bills, and we children followed, scampering up the sides of the truck to peer in at the huge fish lying wide-eyed and stiff on a bed of ice blocks.

Because I grew up during the Depression, when everyone was struggling, I never thought of us as poor. Still, I was aware of economic differences, even as a child. Although I knew we didn't live in a fancy neighborhood, I understood that we weren't "po'" like many families who lived in the Bottom, the run-down, low-lying part of hilly Vicksburg, where Colored folk were crowded into rows of gray shotgun houses — so called because a bullet could go in the front door, pass through all the rooms, and come out the back without touching a wall. And we were certainly not as bad off as the homeless who lived in dirt caves in the neighboring hills.

Social standing was, in fact, measured by the size of one's outhouse. We had four seats in ours, instead of the standard one. In my child's mind, I often imagined four people sitting there together, in deep conversation; that such a communal arrangement was a mark of status escaped me. We also did not have to bathe in the same tub used for washing clothes, as po' people did. Our bathtub, long and oval and suitable for lounging, hung just outside the house next to the kitchen door. When it was time for my bath, Mama would bring it in and set it on the floor next to the woodstove. She'd heat two big kettles of water, pour in just the right combination of hot and cold, and scrub me with Ivory soap, which was considered a luxury and usually reserved for Saturday nights.

One winter, when one of the window panes in the living room broke and we couldn't afford to replace the glass, Mama tried to save us from the cold by covering the gaping hole with cardboard and newspaper — the same materials she sometimes used to extend the life of my shoes when I outgrew them or wore out the soles. The potbelly stove, our only source of heat when we slept, was impossible to regulate, so Mama had to get up several times a night to stoke the fire by adding more wood and coal.

One of my earliest memories of Magnolia Street is of Martha Hoover, my great-great-grandmother, sitting in her favorite spot, a rocking chair in front of that stove. She was a former slave, Mama's grandmother on her mother's side. I have no idea how old Martha was — maybe in her nineties. She was legally blind, but when the stove overheated, as it often did, she could see its red glow.

Grandma Martha was a hefty woman. Nestled in her ample lap, I could feel the soft folds of flesh beneath her housedress as she rocked and patted me on my shoulders and head. The effect was almost hypnotic, and so comforting and safe that whenever I sensed I was in trouble with Mama I'd scamper into the living room and onto her knees. Grandma Martha would swoop me up, hug me, and then just sit there, rocking.

In seconds, Mama would appear with a scowl on her face — my usual transgressions were running in the house or not moving immediately when Mama told me to do something. Grandma Martha just kept on rocking, shielding me with her giant arms, until she got good and ready to lift her head and look up at Mama. Finally, with a melodic but deadly serious lilt to her voice, she'd intone, "Noooooo, Annie, you ain't gonna hit this chile today."

I smile remembering the way that Grandma Martha, and only she, could subdue my grandmother. Of course, that's because she was Mama — the woman in charge — long before Annie had ascended to that role. The term *Mama* dates back to slavery. Even when her men and children were sold, a Mama would find a way to keep going. After abolition, when her man could not find work, a Mama would get a job. *She made a way out of no way.* ⚘

I was five when my great-great-grandmother passed. Only then did Annie Beasley become the undisputed matriarch of the family. My childhood memories are dominated by images of this, *my* Mama. She loved me and cooked for me. She made rag dolls for me that I cherished, and she painstakingly hand-stitched delicate little dresses for them. She held me and read the children's classics to me — *Cinderella, Little Red Riding Hood,* and *Brer Rabbit.* Before bedtime, she sat in a straight-backed wood chair and had me sit on a pillow placed on the floor between her legs, so that she could brush my long hair and bring out its natural shine. I leaned into her as she brushed and brushed, counting aloud until she reached one hundred.

Always the teacher, Mama used that quiet time to correct my diction, to encourage me to speak slowly and clearly — to *e-nun-ci-ate* my words. It is no accident that many Black women of my generation speak so deliberately; it says to the world, as Mama often said to me that "you are a cultured human being." Ebonics would not have met her approval, nor does it mine today. One must be prepared to compete in the real world in which we live. Like Mama, I believe that good speech is a passport to greater achievement.

I started piano lessons at age four; to Mama, learning notes was as important as learning my letters. She made sure that I devoted time (and whatever extra money she had) to my cultural advancement, through books and music. My aunt, who was my first piano teacher, insisted that I listen exclusively to classical music. Mama and Auntie hoped that, with practice and music appreciation, someday I would become a virtuoso.

Mama also reminded me regularly, "There's lots of girls who are cuter than you, with hair longer than yours." She wanted to keep me from getting a "swell head," but her constant doting (and prodding) also let me know how special and talented she thought I was. As a result, two conflicting voices, one of mastery, the other of self-doubt, sat on my shoulders for years into adulthood.

I was expected to follow Mama's orders and to accept her word without question. Whenever I had to dust the furniture, she made a final check, running a finger along the surfaces and in the crevices to make sure I had gotten every molecule. "Come here, Baby Sister," she'd call if the room didn't pass her inspection. "You did not complete your job. Just for that," my taskmaster would order, "clean the room again." I learned to do things right the first time.

Fun did not happen in our home until all chores were done. Mama always said, "Put first things first. Tackle the hardest job at once and get it out of the way. Accomplish that, and you'll feel better, and when you feel good about yourself, so will others." The primary mandate of my childhood was crystal clear: Achieve, achieve, achieve. The themes woven through my days were always the same: Do your best, look your best, *be* the best. Because of my grandmother's and aunt's prodding, I have driven myself for most of my life. I have accomplished a great deal, but I have also been too hard on myself when a task is not done quickly or perfectly enough. I was in my late thirties before I became aware of the crippling effect of extreme self-criticism, and only then resolved to give to myself the leeway I hadn't been given as a child. It took me years to reach the point where I knew that I didn't need to please anyone but myself. However, feeling I can handle it all — that I *must* handle it all, and by myself if necessary — is something I still struggle with. Unfortunately, many women are faced with this challenge. We all need to learn to ease up on ourselves a bit and realize that we can't, and don't have to, take on the world single-handedly or be perfect in everything we do.

Though I rarely disobeyed, Mama kept me in line with the threat of a whipping, not with her hand or a paddle, but with a switch — a branch from the peach or mulberry tree in our backyard that *I* had to go outside and get — and I dared not take too much time finding one. When I reappeared, she held my hand so that I couldn't escape as she struck the back of my legs. The sound, like the snapping of a tiny whip, pierced my ears before I felt the painful sting on my skin. *Will it ever stop?* I wondered.

In fairness, most children of my day were disciplined this way. Wooden paddles hung in the principal's office and in our Sunday school classrooms, reserved for anyone who got out of line. And we also knew that if we were punished at school or church, our parents or grandparents would be notified, and we'd get it again at home.

Unlike the distinctions drawn today among church, school, and home, in my childhood, common standards seamlessly connected these institutions, each reinforcing the same values and indoctrination. My teachers fortified in word and example what had already been drummed into me by Mama and our minister. Roles were clearly delineated; I was never allowed to call adults by their first name. In many ways, that kind of strict environment made it easier to be a child — you knew what was expected of you and how far you could go. Even if our parents and grandparents had had a Dr. Spock to guide them, it would not have made any difference; they had their own rules and regulations for *their* children.

We worshiped regularly at Mount Heroden Baptist Church on Clay Street. Every Sunday, from sunup to sundown, we were there for services, and I attended Sunday school and youth meetings as well. During the week we took part in choir practice and other church activities. There, as elsewhere, I was expected to toe the line, to be respectful at all times and, unless I was singing or reciting, to be seen and not heard. Sitting still through the long service was a tough assignment for a wiggly little thing like me. But sit I did, erect, feet on the floor when I got old enough for them to reach. Whenever Mama sensed I wasn't paying strict attention to the minister — or, God forbid, was falling asleep — she'd either elbow me or pull me toward her, almost as if she were about to give me a sweet embrace. Then I'd feel her fingers dig into my upper arm.

Although I have questioned God at various times throughout my life, the faith that grew from my early upbringing in the church has, I realize, sustained me in my darkest days. But as a youngster, doused in my grandmother's particular brand of religion, all fire and brimstone, I got the message early on: God was to be feared. At revival meetings in the summer, we little children who had not been baptized sat on a "mourner's bench," while the older people hummed a frighteningly ominous dirge, and the preacher delivered his sermon. He sputtered and spouted as he described hell — the most horrible place imaginable — and we listened, spellbound and shaking. "You will burn in hell unless you want to be saved," he shouted. "Do you *want* to be saved?"

"Yes, yes, I want to be saved!" I answered, seeing no other option. "Please save me!" No wonder I was such a good little girl. I was frightened half to death — frightened into goodness! I prayed endlessly, to be forgiven for even *thinking* evil thoughts, let alone for doing anything wrong.

During the service, emphatic but restrained utterances emanated from the congregation: "Yes, Lord!" "Amen!" Now and then, a woman might move rhythmically to the music, even stand up and clap her hands, but always with reserve. Female ushers, dressed in white and wearing little nurse's caps, gave out fans and smelling salts to those who "got happy," as they called it. Mama and her friends craned their necks, frowning and staring; the music would stop, and the minister would say, "Yeah, Sister, we all know the Spirit is in you — don't hurt yourself." The transgressor might be gently shepherded into the vestibule, to sit there until she calmed down.

Of course, we kids looked forward to these moments, because they broke the monotony. There was one lady in particular who often jumped up and down, hands in the air, crying, "Yes, Jesus! Save me, Jesus!" My friends and I, each sitting with equally strict elders, would look at one another and giggle. We knew the price of disobeying them, but we couldn't stop. Tears would run down my face until Mama reached down and grabbed a little piece of flesh from my knee, pinching it, twisting it, until she made sure I got the message.

Church was also where I first learned to stand up and be seen. Members of our community believed that it was part of every child's training to be placed up front, so that he or she wouldn't grow up to be shy or afraid. Even a toddler could be given the responsibility of holding up a poster, or displaying a letter of the alphabet in a church pageant. At age three, I was already singing in the children's choir. Dressed in white with a huge white bow on the side of my head and three long braids in "Sunday style," I dutifully belted out the song "Jesus Wants Me for a Sunbeam."

After I had learned to read, my grandmother made sure I was selected to make the weekly announcements, and she constantly pushed me onstage to recite prayers or poems. Later, I played the piano. I must have been all of four when I appeared in my first fashion show, an annual church fund-raising event. Mama, ever determined to make her baby stand out, made me a "sweet little Alice-blue gown," as she called it, after the song that was popular in her day. It was light blue jersey with little puffed sleeves and trimmed with a ribbon of pink-and-red-flowered embroidery across the bodice.

The day before the show, she took me to have my hair done at the home of Jessie, her hairdresser. Negroes weren't allowed in beauty parlors; our beauticians usually worked out of their kitchens. Walking in, I could smell the hot oil burning and hear the hair frying in the curling irons. Even though it made me feel grown up, the prospect was menacing. But Mama was right there with me. "Her hair doesn't really need that much straightening," she informed Jessie. "Now, don't you make that comb too hot."

That night I had to sleep with my just-straightened hair wound around rolled-up strips Mama had cut up from a brown paper bag. It was sheer torture. The next morning, she coiled and shaped my long hair around a wooden spoon handle, brushing it, smoothing it. When Mama was finished, I had shiny corkscrew ringlets, just like Shirley Temple, whom America idolized. Later, at the fashion show, I imagined I was she, strutting in my pretty Alice-blue-gown dress and beaming a partially toothless smile at the congregation. ⁊

Mama was determined not only to mold me to her high standards but also to separate me from the shame of my early beginnings. She never explicitly banned my mother, but Mama's coldness toward M'dear made it perfectly clear that she wasn't welcome in our home.

Sadly, my mother never really recovered, financially or emotionally, after I was born. She took what work she could get without a high school degree: domestic work, waitressing, a stint as a pleat-presser at a dry cleaner's. With little to keep her in Vicksburg — no access to her child, no family to embrace her — she eventually moved to Yazoo City in the Delta, a good two-hour drive away. There she met and married Lee Mack Sanders, a former Marine who worked at a local plant. I wasn't allowed to visit until the summer I was ten or eleven. Years later, I discovered how much that hurt her.

I never thought that my mother "abandoned" me — not then, not now. I knew that she had no choice in the matter. In fact, by relinquishing my upbringing to Mama, who could afford to raise me, M'dear showed how much she cared. Nor did I think that living with my grandmother was odd, since many children did in those days and, in fact, still do. All the same, I must have felt some longing for my mother, even at that tender age, because on one of the rare occasions when my father was home and my mother had come to visit, I remember taking each of their hands, pulling them together, and pleading, "Why can't we live together?"

Mama's mother-lion guardianship also distanced me from my maternal grandmother, Alice Washington, even though her house was directly across the street. Alice, a short, cocoa-brown woman with skin like silk, was known to me as Big Mama. She had no children, which was why she had so readily taken my mother in and raised her as her own. Warm and jocular, Big Mama was a woman who obviously loved youngsters and had a great deal to give to them.

I felt adored by both grandmothers, but there were stark differences between the two which were apparent to me at a young age, even though I might not have been able to articulate them then. Mama had retired by the time I was born. Her social circle included other teachers and the wives of ministers and postal clerks — highly respected careers in our community. In contrast, Big Mama always seemed to be on her way to or from work. If she had a social life, I rarely saw it. I knew that she had another family to care for, though, the Robinsons, a White family with a little girl named Roseanne, who was around my age.

On the surface, Mama tried to get along with Big Mama. I'm sure she didn't doubt that Big Mama loved me as ferociously as she. But every time I said, "I want to go see Big Mama," Mama said, "Not now," without further explanation. She inevitably tried to come up with a chore, an errand, or some other pressing reason for me to stay on *her* side of Magnolia Street.

On the few Thursday afternoons that Big Mama wasn't working, she came to see me, usually bearing the Robinsons' leftovers, which seemed like delicacies to me. Of course, they were just foods we couldn't afford, like steak and braised lamb shanks, smoked turkey, different kinds of cheeses, puff pastries, and huge strawberries from the supermarket that dwarfed the tiny ones we grew in our backyard.

On holidays, Mama reluctantly allowed me to go with Big Mama to the Robinsons' immense brick mansion, which was located in one of the more exclusive enclaves of Vicksburg. It was the only time I ever saw Big Mama in her uniform of black dress, white apron, and little pleated starched hat. She cooked and served while I sat in the Robinsons' windowed kitchen, filled with modern appliances and shiny pots and pans, the likes of which I'd never seen. I wasn't allowed to play with Roseanne, of course, so I ate leftovers or just sat there quietly, watching Big Mama cook.

Mr. Robinson was a successful and highly respected businessman in Vicksburg, and his wife was a local socialite. Occasionally, Mrs. Robinson floated into the kitchen in her finest frippery to ask my grandmother if I could come in and play the piano for her and her guests. "Oh, Alice," she would coo afterward, "what a doll she is — soooo cute. She plays so well. And Alice, look at that lovely, long hair."

Some would call Mama snobbish for her attitude toward Big Mama, but as I got older, I understood that both women were victims of the strict pecking order among the Negroes of their day. Not only were one's family and occupation indicators of status, so were physical attributes. A narrow nose, a light-toned complexion, and long, straight — and, ideally, silky — hair were precious commodities in our community. Big Mama had doled out her own share of class discrimination, preventing my mother from associating with her half-sister, Frances — M'dear's birth mother's other "tainted" child. But Big Mama certainly didn't like being on the receiving end of such practices, and years later, she finally acknowledged her feelings. I had stopped in to see her during one of my college breaks, and when I was leaving, she said, "You're rushing back, aren't you? *They* never have wanted you to stay with me, and *they* are still at it." ℘

It's no wonder that Big Mama often referred to Mama and Aunt Myrlie as a collective "they." Like twin sentinels, the two of them held unchallenged sway over my life. Indeed, in many ways I was more like Aunt Myrlie — for whom Mama insisted that I be named — than my own mother. Physically, I was Auntie's spitting image, the same coffee-and-cream complexion, the same slender build that broadens with age, the long face, high cheekbones, and thick lips.

Myrlie the First was twenty-six when I was born, solid and accomplished in her own right, a respected member of the community. When she married John Decatur Polk, an agent for the Mississippi Agricultural Department (serving only Blacks), they moved into a wood-framed house on Farmer Street, in one of the better mixed neighborhoods of Vicksburg, directly across the street from the homes of White working-class families. Aunt Myrlie and Uncle John also owned three smaller houses in back, which they rented out.

One of my most vivid, and telling, images of Auntie is at Mount Heroden, where she held forth as the church's esteemed organist. The gray stone building with its prominent steeple and brilliant stained-glass windows boasted among its parishioners many of the best Negro families in Vicksburg. And there Aunt Myrlie was, perched high above the congregation, the first person I saw as I walked into the sanctuary. She sat straight and poised at the huge pipe organ, which rested on a raised platform at the back of the room, spanning the width of the church.

If Mama shaped me, it was Aunt Myrlie who applied the polish. Myrlie was a conservative, elegant dresser. Almost every Saturday, she took me shopping at the Valley, a downtown department store half a block wide and six or seven stories high, which was enormous for Vicksburg. We Negroes had to use the side entrance and weren't encouraged to try on anything but hats and shoes, providing that we lined them with tissue paper first. All of the sales clerks were White, but several Black women, friends of Aunt Myrlie's, unpacked the merchandise and cleaned the store. When an item went on sale that they knew Auntie was interested in, they'd telephone her: "That dress you admired is reduced, Mrs. Polk. Should we put it aside for you?"

Auntie often guessed at my size and brought apparel home for me, sometimes upsetting Mama with her extravagance, but my aunt always had a good reason for her purchases. Once she gave me a pair of high-quality crepe-sole oxfords that cost eight dollars. When Mama exploded, Auntie explained calmly, "But Mama, they were on sale. How could I pass up such value?" Another time, when she brought home a coat Mama thought impractical, Auntie pointed to the broad seams and said, "Look how many years this child can use this coat!"

Although Auntie sometimes wrangled with Mama, the two women's common standards and goals overrode whatever differences they had. Indeed, they were always in alignment where *I* was concerned. 🐶

My mother was as different from my aunt as Big Mama was from Mama. M'dear, who was ten years younger than Aunt Myrlie, chain-smoked, and wore bright clothing in oranges, reds, and yellows — colors that were disdained by my aunt. M'dear also was more openly affectionate and playful than my aunt or my grandmother, who were loving but far more reserved. And she was a gracious hostess and a fabulous cook, just like Big Mama.

I also valued — and ultimately embraced — M'dear's relationship with God, which was far different from Mama's and Aunt Myrlie's. Though she too believed that faith and the Spirit carried you through hard times, in her view God was a forgiving being who understood your frailties and absolved you if you fell by the wayside. Given her life, one could assume she had to think that way. But to me, her pragmatic approach was a welcome relief from Mama's hell-and-damnation religion.

For all that Mama and Aunt Myrlie meant to me, the older I became, the more I realized that it was my mother who truly understood me. My grandmother and aunt gave me so much of what I needed in the world, but M'dear gave me so much of what I needed in my heart. We were more like sisters than mother and daughter. Poor as she was, she was always generous. Whenever she visited me at college, she brought gifts of nylon stockings or something of hers, perhaps a dress she thought I might like.

My mother was also the only one who wholeheartedly supported my marriage to Medgar, a prospect that frightened my grandmother and aunt because he talked foolishness, wanting to change the status quo in Mississippi, which Mama and Aunt Myrlie believed was unchangeable. They feared for my safety and worried that, if I married him, I would not complete my education. After meeting Medgar for the first time, M'dear simply asked me, "Do you love him?" I was a college freshman, and he was a junior, only eight years younger than she.

"He makes me quiver," I told her. I blushed, and she let out a knowing laugh. She was the only one to whom I felt free enough to confide even that.

"Do you think he loves you?" she asked. The tears in my eyes answered yes, so she continued: "I know, I know. They want you to wait. They want you to finish college. But you have something good here. Grab him. You can still finish college."

I remember getting a wonderful, lighthearted letter from her shortly after our son Darrell's birth, telling me she had entered his picture in an NAACP Mother's Day contest — ironically, a fund-raising idea initiated by Medgar, who was then doing volunteer work for the organization. She happily rattled on about how proud she was to be Darrell's grandmother, how beautiful he was, and that she was sure he'd win. I still have that letter in my vault, one of the few mementos I have of my mother.

The last time M'dear and I were together was when I took Darrell and Reena, who was just a baby at the time, to visit her one weekend. After Medgar dropped us off in Yazoo City, he drove to Jackson, where he was to sign the contract naming him the first field secretary for the Mississippi NAACP. He would pick us up on the following afternoon, which was a Sunday. Only a few minutes into our stay, it became clear that something was wrong with my mother. She had always been a heavy smoker, but now she was lighting each cigarette from the one before, all the while bemoaning everything she considered she had done wrong with her life.

That night, M'dear stopped her smoking and sat up rocking and humming to Reena, who was a good baby and rarely needed the attention. Sunday morning, my mother continued to review her life. When I asked why she was taking such huge amounts of BC — a headache powder — to my surprise, she told me that she had a heart condition. Her doctor had warned her to stop working, she admitted, but she needed the money.

When Medgar returned from Jackson, M'dear made dinner for us. We ate, talked for a while, and, as we prepared to depart, she suddenly began crying. Never had I seen my mother break down like that. I left her house sad and confused.

The next day at noon, her husband, Lee, called me at work and said despairingly, "Boots is gone, Baby Sister, Boots is gone," using his pet name for her. I assumed their marriage had gone sour, and my first thought was, *Oh, she's left him — that's why she was telling me all that.*

"Oh, Lee, I don't know what the problem is, but," I reassured him, "I'm sure she'll be back."

"No, Baby. Boots is *gone*," he said more emphatically.

"She'll be back," I said again, still not understanding.

"Baby, she's dead," he finally explained, leaving no room for misunderstanding. I suddenly understood her tears — she obviously had had a premonition that her time was near. I screamed, and a coworker in my office took the phone. Apparently my mother had gone to her job still complaining about her horrible headaches. She asked a friend for an aspirin and water, put the glass to her mouth, and was dead before she hit the floor.

M'dear died a few weeks before her thirty-eighth birthday; I was only twenty-one. I couldn't cry for a month. When I finally did, I sobbed for two days and two nights; my eyes all but closed they were so swollen. "We just found each other," I said to Medgar when he tried to console me. "I was just getting to know her, and now I've lost her."

My mother didn't have many material possessions, but she had dignity. I thought of how my father had rejected her and how Lee, good as he was to her, had never been able to make her life easier. She owned no property and constantly struggled to make ends meet. She lived her whole life in houses without running water.

I often think of M'dear, regretting that we never knew each other as adult women. Even today, I wish that I could lie across her lap, so that she could pat my head and soothe me. I could talk to M'dear, I could cry, I could laugh. She guided me and reassured me.

In fact, one of the most resonant chords in the symphony of my life has been the support of women. Many of my female friends have discovered this as well. Long after our mothers are gone, we get mothering from one another. We seem to have the power to reach into the deepest parts of our sisters — parts we rarely if ever allow men to see — and find solace in our common threads. We are "sisterfriends" who understand the agony, despair, and disappointment, as well as the success, joy, and hope. Though there may be times when we deny or try to control our feelings, we know each other's emotions. I've seen men who feel threatened by their girlfriends' and wives' "best friends." It's understandable; women find with other women an important and very special kind of support that no marriage, no love affair, can equal. Luckily, after our mothers are gone, we still have our friends. ℞

When I was ten, Uncle John, Auntie's husband, died, and Mama and I moved into her house, both because it was the economical thing to do and because Mama wanted me to grow up in a better neighborhood. We now had not only running water and a porcelain tub, but also indoor plumbing. Aunt Myrlie's home was beautifully furnished with matching custom-made drapes and upholstery, and an upright piano. I listened to *The Shadow* and *The Lone Ranger* on the Philco radio and delighted in my aunt's books and magazines, from *Good Housekeeping* to *National Geographic*. I rarely had seen a newspaper on Magnolia Street other than those Big Mama brought home from the Robinsons'; in our new home, we had the local newspaper delivered daily, and we discussed current events. The summer I was twelve I discovered Auntie's set of encyclopedias, and I became obsessed with the idea of getting through every volume. After dark, I was not allowed to turn on a light for reading, but I used a flashlight to read in the dark. I managed to get through the entire set and, that fall, was fitted with my first pair of eyeglasses.

If one ranked the homes in our community according to strictness, ours, not surprisingly, was at the top. Even though the house had three bedrooms, I slept in bed with Mama until I was in high school, when I finally begged for space of my own. Auntie gave me a sixteenth-birthday coming-out party, which meant that I could officially date and that I was finally allowed to wear lipstick — but only light colors, blotted three times until merely an illusion of pink remained. Being permitted to wear stockings and shoes with a little bit of a heel represented the ultimate freedom to me, but even that didn't happen until my high school graduation.

In junior high, my aunt or grandmother went with me to church or to school dances. How well I remember my embarrassment when Aunt Myrlie rode in the taxi between my date and me. During the dance, she was not alone in her vigilance. "Let's see some light between you — now!" barked the chaperons when a couple danced too close. "What are you trying to do, dance on a dime and get nine cents change?" Little did they realize they had nothing to worry about in my case. I had no desire to experiment with boys. The fear of pregnancy that Mama instilled made me reluctant to even allow an innocent kiss. ⤳

I went to elementary school and high school at Magnolia High, a large, old redbrick building that housed both lower and upper grades; in between, in seventh and eighth grades, I attended McIntyre, the junior high. Our schools, such as they were, represented our hopes of advancement. Our teachers were deeply committed to giving us what they had been so fortunate to have themselves — a thirst for knowledge and an education. But they had precious little to work with. Our segregated schools were not even close to being equal to the White facilities. We used textbooks that were years out of date, all marked up, and had pages missing. In chemistry class, we had Bunsen burners but no test tubes.

All the same, our teachers made the best of what they had. They inspired us to think and embraced us in our desire to learn, offering special help to the slower students. Those wonderful women — and a few men — cared for us and worked with us as individuals. They acknowledged the evils of society at the time, the unfairness, the savage treatment of our people, but they told us, "You can't let these things hold you back." I repeat that same message to children today.

Discussions about education are ongoing in the African-American community. In the fifties and sixties, we fought hard in the courts to eliminate the "separate but equal" system, which, in practice, is contradictory. Originally, integration was viewed as opening the door to skills and knowledge *all* children needed to succeed. However, some of those early promises have not been realized. In many communities in America, the mandate for equal education is ignored. In some integrated schools, African-American children are treated unfairly, overlooked, made to feel inferior. Understandably, there are those within the African-American community who believe that the remedy is separate schools where our children would get the attention they need and, not so incidentally, be exposed to their own history and the accomplishments of their people. I know children who have graduated from such schools and they have, in fact, thrived in this rarified environment. But I also believe that children must be exposed to, and learn to interact with, all races in our society. In short, we live in an integrated world, and we must prepare our children for this reality.

The consciousness of educators of all colors must be raised; our schools must teach tolerance as routinely as we do other "core" subjects, and make history reflect the experiences of all races. And we must give our children a sense of who they are, instilling pride and self-worth in them from infancy. Every child needs to be encouraged. Indeed, long before Jesse Jackson thrilled thousands with the chant "I am somebody," our parents and dedicated teachers in Vicksburg compelled us to believe that we *were* somebodies who had talent and a future, and through education we could take our rightful place in American society. Where are those sentiments today? I see heartening signs, pockets of hope, throughout America in communities where citizens band together to protect their children and to bolster their schools. But we need more of this kind of grass-roots dedication to ensure the achievement and hope of future generations. ♣

I don't remember a time when I wasn't aware of race; living in Mississippi, it was an unavoidable fact of life. However rigid the class structure within the Black community, in the eyes of White Vicksburg, we Negroes were all the same: inferior. Throughout my childhood, I instinctively took offense at how Blacks were portrayed in the media — women as fat, jovial mammies, men as bumbling Stepin Fetchits or uncivilized savages. We didn't talk about these things, but I saw no such shuffling in *my* family, no one who said, "Yasem, ma'am." In fact, in both subtle and obvious ways, I was taught not only to reject but to disprove stereotypes. It's no accident that today I am always conscious of posture and presentation. I was told to carry myself like I was *someone*.

When Mama read *Little Black Sambo* to me as a child, she informed me that I was never to look disheveled, wear little pigtails all over my head, or in any way resemble a "pickaninny" — a pejorative term even then. When Big Mama came home with Roseanne Robinson's hand-me-down clothes, I instinctively resented them, preferring the dresses Mama and Auntie sewed for me out of cloth flour bags to castoffs from what might as well have been a Big House. And when M'dear worked as a waitress at the Old Southern Tea Room in Vicksburg, I remember feeling proud of her for quitting. She refused to wear an Aunt Jemima kerchief on her head, she told her employers, because to do so would be demeaning to her and to her race.

I avoided buses as much as possible, preferring the inconvenience of walking to the indignity of segregated transportation. Taking a bus meant getting on at the front, paying your fare, stepping off, going to the back of the bus, and entering a small section cordoned off with wire fencing where Negroes crowded together like chickens in a coop. I remember on more than one occasion the bus chugging up a hill and, suddenly, just for the "fun" of it, the driver would slam on the brakes. Like dominoes, each of us would fall one onto the other, as he grinned into the rearview mirror. It was only one of many everyday insults in Vicksburg.

Mama was right to teach me to be cautious. By junior high school, I had already been exposed to the hatred, dangers, and indignities from which she had tried to shield me. McIntyre was a good three-mile walk from home. Because of serious overcrowding, the school day was split into two sessions, which meant walking to school before sunup to get there at six-thirty. For safety, I walked with my girlfriends. Unless we went several blocks out of our way, we passed the courthouse, where we were tormented by a group of White high school boys — "the courthouse gang" — who seemed to make it their life's work to threaten us, spit on us, call us names, hurl rocks and sticks at us, shove and hit us. Whenever we gathered at one another's houses, we talked about fighting back, but we knew that those boys had the power of the White community on their side. Our parents had warned us to turn the other cheek when Whites taunted us or to try to avoid them altogether. To be sure, most of us had experienced a parent or grandparent quickly steering us to the other side of the street when a White person was coming from the opposite direction.

For months we followed our elders' example, picking up the pace when we neared the courthouse, breaking into a run when we saw the boys. One or two of our parents had gone so far as to register a complaint at the (all-White) police department; not surprisingly, their protests weren't taken seriously. No one said it out loud, but everyone knew that picking on little Black girls was considered sport in Mississippi.

Disgusted and tired of running, we secretly cooked up a dangerous plan with one of the girls' older brother and his friends. On the specified day, we walked by the courthouse as usual, but this time, when members of the gang taunted us, we taunted back; we even threw rocks at them. Naturally, they took off after us. We ran as fast as we could and lured them into an enclosed courtyard behind a store, where the older Black boys — brothers, cousins, and friends — were waiting for them. The element of surprise, not to mention a cache of old building materials that made excellent weapons, worked in our favor. All of us joined in the fray, and it was over in minutes, well before the police could arrive.

Our families were appalled when they heard what we had done. Many Blacks had been killed for less in Mississippi, a state known for its unmitigated violence against Negroes. Between 1880 and 1940, nearly six hundred Mississippi Blacks were lynched; and no jury would convict a White man for killing a Negro. As it turned out, the boys never bothered us again, but the scars remained there all the same. The color of my skin made it necessary to fight for my life. I learned early to depend on myself and perhaps a few trusted others to get a job done. In retrospect, the incident was my first experience in organization and activism; we conceived and executed a strategy that would, we hoped, lead to change. ⁊

When I was in high school, Mama finally stopped sitting at my side as I did my homework. But by then I wanted to excel and make something of myself. I had internalized her dreams for me, by that peculiar trick of life whereby we inadvertently turn into the people who made us who we are. It's a subtle process, and we often don't realize its power until we are far into adulthood.

Just as Mama had, I began to imagine myself a concert pianist, an idea I had scoffed at when Mama first planted it. Aunt Myrlie gave me piano lessons for the first year; later Ruth Rowan Sanders, a graduate of Fisk and the Juilliard School of Music, took over the job. Mama insisted that I practice for at least two hours a day, and at first I took no joy from the hard work, especially since I was only allowed to play classical music. "It will carry you forth," Mama reminded me when I protested or broke into "Chopsticks."

I sat there day after day, year after year, at Aunt Myrlie's upright, and eventually I found myself able to play the concertos and etudes that made Mama smile. Two of her favorites were Debussy's "Clair de Lune" and Rachmaninoff's Prelude, Opus 23, Number 9. Whenever I practiced Czerny's Opus 74, "The Art of Finger Dexterity," Mama would just sit there, positively beaming with pride at my discipline and skill, her mission accomplished. Music had been part of my life from birth, but now I could produce it. I was becoming proficient, and with mastery comes pleasure. I tell young mothers today: Help your children develop a passion in life. Too often I see children who laze in front of the television set or dawdle on street corners with their buddies. So much in life distracts young people today, they need an abiding interest to occupy their minds and keep them from the many devastating temptations of our society. It could be a sport, a hobby, music, or an intellectual activity that absorbs them; what matters is the child's enthusiasm and dedication.

One day Mrs. Sanders gave me an article from the *Chicago Defender*, a Black newspaper, about Phillipa Schuyler, the publisher's daughter. She was a young woman of mixed heritage, not more than a few years older than I, who gave concerts throughout the world. I studied the photos of her and scoured the papers for others. I wanted to *be* her, dressed in elegant evening gowns, wearing delicate, dangling earrings. Secretly I told myself, *You can do that. You will do that.*

But this was Mississippi, and while Mama clearly wanted me to be somebody, she meant somebody by *her* definition. Her vision was limited by her beliefs about how far a pretty, smart, well-educated, talented Colored girl could feasibly go. Though she had talked of my being a concert pianist someday — probably to encourage me —

when she saw that I might actually aspire to such a lofty goal, she was frightened. This same unrelenting dynamo of a woman, who had driven me relentlessly, now warned, "Baby, don't get your hopes up too high or you may be disappointed."

The system proved her right. Only 17 percent of White women and 6 percent of African-American women in 1950 sought an education beyond high school. While there was never any question about my going to college, the only two public institutions for Blacks in Mississippi were Alcorn and Jackson State, neither of which offered a music major. I didn't have the money to attend a private Negro college, so I applied for scholarships at Fisk and Talladega Universities. I was turned down, because only the very light-skinned girls received such awards.

I knew from my aunt that the Mississippi Board of Higher Learning had funds earmarked to financially assist Negro students who could not pursue their desired major in the state. I applied. My grades were excellent — I ranked second in my senior class — but I also needed letters from the presidents of Alcorn and Jackson State confirming that they did not offer the music major I wanted. The president of Alcorn quickly and willingly complied, but President Reddick of Jackson State refused. He explained in his letter, "Jackson State offers enough music education for what Miss Beasley needs to pursue her goals in life." In other words, Reddick assumed that I was going to teach music, not become a concert pianist.

I was terribly disappointed and then enraged. This was the first time I truly became angry with the way things were and, worse, angry with one of my own. Then, a man like Reddick was called an Uncle Tom. Reddick was sexist as well, although I didn't have the consciousness at the time to understand that. I can't prove that he would have denied a young Black *man* a chance at the career of his choice, but I'm certain that my gender influenced his decision. Though I was hardly an activist at that juncture in my life, I knew his bias was inexcusable. And in the years to come, when Medgar spouted his subversive ideas about racial equality, though they sometimes scared me, I understood all too well his frustration. ℞

This brings me to the final piece of my childhood puzzle, my father, James Van Dyke Beasley. He was twenty-four when I was born, an irresponsible rascal who could charm the birds out of the trees. Before he moved to Detroit in the late 1940s, joining the Great Migration north, Dad drove an ice cream truck and was also the delivery man for a hardware store. He had grown up around women who catered to him and made him feel important, but that illusion crashed down on him in the real world. During World War II, when he was drafted into a segregated army, he felt, as he put it, like "a grain of sand on the beach of life." In India, where he was stationed, the women ran from the Negro soldiers, believing that their tails came out at night and that they turned into monkeys.

Though he wasn't there for me much more than he had been for my mother, my father did leave his imprint on me. My relationship with him was more problematic and painful than any I had with the women in my life. Daddy wasn't exactly a con man, but he was clearly a genius when it came to talking himself into or out of a situation. He loved literature and wrote short mystery stories. He was a marvelous raconteur, telling tales and twisting words until his listeners were thoroughly absorbed and had no idea whether or not he was telling the truth. My own talent for public speaking is, in part, a gift from him, as is my willingness to do battle. If a playmate taunted me, he would insist, "You get out there and fight, or get back in here and get a spanking." Believe me, this was a confusing directive, because my grandmother told me it wasn't "ladylike" to use one's fists. Today, I choose my battles carefully, use mental rather than physical force, and know there's more than one way to win a fight. All the same, that feistiness definitely comes from Daddy.

On the opposite side of the ledger was my father's brooding nature. Born on a Friday the thirteenth, he was convinced he could never really reach his full potential. He was plagued by feelings of self-doubt and tended to approach life with a negative outlook. "I was born for bad luck," he'd say as one job after another didn't pan out. His pessimism probably infected me, and I've had to fight my own tendency to imagine the worst.

When I married Medgar, and we made plans for a weekend outing, I inevitably worried that something would prevent it. "Myrlie,
get rid of that negative attitude," Medgar complained. In part I was
imitating what I had observed as a child — a constant fear that "the
other shoe" would fall — and in part it was a defensive posture that
shielded me against disappointment. I have since challenged myself
to change my pessimistic outlook. And the more I have dismissed
those feelings, the more positive I have become. If one approaches life
thinking that something bad is going to happen, more likely than not
it will. If, on the other hand, you think positive and act positively, you
become a winner, even when the outcome is not exactly what you
planned.

I also remind myself that I am not my father. If circumstances
don't turn out the way I anticipated, I can, unlike him, change course.
Awareness of my own strengths helps too. I say to myself, *Myrlie,
you've been here before. You've conquered other problems. You'll do it
again.*

On occasion, Daddy took me to the movies, where we sat in the
buzzard's roost — the bleachers farthest from the screen, where
Negroes were allowed — to watch Humphrey Bogart films and war
movies. More often, though, he made promises he rarely kept. When
I invited him to school plays or church pageants, he simply didn't
show up. A particularly painful memory of him centers on one of
those missed dates when he supposedly had to work. Quite by accident, I spotted him in a back alley, on his knees, rolling dice. I cried
dry tears as I ran home that day, and it took me years to build up the
nerve to express that pain to him.

By his negative example, my father did convince me that if I
wanted to find happiness with a man, I'd have to look for someone
unlike him. Luckily, I was blessed, finding not one, but two wonderful
men — Medgar and Walter. And in doing so, I gave my sons a different kind of role model. They, in fact, are living proof that it's possible
to change a troublesome family pattern. Darrell and Van have grown
up to be strong and reliable, sensitive and spiritual, nothing like the
grandfather they barely knew.

Years later, I finally confronted my father, an act I heartily endorse. If someone has disappointed or hurt you, speak your mind — but don't ever expect to change that person fundamentally. I was the mother of three by the time I faced my father, and he was in his mid-fifties. We were in the den in Auntie's home in Vicksburg, and I had asked my aunt for advice on some matter. Daddy interrupted and, in a stinging tone, asked, "Why do you always have to ask *her* for answers?" My aunt started to cry, hurt and shocked by his nastiness, and I became livid.

"And why do you think I always go to her for advice?" I snapped. "Because she was *there* for me — because she's done everything for me that you should have done!"

Dad sat there, astonished, the Camel cigarette dropping from his mouth. Auntie was ashen and speechless, while Mama, shocked as well, said quietly, "Baby Sister, don't talk to your father that way."

It was one of the rare times in my life that I didn't obey. "I will — and I have a lot to say to him." I recounted the gambling incident, and reminded him what he was like back then — his carousing with women, his many broken promises, his neglect.

He interrupted. "You *saw* me? You remember all that?"

"Like it was yesterday," I answered, feeling the muscles in my jaw tighten. "You made me feel like I was dirt, like I wasn't worth anything, like you didn't want me. And you constantly made Mama cry." It all came spilling out of me, twenty-nine years of disappointment and anger.

By the time I was finished, he was crying and my aunt was begging, "Oh, Baby, please don't say any more." I took her counsel and simply told him I loved him but did not like the man he had been.

That encounter marked a turning point in my relationship with my father. By the late sixties, when he lay dying of lung cancer, my anger toward him had dissipated. Seeing my father so small and frail in his sickbed, I flashed back to the last few minutes before I married Medgar, a man who was nothing like Jim Beasley. On my wedding night, as on many other occasions, I waited and waited for my father to appear and to accompany me down the aisle as he had promised.

But once again, he disappointed me. In the splendor of my formal wedding gown and veil, I walked down the candle-lit aisle alone. When I reached the altar, Mama stepped from her seat in the front row, stood next to me, and when the minister asked, "Who giveth this woman to this man?" she proudly said, "I do." As an apt metaphor for my life at that point, it was Mama who took me in, and Mama who gave me away.

2

EMERGING FROM THE SHADOWS

Loving Medgar, losing Medgar

Medgar and I on our wedding day, December 24, 1951.

It is only by risking that we live at all.

            ❧ *William James*

*M*arriage was a door I walked through willingly, promising to love and to cherish Medgar Evers " 'til death us do part." But I was a young eighteen. Little did I know that marriage would bring change beyond my wildest imaginings and my most horrible nightmares. Of course, none of us knows what life holds in store. The best we can do is take whatever comes at us and make the most of it. Even out of bad, there can always come some good, but it sometimes takes a great deal of perseverance and faith to find it. To survive, you have to live for today but be ready for anything — and I do mean *anything,* including the surprising results of your own choices and your own growth.

How did this happen? How did I get here? One night shortly after Medgar's assassination, aching for him, I wondered how I would go on. I was little more than a child when I walked down the aisle, but eleven and a half years later, in June 1963, when my husband was murdered, I had become a woman and was beginning to grasp an important lesson: In the end, it's not what happens to you that matters; it's how you deal with it.

The fact was, I didn't think I *could* deal with Medgar's death. In those first crushing months, I automatically chauffeured the two older children to and from school, took care of three-year-old Van, prepared meals, ran errands. Sometimes I even smiled at people, acting sweet, appreciative, forgiving. I had to carry on. I feared that if I became too abrasive, expressing the true extent of my deep hatred, my family and I would be shunned. I would not have been seen as the "proper" civil rights widow, and worst of all, Medgar might be forgotten. I could not allow myself to believe that his death was in vain.

So I acted the part of the brave martyr's wife and solemnly told reporters, "He really didn't belong to me. He belonged to all the people in the civil rights movement. That's why he died for them." In truth, I had always wanted my husband to belong to *me*; I resented sharing him. And while I insisted, "I don't hate anyone now for what happened — Medgar wouldn't want me to," inside, I was raging, brimming over with deep, dark loathing and despair. Secretly, I imagined my revenge, torturing whoever was responsible for Medgar's death.

As far as I was concerned, everyone was responsible. I screamed at the White policemen who dared to come to my door on the night of the assassination. "This won't stop anything! You'll have to kill me and the children and a lot of others, but you won't stop us!" But I also ranted at my own people — at the Black men in Jackson who rushed to my home allegedly to protect the children and me, and at those in the NAACP headquarters who expressed concern for us. "We don't need your protection now," I shouted. "They got the man they wanted — Medgar. Where were you when *he* needed the protection?"

Though danger had been a constant companion in our lives, though Medgar was so clearly a marked man, though the movement in Mississippi had already claimed the lives of several friends, though Medgar knew that he too would be killed, I still could not imagine life without him. My love for him kept me going before he died; and after he was shot, it continued to propel me. Less than twenty-four hours after his death, I insisted on addressing a mass meeting at the Pearl Street Church.

"Dressed in a pale green dress, she appeared tired but composed," reported Claude Sitton in the *New York Times*. As many people wept openly, I reminded them of what Medgar had died for — that our movement would be one of the most successful that the nation had ever known. I informed them that I intended to take up where he left off. "Nothing can bring Medgar back, but the cause can live on."

Where Medgar once stood, I now took my place at the podium, chanting the new mantra that would echo in the streets of Mississippi after Medgar's funeral and at mass rallies in the months to come: "After Medgar, no more fear." Most historians agree that Medgar's death marked a turning point in the movement, mobilizing numbers of people who were previously unconcerned or too frightened to join.

All the while, I felt as if I were in an altered state — out of my body, and out of my mind with grief. I had never intended to become an activist, and I didn't want the attention now, nor the challenges. I would have traded everything — the outpouring of support, the thousands of telegrams and letters from the famous, the visit to the White House with my children, the posthumous honors given to Medgar, all the money in the world — just to have Medgar in my arms again. ~

When I met Medgar Wiley Evers, in 1950, I was a freshman at Alcorn Agricultural and Mechanical College, a modest school of higher education for Negroes located in rural Lorman, Mississippi. Despite my early aspirations, I had chosen to major in education with only a minor in music. The campus, formerly a White military school built by slaves, was set back in a glade of enormous trees, and its redbrick buildings with a smattering of ivy would impress no one but a shy, green girl from Vicksburg who'd never even seen a tennis court up close. Going to Alcorn was a monumental event for me; at the time, I couldn't imagine taking a more exciting or a more terrifying step.

After delivering me to Alcorn, Mama and Auntie reached out to embrace me before climbing into the car for the trip home. "Baby, now you be a good girl," Mama warned, "and don't get involved with any of those veterans." Some eighty-five thousand Blacks from Mississippi had served in World War II, and several were now at Alcorn, thanks to the GI Bill, which paid their tuition.

"Yes, Mama," I replied, ever the dutiful child. My heart raced as their car disappeared over the horizon.

A short while later, I found myself leaning on a lamppost near the student grill, amidst a group of other freshman girls. It was an Alcorn custom for the football team, which arrived a week before the rest of the student body, to look over — and get first pick of — the new crop of freshman girls, who were also on campus early for orientation week. There I stood, hoping to appear nonchalant and sophisticated, when Medgar trotted by with the rest of the Alcorn Braves. He was six feet tall, strikingly handsome in a non-Hollywood way, magnificently built, and, I would soon discover, intelligent and serious-minded. He spotted me, too, and slowly approached me.

"You shouldn't lean on that electric pole. You may get shocked," he said with a devilish smile.

Employing my best Vicksburg manners, I tried to look unfazed, but of course I was immediately and thoroughly smitten. I tossed my head, so that my long hair fell provocatively over one shoulder, and raised an eyebrow, just as I had seen Veronica Lake do in the movies. "Oh, I'm not worried," I retorted, in as blasé a manner as I could. He laughed and ran off to join his teammates, leaving me more than a little intrigued.

In the weeks ahead, I spotted him again in the dining hall, thinking his name was "Edgar Evans." Our eyes met only in passing until one day he finally came over to the table where I was eating with some girlfriends.

"Would you like to sit with me over there?" he asked with an air of confidence, pointing outside to a large oak tree. My heart was racing, and my last bite of food was lodged in my throat. One of my friends kicked me under the table, and I managed to squeak out a barely audible, "Okay." I excused myself and walked out with him, praying that I wouldn't fall flat on my face.

From that first conversation in the shade of the oak tree, I learned that he was a returning veteran, eight years older than I — precisely the kind of man I had been told to stay away from. He was editor of the school newspaper, a member of the debating team and the glee club, and president of the junior class. I could *not* get him out of my mind. He was so unlike the boys back home — sophisticated, intuitive, smart about money, knowledgeable about current events, and possessing a vocabulary that invariably sent me scurrying to the dictionary in my dorm room. My God, he had seen the world, and I had barely seen Vicksburg!

During my freshman year, I practiced piano for hours every day in the "music hall," which was really just an ordinary building with tiny rooms, each of which had a small window and a piano. Unbeknownst to me, Medgar passed by the hall every day on his way to football practice. One day he knocked on the outside wall. I stopped playing and looked out the window. When I saw my handsome Romeo — who, it was said, dated a new girl every week — I felt like Juliet.

"Sounds nice," he said in his smooth, resonant voice. "The music is beautiful, and you're very good."

I barely managed a shy thank-you before he ran off. A day or two later, he appeared again, but this time he came into the room. "I really enjoy classical pieces," he said. "Do you play any other kind of music?"

"No, not really," I said hesitantly, wondering what answer would appeal to him. "I was never allowed to." I found out later that Medgar really didn't care much for classical music, but that was as good a line as any to flatter a naive girl who played nothing else.

Medgar stopped by every day after that, only staying a few minutes. He asked about my aspirations, and what I was studying. He talked about ideas I'd never heard anyone express — the struggle of our people, the need to register and to vote and to challenge the system. Some of the other students at Alcorn, who only wanted to party, thought him a nuisance because he continually brought up such serious issues, but that was precisely what I found so fascinating about him.

After we'd dated a few weeks, he announced bluntly, "I'm going to shape you into the kind of woman I want you to be." I had no idea what he meant, so I let the remark pass. I was mesmerized, at once scared of and attracted to him. And, before he even kissed me, he informed me I was going to be the mother of his children.

"You haven't even told me you love me," I replied.

"I will tell you I love you when I do," he retorted without missing a beat. That was classic Medgar: *I* was to be the honored one in the relationship.

During one of his visits to the music room, he stood unusually close, leaning on the piano as I played. I could feel his eyes on my face, but I dared not look up. I didn't want to hit the wrong keys or appear too forward. As I finished the last note of Lassen's *Crescendo*, he bent down and gently lifted my head and kissed me — a moment that reminded me of that old Tabu perfume ad. I just melted. I remember thinking how sweet he was — his breath, his person — and how wonderful it was to be kissed like that instead of having some teenage boy plant wet, awkward, and unwelcome smooches all over you.

But in seconds Medgar took the thrill out of it. Dramatically swiping his lips with the back of his hand, he looked down at the results and showed me his hand. "You wear too much lipstick," he said disdainfully. However, that didn't stop him from kissing me again. Medgar knew how to woo a tender young soul like me, but could that man sting!

He was right, of course. Like many Alcorn coeds from strict homes, freed from our parents' critical eyes, I wore bright red lipstick, put on far too thick and heavy. After Medgar's stern rebuke, I wore less, and always paler, more conservative shades. ~

That summer, after we had been dating for several months, both of us took jobs up north. Medgar, who had siblings in Chicago, had worked there every summer. My mother's half-sister, Aunt Frances, also lived there. Being in a big northern city would be a new experience for me, but I had other motives for going. I wasn't interested in letting Medgar out of my sight for three whole months, creating a void that other girls would certainly fill. When I told Mama my plans, she insisted on accompanying me. She left Chicago only after she saw that I was safely ensconced in Aunt Frances's apartment and that I had secured a bona fide job. I worked for an automobile sales and service company, where I was paid per day based on the number of envelopes I typed. I saved every penny, enjoying an even greater sense of independence and feeling relieved that I could supplement the meager scholarship dollars I'd have when I returned to school in the fall.

On one of our days off, Medgar suggested a trip to Lake Michigan. "I can't swim," I confessed, but either he didn't believe me or he saw the outing as yet another opportunity to toughen me up. We were wearing summer clothes, he in khakis and T-shirt, me in a sleeveless top and a light blue flower-print broomstick skirt — the kind with a wide waistband and full cut, which when washed, starched, and ironed properly could stand on its own. Underneath, we wore our bathing suits. I remember being shy about taking my clothes off and feeling half-naked in front of him. When we got into the water, Medgar led, and I trailed close behind, splashing, giggling, acting the coquette. Without my realizing it, he was luring me into ever deeper water.

At one point, Medgar swam away from me, and I, fool in love that I was, tried to follow. Suddenly, the sandy bottom of the lake disappeared beneath me. I panicked and went under. Though I managed to struggle to the surface long enough to gasp for air, I went under again. Finally, Medgar came after me and pulled me toward the shore.

As much as I had accepted just about anything he did, I was furious with Medgar. He hadn't warned that if I tried to go out farther, there would be nothing under my feet. What a foreshadowing that was: Medgar leading me into the unknown, leaving me to test my survival skills.

I remembered that outing periodically during the later years of our marriage. While I often didn't appreciate his method, I came to understand Medgar's intention and the wisdom behind it. Life is full of false bottoms, and one must be ever alert and resourceful. I'm sure it's no accident that "sink or swim" is a motto I taught my children, or that we all continue to live by it today. Indeed, if there is one lesson that my life with Medgar taught me, it's that we often have more strength and endurance than we think we do. Hard times and tough challenges can turn a meek person into a tough one, an endangered person into a survivor, a passive person into an activist — as long as you never give up on yourself and allow yourself to keep growing.

True to his promise, Medgar continued to mold me and to force me to be more independent; and I was, for the most part, a willing pupil. But even as I wanted to embrace whatever he had to offer, a part of me resented his ability to dominate me. At the same time, I was flattered by this kind of attention, and relieved, because I had always longed for the guidance of a strong man. One hardly needs a degree in psychology to see that in Medgar I had found the benevolent, reliable father I'd never had. In only one respect was he very much like my own father: He constantly urged me to fight back.

This often left me feeling angry and frustrated, but upon reflection, I realized that Medgar was strengthening me, and not simply because he thought his days were numbered. You can't overprotect a partner (or a child, for that matter) and then expect her to feel confident about being her own person. I never saw myself as having Medgar's wisdom, strength, or cunning, and in those days, my scant experience didn't compare to his worldliness. But he saw my potential; I just needed time to blossom. Time obviously proved him right, but in the early years of our relationship, I tried to hold my own with him because it was what *he* wanted and needed. To stay with Medgar Evers, I knew that I must keep up with him.

Medgar goaded me constantly. I'd say, "What a beautiful day," and just to argue, he'd come back at me: "No it's not." I hated arguments, so I'd immediately back down, at which point, he'd reprimand me. "You're too timid. You've got to learn to fight back."

I did. We sparred constantly — up to the night before our wedding. For the life of me, I have no idea today what that particular fight was about. No doubt I was nervous, because as much as I loved Medgar, somewhere deep inside me I knew he would control my life. But he was my Prince Charming, I his Cinderella, and there was no turning back.

Not surprisingly, Mama was furious when she found out about Medgar. The only reason she grudgingly consented to our marriage was that she feared I might lose my virginity to him and, God forbid, get pregnant. She remained fiercely protective even after our nuptials, certain that Medgar was taking advantage of me and sure that I'd never finish college. She also feared for my safety; hers was an Old South mentality in which Negroes knew their place.

For a long time, I felt caught between the two people I loved most in the world — and the two who had the most control over me. I didn't want to lose either of them. But I finally realized it was not a matter of taking either one's side. Growing up meant I had the right to make my own decisions, for better or for worse. If Mama turned out to be right and Medgar was in fact too old and worldly-wise for me, *I* would have to live with my choice. ⱬ

Medgar and I married on Christmas Eve, 1951, and returned to Alcorn after winter break, moving into an apartment with another couple. He was to graduate in June. Our relationship was standard fifties fare, and marriage had a vastly different effect on each of us. He, the young husband, was now free to pursue his work unencumbered by domestic responsibilities; in me he had a personal assistant who helped research and type his papers, and he made dean's list for the first time. I, on the other hand, added household chores to my studies; though I kept up my grades, the results were otherwise disastrous: burned grits, soggy fried oysters, an eternally smoke-filled kitchen. Not surprisingly, I lost weight, once again becoming the familiar "stack of bones" I had been in elementary school.

My sheltered life had led me to the altar with absolutely no sense of what it really meant to be a wife. I knew she cleaned and cooked and entertained for her husband; she was supportive and eventually bore his children. And of course, there was sex, a subject about which I knew less than nothing! I realize now that I was quite typical in that respect.

On our wedding night, I was not only chaste, I was painfully innocent and very scared. I had no information and no role models, just horror stories from a few outspoken older women, who made sex sound dirty and ugly. I was also excruciatingly modest. For months, I undressed in the bathroom. One night I had just slipped my pink rayon nightgown over my head when Medgar walked into the bathroom and startled me. He took one look at that gown and ripped it off my body. "You shouldn't be ashamed of your body," he said. "It's beautiful."

Luckily, Medgar was a dedicated, gentle, and wonderful teacher. His patience saved me from being a woman who believed that sexual pleasure was only for men. Still, in terms of the overall relationship, I remained incredibly immature, with nothing but the stories I read in *True Romance* as a model. I cried regularly, because our experience didn't fit their storybook image.

"I want you to love me," I wailed when Medgar questioned my tears. "Do you love me? Do you *really* love me?" We were still living on campus, surrounded by girls Medgar had once dated who resented my taking him out of circulation. I wondered if he was truly mine. I wanted Medgar to make me feel secure, to constantly cuddle me, so that I'd know I was special. I wanted my very being reassured, and I truly believed that that was his job.

It would take Medgar's death and the experience of many years for me to learn the truth: No one, no matter how much he loves you or you love him, can make you feel confident and secure. You have to feel that way about yourself. That's why it's so important to work on your own growth — get an education, acquire skills, develop your own interests, and have a network of friends who support you — rather than count on another person's love to make you whole. Unfortunately, our culture sets us up for this expectation, our love songs, our romantic myths, even the phrases we use, like "my better half." Is it any wonder that so many young women still go into marriage thinking their husbands will complete them?

On several occasions, Medgar said in response to my tears, "Come on. Let's go for a ride." Buoyed at first, I panicked when I realized his intention. "I'm taking you home to your family," he'd say, like a father scolding a recalcitrant child, which I guess I was.

"No! No! No, you don't!" I screamed. Most times, he drove only a few miles away from campus and stopped the car. We'd argue and make up — which was always the best part. One time, though, he drove the entire fifty miles to Vicksburg and parked outside Aunt Myrlie's. "Go in," he ordered. "I can't deal with you."

When I didn't move, Medgar got out of the car and demanded that I do the same. I refused. He walked a few steps to the front door and knocked. Aunt Myrlie answered, and after a short conversation, they both came back to the car.

"Baby," Aunt Myrlie said softly, leaning down and poking her head through the car window, so close I could feel her breath on my face. "What's wrong?"

"Nothing," I replied, trying hard not to cry.

"I'm bringing your child back to you," he announced to Auntie. "I can't deal with her."

Of course, Medgar didn't leave me with Auntie that night; he just wanted to make a point. Looking back, it's something of a miracle that we managed to get through that first year, limping as we did over the hurdles. But for all the emotional turmoil, both of us remained on dean's list and, despite a rash of domestic mishaps, I was overjoyed to be with the man I loved. Medgar, meanwhile, discovered the downside to molding a young woman. In fact, years later, when we talked about that period, he admitted, "Honey, you dried my soul." ☙

I had hoped we'd move to Chicago after Medgar's graduation, but Medgar preferred Mississippi. An offer of a job at Magnolia Mutual Insurance, one of the few all-Black companies in Mississippi, clinched it. Even worse for me, Medgar insisted on our settling in Mound Bayou, a historic but tiny town in the Delta that made Vicksburg seem like the big city. We moved into a dingy, cramped, two-room apartment with a shared bathroom. I made a few acquaintances but no true friends and had no respite from a dreary daily routine.

We had agreed that I'd go back to Alcorn in the fall, an idea I embraced only halfheartedly because I didn't want to be separated from Medgar. He secured a summer job for me as a keypunch operator at the Magnolia Mutual headquarters, which was within walking distance of our home. In the sweltering Delta heat, I suffered through boring days at work and, because Medgar worked late most nights, long, lonely evenings at home. I felt as if I had reached a dead end. He was excited by his new job, but I could barely remember my dreams. My crying jags, though more infrequent, continued, and I became smart enough not to allow Medgar to see my tears. I was learning to cope. I was growing up.

That July, I was thrilled to learn that I was pregnant, but two months later, I became very ill. Medgar had been out selling insurance, returning home late that afternoon to hear Mrs. Porter, the kindly older woman who lived in the adjoining apartment, calling out to him.

"Hurry! Hurry, Mr. Evers!" she urged the minute she heard his car in the driveway. "Your wife is sick, so sick." All day long, she explained to Medgar, she had been hearing my moans and groans through the paper-thin walls, but being a proper woman, she hadn't wanted to intrude.

Medgar came into the house to find me barely conscious. He gathered me up in his arms, and the next thing I remember is waking up in a hospital. I heard the words "spontaneous abortion," and because I didn't know what the term meant, I thought somehow I was being held responsible for my baby's death. I was devastated physically, because I had lost so much blood, and emotionally, because I had wanted a child so badly. Medgar tried to assure me, "It wasn't a baby, Myrlie, it wasn't a baby. We'll have children, I promise."

My illness drained what little savings we had, so my going back to school that fall was out of the question. Although the doctor advised us to wait before trying to have children, and the old wives in the neighborhood warned I'd never get pregnant after a miscarriage, within a few months I was expecting again. ⅋

Mound Bayou was distinguished only by the fact that it was the oldest all-Black township in Mississippi, founded in 1887 by three slaves, one of whom had been the property of Jefferson Davis, president of the Confederacy. Medgar had been drawn to Mound Bayou because of Theodore Roosevelt Mason Howard, the highly respected businessman who owned Magnolia Mutual and was easily among the wealthiest Negroes in the state, if not the wealthiest. In many ways, he was a role model for Medgar, a man who could have easily and quietly enjoyed his wealth, but instead sought to better his people and change the system. During World War II, Doc, as we called him, founded the Friendship Clinic in Mound Bayou and also built the state's first swimming pool for Negroes. Though some criticized his flamboyant ways, T.R.M. Howard was an outspoken critic of Jim Crow and an early pioneer of civil rights. In Medgar he saw a young Black man who wasn't afraid to buck the system.

Medgar had been inclined toward activism since childhood. Growing up in Decatur, a small Delta town where little Black boys were routinely humiliated and beaten, Medgar had always been at the center of racism. He saw bloody clothes rotting on the ground for weeks after a friend of his father's had been lynched. And whereas my family tried to accept the southern way of life, Medgar's family taught him early on to stand up to it.

Medgar's mother — Mother Jessie — worked for a White family, took in ironing, and was also deaconess of her church. A dedicated homemaker, she had had three children by a previous marriage and four with Medgar's father. She was the quiet force that held the Evers family together. Medgar's father, Jim, owned a small plot of land but was unable to sustain his large family from farming alone; over the years, he held a series of jobs at the sawmill and on the railroad as well. The local townsfolk called him Crazy Jim, because he was so bold, refusing to move off the sidewalk when any White person was approaching. One time, when he was in town with Medgar and Medgar's brother, Charles, Daddy Jim questioned the amount of his grocery bill. Shocked by the Negro's audacity, the indignant store owner threatened to throw him out, but Jim Evers would bow down to no man. He told his sons to step outside, broke a bottle on the counter, and threatened the man right back. The sum was corrected, and Jim backed out the door, broken bottle in hand. Few Black men had lived to tell such tales.

Medgar and Charles, who was two years older, were chips off the old block, always testing the limits of the system, always in danger. Even as a teenager Medgar deplored the treatment of his people and the inequities in their lives. In 1946 he and Charles faced an angry, armed mob of White men who were determined to keep them from registering to vote. Unsuccessful that day, Medgar vowed he'd return.

If his boyhood in Decatur sowed the seeds of discontent in Medgar's soul, his new job made them grow. Traveling the long, flat stretches of two-lane highway connecting the various towns on the Delta, Medgar saw firsthand the utter poverty and miserable living conditions of Black people. "They might as well still be slaves," he said of the dirt-poor sharecroppers who died young and penniless and could ill afford the insurance Medgar was supposed to be selling them.

I listened, and I was sympathetic — I had seen glimpses of such poverty in Vicksburg — but I didn't think there was much anyone could do. I cared desperately about my husband, but I certainly didn't share his zeal for the cause. To the contrary, I found Medgar's tireless enthusiasm threatening. It was almost as if he had another wife, another love — his work.

For most people, "the sixties" is synonymous with the civil rights movement, but behind the cotton curtain, a quiet insurgence had been taking place throughout the late forties and fifties — the "forgotten era." The National Association for the Advancement of Colored People, established in 1909, was the original civil rights organization, dedicated to fighting through the courts for equal housing and education and, most important, the right to vote. Although the first Mississippi branch was started in 1918, it wasn't until after World War II that the organization became an increasingly important presence in our state. Being a member meant putting one's life on the line. Not surprisingly, racist Whites in Mississippi, determined to keep the Negro in his "place" through the passage of so-called Jim Crow laws, abhorred the NAACP and accused its members of Communist leanings. According to them, the initials stood for "Niggers, Alligators, Apes, Coons, and Possums."

Medgar, who had fought for freedom on foreign soil only to find himself denied full citizenship in his own country, joined the NAACP in 1948. By the early fifties, he had started giving even more time to the organization and, on a strictly voluntary basis, revived an office in Mound Bayou that had been closed years before. He later opened a new branch in Cleveland, some twenty miles south. He and T.R.M. Howard launched a boycott against filling station owners in the Delta in 1952. In those days, it took a great deal of courage to drive a car bearing the bumper sticker, "Don't buy gas where you can't use the rest room."

Medgar read voraciously and was particularly struck by accounts of Jomo Kenyatta's Mau Mau uprising in Kenya. For a while, he considered that violence might be the means to freedom for Mississippi Negroes. But his mother, a very devout Christian, talked him out of that idea. Still, Medgar was interested in his African heritage. Long before Afrocentrism became fashionable, he urged me to let my hair be "natural," and when our first son was born in June of 1953, Medgar wanted to name him "Kenyatta." I, in a rare show of defiance, ordered "Darrell" to be placed on the birth certificate, with "Kenyatta" as a middle name. I was no activist, and I was almost as appalled by the thought of my son's having an African name and being called a little Mau Mau as I was by the idea of having nappy hair.

On January 22, 1954, as much to test the system as to study to become a lawyer, Medgar made headlines. "Negro Applies to Ole Miss," reported the *Jackson Daily News*. I was horrified by his action, frightened of the repercussions, especially since I was pregnant again. Our families were equally dismayed, but none of us could dissuade Medgar, not even Daddy Jim.

While Medgar was waiting for a response from the university regarding his application, the U.S. Supreme Court handed down its landmark *Brown vs. Board of Education* verdict, which declared that "separate but equal" schools were unconstitutional. Thurgood Marshall, who argued the case on behalf of the NAACP, celebrated the verdict as a national victory for civil rights. Die-hard segregationists declared the day Black Monday, and no southern state reacted as fiercely as Mississippi.

The Citizens' Council, a powerful anti-integration organization, was formed in reaction to the Supreme Court decision. The all-White organization, comprising bankers, lawyers, congressmen, mayors, businessmen, and other "respectable" leaders of the community who vowed to stem the tide of desegregation, had chapters throughout the state. Its members may not have donned white sheets, but their goal was similar to the Klan's. At the same time, the state legislature created the Sovereignty Commission, whose sole purpose was to preserve the state's "sovereign right" to a segregated society. Overall, resistance to the Supreme Court decision was so virulent in Mississippi that it would take more than a decade after *Brown vs. Board of Education* to enroll even one Black child in a White school.

Given such a climate, it's no wonder that Ole Miss refused to admit an "uppity Nigger" like Medgar Evers to its law school. The letter arrived on September 16, a few days after our daughter, Reena, was born, citing a technicality as the reason for the decision. Medgar had submitted the requisite references from Whites, but, as the board informed him, the men who wrote on his behalf lived in the county of Medgar's birth, not where he now resided.

After conferring with Thurgood Marshall and other NAACP leaders, Medgar decided not to go to court and instead accepted the position as Mississippi's first NAACP field secretary. He would continue the work he had been doing on a volunteer basis — signing up new NAACP members, urging voter registration — but now he also would be responsible for reporting incidents of brutality and violations of civil rights.

Medgar had his work cut out for him. In the wake of the *Brown* decision, lynching and other violence against Negroes escalated. Of the forty martyrs whose names would later be inscribed in the national civil rights memorial in Montgomery, Alabama, nineteen — almost half — were killed in Mississippi. ∾

While I recognized that Medgar's new post would pose dangers to our family, and I initially argued with him about taking the job, I was thrilled that it enabled us to relocate to Jackson. We lived in a two-bedroom apartment for our first three years there and, in 1957, moved to our home on Guynes Street in a new, middle-class subdivision. Our neighbors were Black professionals, many of whom had served in the army and qualified for Veterans Administration loans. We borrowed the down payment, but buying a $10,500 house, which required a $56 monthly payment, was a struggle. Still, owning our own home meant we were on our way to "making it." The tiny house, cream-colored brick and light green asphalt shingles, had three small bedrooms, a bathroom, a minuscule kitchen, and a living/dining area. Our modest lot had a green front lawn and, in the backyard, a medley of graceful trees — oak, mimosa, and plum.

We learned later that several neighbors had signed a petition to keep us out. Medgar was by now a well-known figure — the most visible civil rights activist in what was clearly the most racist state in the Union. Margaret Walker Alexander, the renowned African-American poet, lived a few doors down from us on Guynes Street. Now well into her eighties, she recently recalled, "Many of them had the attitude that White people in Mississippi knew what they were doing, and they believed that Black people weren't going to get anywhere making trouble like that." It was feared that our presence would bring undue attention to their model neighborhood. Accordingly, Medgar was shunned by some, scorned by others.

Although the petition was unsuccessful, our neighbors' anxiety was based in reality. The previous year, the Mississippi House of Representatives, aiming at the NAACP, had passed a bill that imposed a jail sentence and/or a fine for "advocating, or urging, or encouraging disobedience," not only to any state law but also to "established traditions, customs and usages" of the state. Assaults on Black business owners who were too vocal about their rights were also common. Worst of all were the night riders. What if they went after Medgar, some of our neighbors wondered, and burned down the wrong house?

There is no question that the danger heightened as Medgar pursued equal rights for Blacks. Still, I felt as if my life started anew in Jackson. I made good friends on Guynes Street, my children flourished, and I became more confident than ever as a wife and mother. And we had an upright piano, which provided hours of pleasure for me.

The competition in our neighborhood was fierce but all in good spirit — and, to me, very familiar. Just as my grandmother and her friends had done, we compared gardens, children, clothes, even outdoor Christmas decorations. Every December, we would all take part in a citywide contest and would exhibit large plywood greeting cards on our lawns, along with Nativity scenes and other holiday ornaments. Our little enclave was unbeatable, repeatedly judged best in the Black community; and each year the displays grew more elaborate. Guynes Street eventually became an attraction for all of Jackson — including Whites — to enjoy. In fact, during the fifties, our Christmas contests were one of the few Negro festivities that the mainstream press would cover.

Medgar and I spent little on furnishings, but in the corner of our living room sat a thirteen-inch Philco TV. Medgar was a news addict; he especially enjoyed Edward R. Murrow. We watched Ed Sullivan's *Toast of the Town* together and, during the day, I was drawn into the saga of *As the World Turns*. Our house was also full of books and magazines, sheet music and records — not just classical but jazz, rhythm and blues, and by the early sixties, Motown.

We had fun in those years, particularly when we went out and could avoid the constantly ringing telephone. There weren't many public places open to us, except on the rare "Negro days" at the zoo or the fairgrounds. Most often, we went to friends' homes for dinner. Medgar and I even had a few White friends, although whenever we paid a visit we had to park our car a block away and slink into their homes. We took the children on family picnics and Sunday drives, or took trips to Sterling Lake, where we barbecued hot dogs or munched on peanut butter and jelly sandwiches. Medgar often took them out in a rowboat and fished, while I sat on the shore, safe from drowning and snakes, of which I was deathly afraid.

Medgar was a wonderful father, different with each of our three. Darrell — his "big boy" — was the child Medgar raced with, the one he knew would grow up to be a football player. Medgar pushed Darrell, and pushed hard. He taught him how to cut our thick St. Augustine grass when Darrell was barely tall enough to reach the handles of the lawn mower. I often argued, "Don't force all of these man things on him right now — let him be a child. He'll have to deal with life's hardships soon enough." But Medgar was determined that Darrell be "prepared."

Medgar called Reena Denise "Punkin" and "Sunshine," and she was, without a doubt, Daddy's darling daughter. Anything Reena asked for, she received. Medgar simply couldn't say no to her when she looked at him with those big eyes. When Medgar sat on the piano bench and did leg lifts, Reena would say, "Please, Daddy, let me sit on your feet." And he did, delighting her as he strengthened his abdomen.

Van was clearly our baby. Six and a half years younger than his siblings, he was the child I schemed to conceive. Even though I knew Medgar had no plans for another child, I stopped using birth control because my body cried out for another child. "You are *what?*" he said in disbelief when I told him I might be pregnant. He left the house and didn't call all day. When he came back that night, no words were spoken between us. The next morning we ate in silence, and then he went to work, forgoing our customary kiss, ignoring the pact we'd made never to part in anger.

A few hours later, the phone started ringing, friends and NAACP workers in Jackson calling to congratulate me. I knew Medgar couldn't have been that angry if he'd shared the news so quickly. Still, when he came home that evening, he continued to act as if he were.

"Cut the nonsense," I finally said to him after an hour of his impenetrable silence. "You might as well stop acting, because I know you've already told everyone in town that I'm pregnant." All was forgiven and forgotten, and Medgar enjoyed feeling my bulging middle as he did with the first two — we were both sure it was a girl, and even referred to "her" as "Wendy." I cherish one of Medgar's letters from the road, written a few months before Van was born, in which he asks, "How are you and the little one?"

Although we tried to give the children a normal life, ours was anything but, and I knew they felt the danger. They saw college students who dared to sit at the counter in Woolworth's covered in ketchup and syrup by angry Whites. They saw images of police brutality and mass arrests on TV. They sat at our dinner table and listened as Medgar and others engaged in heated discussions about church burnings, the Ku Klux Klan, lynchings. They knew that whenever someone was in danger, Medgar would leave our house dressed in "come down" clothes — tattered overalls and a straw hat. Medgar told them he needed his disguises to help people and that he and others had formed a kind of underground railroad, transporting people — sometimes, in the trunk of our car — to safe houses and, eventually, out of Mississippi.

Medgar patiently and expertly helped the children understand that we lived in a state and in a country where people of our color were severely mistreated. On our Sunday drives, he often made a point of passing by parks, swimming pools, libraries, stadiums, or restaurants — places we weren't allowed to go — explaining that he was working to change things. He watched the news with the children and talked to them about what they saw. Medgar acknowledged that, yes, there were some bad people who might try to hurt them, but he would do all he could to protect them. 🕭

Medgar's starting salary as field secretary was $4,500. I had stopped working after Reena was born, but helped out as Medgar's secretary at the NAACP office. The minute we walked into that building, I became "Mrs. Evers" to him, he "Mr. Evers" to me. That was Medgar — formal and determined to keep our personal life separate from our public life, and thereby to present a proper image to the world. After Van was born, I continued to be a part-time volunteer, helping Medgar with his speeches, typing, and answering phones. I was also the chauffeur, called into service whenever anyone needed to be shuttled to or from the airport. But I began to resent the growing responsibilities of the movement that, increasingly, impinged upon our family life. There was never an evening at home without the phone ringing through dinner and, sometimes, throughout the night — always threats to be dealt with or some need to be met.

And I worried constantly. We couldn't open the newspaper or turn on the TV without hearing that another body was found floating in a river or hanging from a tree or burned beyond recognition. We kept guns in every room; I slept with Medgar's Luger on my nightstand; Medgar had a shotgun poised at his side of the bed. Hanging in the hallway, ironically positioned over a prize bass he once caught at Sterling Lake, was a rifle. Our German shepherd, Heidi, slept outside, ever watchful for intruders.

The greater the demands, the less I saw of Medgar, the heavier the toll on our family, and the angrier I became. The situation began to erode our relationship. And because it took time for me to learn to talk about matters of concern when they happened, my emotions often festered until I lost my temper. My inability to communicate was certainly not Medgar's fault. In fact, he repeatedly urged me, "Myrlie, don't hold things in for months and then explode. Express your feelings, and get it over with." But I couldn't.

My frustration came to a head one day when Medgar called to ask me to prepare an impromptu meal for some NAACP officials from New York, who were in Jackson to attend the annual state conference. "I can't prepare lunch for anyone," I snapped, "because I don't have anything except a roast in the freezer."

"What do you mean, you don't have any food?" Medgar snarled at me through the phone. I could just imagine the veins popping in his muscular neck, beads of sweat on his forehead. Requesting a spur-of-the-moment meal wasn't unusual for Medgar, nor did he think it odd. Mother Jessie was a fabulous cook and often created a miraculous meal out of nothing. Moreover, we frequently entertained officials from the NAACP headquarters in New York, as well as celebrities like Lena Horne and Dick Gregory who came to Mississippi to lend their support. Unwelcome in restaurants or clubs, we had nowhere else to host them except our own homes. On this particular day, however, I balked at the idea of an impromptu feast.

"You heard me," I repeated through my teeth. "I don't have any food."

"Well, what did you do with the money I gave you?"

"What money?" I asked, sure that he couldn't be referring to the meager twenty-five-dollar allowance he passed along every two weeks to provide for our children and run a household. I had spent the morning on my hands and knees, scrubbing and waxing our hardwood floors in a house with no heat. If it rained hard, the heating unit under the house often flooded. I had taken the children to Vicksburg so that they could be warm. Hearing Medgar's tone was like having salt poured into an open wound. I slammed down the receiver.

Medgar, who seldom left the office during a workday, especially in the midst of important meetings, appeared in our kitchen minutes later, demanding an explanation for my attitude. To his amazement, I was ready with another question. "Now, why would you ask me what I did with *your* money?" I asked curtly.

Unfazed, he retorted, "There's no evidence that you've spent it wisely."

"A lot you know," I said. "You know nothing about running a household. We're poor, and I'm stretching *our* money as far as I can."

Medgar raised his hand, his face red with anger. I thought he was going to slap me. I remembered what Daddy had taught me: Always strike first — and hard. I reached for the closest weapon I could spot — the empty cast-iron skillet on the stove — and I swung it in

Medgar's direction as hard as my five-foot-six, 120-pound frame would allow.

The small but heavy pan connected with Medgar's temple. Astonished, he tripped backward, his eyes wide as globes. Shocked, each of us stood there in dead silence, staring at the other. He had questioned my honesty and my abilities; I had challenged his authority. Then, suddenly, Medgar retaliated, landing a large open palm on my left cheek. Every pincurl in my hair went flying. I stumbled against the washer and dryer, stunned more emotionally than physically.

Medgar and I looked at each other in disbelief. How had we let the growing pressures and personal tension reach this point? Finally, he turned around and left in a daze, returning to his meetings with a large knot on his head. I wondered how he would explain his appearance to his colleagues. I was worried about what people might think and that I might have hurt him physically. My striking him happened in a moment of sheer madness; his striking me was something he would never have done without provocation. I realized I needed to reassess my life and my marriage.

That evening, after crying and praying and crying some more, I sat in the back of a Greyhound bus to Vicksburg, full of dread. I was Black and a woman, and it was late at night, which made for a very dangerous situation, but all I knew for sure was that I needed to be with my children. It was close to midnight when I arrived, and my aunt and grandmother knew something was wrong. But I said little, for I remembered Mama's warning me many years before: Don't ever talk to family about the state of your marriage; you'll make up with your husband and perhaps forget about it, but they won't. It was good advice. Partners need to work out their own marital problems — with each other.

Medgar called the next day. "How are my children?" he asked coldly. "I want to speak to them." Without another word, I handed the phone to Darrell. Mama and Auntie watched the drama silently, but the look they gave each other told me exactly what they thought.

The following night Medgar appeared at the door with Clarence Mitchell, then director of the Washington bureau of the NAACP.

Naturally, everyone was polite. My aunt and grandmother were honored to have Mr. Mitchell, whose reputation preceded him, in their home. He was so influential that he was known on Capitol Hill as "the 101st senator."

While Medgar played with the kids and chatted amiably with Aunt Myrlie, Mr. Mitchell deftly ushered me into the kitchen for a private conversation. To the young marrieds in the movement, he was like a father, always there to counsel us and to commiserate, for he truly understood the burden of our dedication — low salaries, coupled with so little time for family.

"I know what you're going through," Mr. Mitchell said sincerely. "I'm so sorry that it has reached this point." He paused and then asked, "You know how much you mean to Medgar, don't you? You know how important your marriage is to him?"

"Well . . . ," I answered hesitantly, "he has an odd way of showing it." Tears formed in my eyes, but I was too proud to cry. "I love Medgar, too," I admitted, "but maybe that isn't enough."

Mr. Mitchell called Medgar in. "It would be criminal if you two fine people, who love each other as much as you do, let the stress of this job tear you apart." (Years later, speaking at Clarence's funeral, I credited that dear man for his clarity and wise advice.)

We knew he was right. But at that moment Medgar and I were still too angry to reconcile. I, for one, needed time to think. What was it I wanted from our marriage? And what did I want for my own life? Those are questions every woman must ask herself. Until that point, I had deferred to Medgar — his ideas, his visions, his decisions. Granted, he had helped me mature, and I was grateful for that. But when would it be time to honor *my* needs? I didn't want to be the helpless little woman anymore. I wanted my name on the checkbook. I wanted to manage the bills. I wanted time set aside for the two of us so that we could nurture ourselves as well as our family. I wanted privacy, and a break from the daily demands of the movement.

"Some changes will have to be made here," I informed him a day later, when we were back in Jackson. "On both of our parts. Otherwise, we may have to go our separate ways." Would I really have left?

At that point in the marriage — four years before he died — maybe not. I was only twenty-six and still dependent on Medgar, but that discussion was clearly a turning point for both of us.

"Myrlie, I can't fight White people, fight with my own people to get them to challenge the system, and then come home and fight with you," said Medgar. "Either you are with me or you aren't. That's your decision." I knew what he needed from me, and I had finally articulated what I needed from him. Clearly, I was aware of the pros and cons of our situation, but my abiding love for him and our children made the decision easy. We would work together as a team, both of us giving and taking as we grew together.

In truth, during the early years of our marriage, I had been a bit frightened when Medgar urged my independence. He repeatedly reminded me, "You must get a degree," always adding, "I have to keep the promise I made to your grandmother." As in our Mound Bayou days, money stood in the way; by the time we moved to Jackson, I also had two very young babies at home. But gradually I began to want to stretch for myself, not just to please Medgar. For years I had been content to sit in the shadow of my husband. Now, at last, I was ready to step out — an equal in our relationship.

On the surface, our marriage didn't change much after our brief estrangement. I was still ironing the white shirts he wore daily, managing our home, caring for the children, and forever being hostess and chauffeur. Medgar's work still came between us — in fact, more than ever. But I was more in control and therefore *felt* different about myself and my marriage. Also, Medgar was constantly evolving — that was one of the things I had always loved about him. Because we loved each other dearly, we worked hard to make our marriage succeed.

I have no idea what the future might have held for Medgar and me. I do know that marriage causes both parties to grow, sometimes together, sometimes apart, but always changing and expanding. In the mix of two lives come joy and pain, blessings and tragedies, advantages and loss. Especially when it comes to the rough spots, we can't control what happens, only how we react. Ultimately, we all must choose: to sink or to keep swimming. ⅔

By 1960, when Van was born, Medgar had begun to achieve considerable success. Not so incidentally, in the same year John F. Kennedy was elected president and the first lunch-counter sit-ins were launched. Two years later came one of Medgar's sweetest victories: James Meredith was admitted to Ole Miss, the school that had refused Medgar in 1954. Meredith, a sophomore at all-Black Jackson State, had come to Medgar in 1961, saying that he wanted to transfer. Medgar, in turn, contacted Thurgood Marshall and Constance Baker Motley, the principal trial lawyer for the NAACP's Legal Defense Fund, who during her distinguished career argued ten civil rights cases in the Supreme Court, winning nine of them. The resulting confrontation was as close to war as a civil action could get, but in September of 1962, after the beatings and the tear gas, the federal troops and the mass arrests, Meredith was enrolled.

Medgar Evers had long been a force in Mississippi, but with this victory, a clear defeat for Governor Ross Barnett and the Citizens' Council, he earned the renewed respect of his peers and the formidable, ever-spiraling hatred of segregationists.

By now I lived with constant apprehension, often in terror. When I went out, I felt only slightly safer when our dog, Heidi, was in the car with me. The police constantly trailed me, almost bumper to bumper, with their own snarling dog — pure and simple harassment. I could not allow the children to play outside without fear, and could not even let them answer the phone. It was difficult enough for me to hear taunts like, "Black bitch — you got another one of them niggers in your belly?" Worse than the obscenities, though, were the anonymous voices, threatening to blow the house up or to cut Medgar into little pieces. Those calls always ended with some version of the same warning: "If he don't stop it, you're never gonna see that so-and-so nigger again."

When real emergency calls came in the middle of the night, Medgar dressed in one of his disguises and left us to investigate yet another horrible brutality or to shepherd some poor soul out of Mississippi before the Klan found him. He averaged thirty-five or forty thousand miles a year in his pale blue '61 Oldsmobile.

If Medgar was frightened, he never showed it, but he was clearly exhausted by it all. His nerves were so frayed that one evening, thinking he heard a prowler, he jumped out of bed and grabbed his shotgun only to find himself aiming it at Darrell, who had gotten up to go to the bathroom. After putting our son back to bed, we wept together, overwhelmed by how close to tragedy we had come.

Regardless of such scares, Medgar was resigned to the fact that changing Mississippi was his mission in life. Nothing could make him quit. "If I go tonight, if I go next week, if I go next year, I'm ready," he told me late one night when he couldn't sleep. Our last months together were punctuated by talks of the inevitability of his being hunted down. He knew he was a wanted man and, in the minds of Mississippi racists, better off dead.

Medgar felt that the best he could do for his family was prepare us for the worst. And prepare us he did. One day he came home to find me on our brown velveteen couch with my back to a window. "Keep sitting there," he said, "and you're going to have your head blown off one of these days." He repeatedly stressed how important it was for me to be vigilant about security. (How right he was; that was the same window the assassin's bullet tore through after hitting Medgar.)

With the children, Daddy's "training" was turned into a game. I still remember their wide-eyed innocence as Medgar put them through their paces, teaching them to listen for the sound of cars passing by and to fall to the floor when they heard loud noises. He showed them how to crawl on their bellies, like he did when he was in the army.

"Where is the safest place in the house to go if you hear gunshots?" he asked Darrell and Reena. "How do you get there?" Then he took them by their little hands and explored every nook and cranny of our small home.

"The bathtub, Daddy," Darrell said proudly. "The bathtub," Reena mimicked.

"That's right!" Medgar replied. "Now remember, both of you, look out for your little brother. Whenever you hide, always take him with you."

Late one night, I heard the sound of a familiar car that frequently paused in front of the house. I turned out the bedroom light and waited, as Medgar had instructed. I thought that in a few minutes, the car would leave, just as it had in the past. But this time the silence ended with an earsplitting blast. Someone had thrown a Molotov cocktail, which crashed into the carport and burst into flames only inches from our doorstep, where poor Heidi was on guard, waiting for Medgar to return.

Instinctively, I rushed outside in my slip, grabbed the hose, and tried to extinguish the fire which, mercifully, was not spreading. I wondered if the children were awakened, and then shuddered at my own vulnerability. What if the bomb had been intended to lure me outside? Killing me would certainly send a potent message to Medgar.

When he got the news, Medgar called our next-door neighbor, Houston Wells. Learning that we were all right, my media-savvy husband stayed at the office long enough to call his contacts, so that the incident would be covered in the press the next day. To Medgar, every event, even this one, was an opportunity to bring attention to the cause. Ironically, I often nagged him because he never put himself in those reports. This time, although I was annoyed that he didn't come straight home, I was secretly pleased that finally *his* name would be in the headlines.

When Medgar at last arrived, the police were still in the driveway. He got out of the car, walked to me, and enveloped me with his strong arms. "Are you sure you and the children are okay?" he asked.

I nodded, squeezed his waist tightly, and put my head on his shoulder. "Please, just talk to *them*," I said, gesturing toward the two White police officers in our carport who, allegedly, were looking for more "evidence."

Medgar walked over to the police, and I could tell from their body language and gestures that they were saying something to him about me. When they left — declaring the incident "a prank" — Medgar and I went inside to check on the children, who miraculously had slept through the whole traumatic event.

"The police told me you cursed them," Medgar said, as he closed the door to the children's room. I explained what had happened — how the policemen had found the remains of a broken brown half-gallon bottle, a charred kerosene-soaked rag in its neck. "Seeing the gasoline we used for our lawn mower, they practically accused me of setting the fire myself!" I exclaimed, bursting into tears, the enormity of what had happened finally hitting me. "The children were here in the house. Yes, I cursed them, and I wanted to do more."

I looked up at him, only to see a smile break across his face. With a slight chuckle, he said, "Curse? But you can't curse." In the best of times, and in the worst of times, Medgar loved to tease me. The diversion worked, and, remembering our early marriage when in anger I had unsuccessfully tried to curse at *him*, we both erupted into gales of laughter.

Our life changed in the wake of that firebomb. Poor Heidi was never the same, becoming jumpy and mean. And although the children didn't witness the incident, they had to walk past the scorched exterior walls and charred concrete and smell the lingering odor of gasoline for months after that. I'd try to pretend it was business as usual, but in truth the incident stripped my last shreds of denial. It also showed Medgar that his wife had, indeed, learned to speak up for herself. Although we didn't know exactly when he would be killed, we knew his life was in danger. During the early years of our marriage, Medgar had asked repeatedly, "Myrlie, isn't there *anything* you believe in strongly enough to stand up and fight for it?" Now, when the enemy stood at our door, putting our children's very lives at risk, I could finally answer, "Yes."

Perhaps I was also getting bolder because I realized that more was at stake. I was pregnant again. If Medgar was worried about the burden of bringing a fourth child into this world, that concern was overshadowed by the terror that blanketed our lives. So much else was happening, we barely had a moment to talk about a new baby. We weren't living a day at a time at that point, we were living a minute at a time.

One night in early June of 1963, Medgar came home from the NAACP office looking particularly tired and dejected. The tension was intensifying in Mississippi, with Blacks becoming increasingly aggressive and Whites digging in their heels to uphold segregation. Medgar had been under tremendous pressure from all sides. A successful boycott of all the shops on Capitol Street — the downtown shopping area — had inspired college students to stage a series of lunch-counter sit-ins. Although the NAACP had already defended a number of these cases, the organization had been founded on the belief that abuses are best remedied through the courts, not in the streets. The New York office questioned the wisdom of such tactics, fearing that the young people's need for bail money would overtax the organization's budget. Gloster Current, then director of branches, was sent from New York to discuss this issue as well as the infighting among the various civil rights organizations. It was feared that the NAACP's staid approach was being overshadowed by the more visible tactics of CORE (Congress of Racial Equality) and SNCC (Student Nonviolent Coordinating Committee), the younger, more vocal groups behind the sit-ins.

Besides politics, the meeting with Gloster Current had another item on the agenda: to request protection for Medgar, who had made it to the top of every racist hit list in the state. Medgar's close friends who had volunteered to be his security force, particularly at night, felt the heat rising in Jackson and knew that Medgar needed a full-time bodyguard. They were willing to take money out of their own pockets to help hire someone, and they asked Current if the national office would allocate funds to match whatever they put up.

"No," Gloster replied flatly, "the NAACP has more important things to do with its money."

Medgar was more despondent that night than I had ever seen him. He had aged ten years in the preceding months. As he related what happened at the meeting, tears trickled down his cheeks. I was livid that the NAACP put so little value on Medgar's life.

"It's okay," he reassured. "When my time comes, I'm going to go regardless of the protection I have. Besides, I don't want anyone to get hurt trying to save me."

A few days later, Medgar was murdered. ⟡

I wanted to die too. For the first year after Medgar's assassination, I didn't think I had the strength to keep going. In my darkest moments,

I floated through my day, barely keeping my life on track. Friends cooked for us, did errands, helped out with the children, and most of them believed I was holding up miraculously well.

I made myself available to the NAACP, exhorting others to join the organization and giving speeches that inspired people to dig deep into their wallets. In that first year, I brought thousands of dollars into the organization — the 1963 effort still stands out as one of the NAACP's most successful fund-raising and membership drives. However, the work involved my traveling a great deal. Mama came to Jackson to help out with the children, or I'd take them to stay with Aunt Myrlie and her in Vicksburg, but I was away from home more than I wanted.

On more than one occasion, alone in the car on the way back to Jackson, I sped heedlessly over Highway 80, which was then a steep, winding, two-lane road. I'd pass cars, weave in and out of traffic, endangering myself and, I'm ashamed to admit, putting other people's lives in jeopardy as well. I'd press my foot to the pedal, watch the speedometer climb to 80, 85, 90, and imagine myself crashing over an embankment or into one of the huge pine trees that lined the narrow shoulder of the road.

I believed my loss was simply too painful to bear.

I seriously contemplated taking my life, but I also worried about what losing another parent would do to Darrell, Reena, and Van. *Someone will take care of them,* I rationalized. I was thankful that within a month after Medgar's murder, I had miscarried; at least I didn't have an infant to consider. Aunt Myrlie and Mama were getting on in years, so I decided that the best place for the children would be with my sister-in-law Nan, Charles's wife, who was closer to my age and had three children of her own. I even talked to her about caring for them if "something happened."

That's the way I phrased it, but Nan was savvy; she knew how depressed I was. "Yes, I'll take care of them, but only if I have to," she said. "In the meantime, you have to take care of yourself and handle your pain. Your children need *you*, not someone else, to rear them."

I heard her, and I knew she was right. I had promised Medgar as much. All the same, I had no control over the shroud that enveloped me. I kept taking foolish risks on the road, and I also began stockpiling the sleeping pills my doctor had prescribed for what we then called "nerves." He had wisely doled them out one at a time. "Have a cocktail or two in the evening," he suggested as well. "That also might help you sleep." But I wasn't a drinker, and I knew alcohol wouldn't dull my grief. Drink or no drink, whenever I closed my eyes, I saw Medgar, I felt his body, I felt the warmth of his kisses, and I relived his death in all its terrible vividness — the shot, the sight of his body, his blood oozing into the armful of white "Jim Crow must go" T-shirts he had been carrying, my screams, the lights, the sirens. I saw it over and over in my mind, a nightmare that just wouldn't quit.

Every now and then, I'd pull out the little container hidden in my lingerie drawer, empty the growing stash of pills into my palm, and count them, wondering, *Do I have enough?* I told no one of my pain or my plan. Instead, I continued to smile and say I was fine. I thanked people for being there, and assured them that if I needed help, I'd call.

One day, after I dropped the two older children off at school, I put Van, who had fallen asleep on the ride home, on the bed and opened the top drawer of my night table. I poured the pills into my hand and raised the hand to my mouth, but I could go no further. For some reason — divine intervention, I'm sure — I simply couldn't act on my intention. More important, I then looked at Van, adorable, peaceful, just lying there in all his three-year-old innocence.

"I can't do this," I said out loud. If I were to kill myself, Van would be the one to find me. I pictured him trying to wake me up, crying because I wouldn't move. Imagining that and then thinking of the pain my older two would suffer, I shuddered at my own cruelty and selfishness. I couldn't do this to them either. Or to Medgar. Or to myself.

From that day forward, I vowed that I'd stop courting danger on the road and that somehow I would go on. I knew I had to be strong. But the devastation and the depression were far from over. I was at the bottom of a deep, dark pit, struggling to climb out, and life kept battering me downward. But the public could not know. The strong widow image had to prevail. ❧

Among those of a certain age, who doesn't remember where he or she was on November 22, 1963? I was at the hairdresser's; it was barely five months after Medgar had been shot when an announcement interrupted the music: "President Kennedy is dead." I gasped, covered my mouth with my hand, and slumped forward, cradling myself with crossed arms. I couldn't even drive myself home.

Only weeks before, giving a speech in front of a crowd of civil rights sympathizers, I had said, "This country is out of control. Where are we heading?" Pausing, I then uttered a slow, deliberately dramatic line that several newspapers and magazines across the country reprinted: "If this happened to Medgar, it could happen to anyone, including the president of the United States."

The night Medgar was killed, the children and I had been watching the president on television, as he assured the American public that he intended to pass legislation guaranteeing Negroes the full rights of citizenship. Civil rights hadn't been a big priority when he came into office, but Kennedy slowly became our hope, the first American president to promise such sweeping reform. I had met him the day after Medgar was buried at Arlington, Virginia, when he invited the children and me to the White House, where he paid us his respects. I remembered thinking to myself that he looked so much older in person. *He's aged in his job,* I thought, *just as Medgar did.*

When I arrived home the day of Kennedy's assassination, I pulled out the letter he had sent after Medgar's death and found myself reading and rereading the poignant handwritten postscript: "Mrs. Kennedy joins me in tendering her deepest sympathy." Now I had to send a note to her.

I watched television almost constantly during the next days, and while I wept, many in Mississippi rejoiced. The "nigger-lover" was dead. Shouts of jubilation rang in the schools, echoing in the hallways and out into the yards. The principal of the local high school announced over the PA system that everyone could go home, as if a holiday had been declared. Radio stations played Dixie, the anthem of the Confederacy. Seeing people pouring into the streets, cheering and glorifying Kennedy's murder, only made the horror more painful.

What a cruel irony that neither he nor Medgar lived to see the passage of the Civil Rights Bill in 1964.

Two years later, Malcolm X was murdered and three years after that, Martin Luther King and Bobby Kennedy. When their husbands were killed, I was a distant admirer of Coretta Scott King and Betty Shabazz, never having met either woman in person. I remember seeing Betty on television in 1965 after Malcolm was shot. Her children had witnessed their father's assassination, just as mine had heard the shot and seen Medgar lying in a pool of his own blood. Betty was pregnant, as I had been when Medgar was killed, and she instinctively fell over her children in the seconds prior to the shooting. "I heard the footsteps of men running up toward him," she said.

I knew exactly what she meant. The commotion first, and then the shots. When you lived the way we did, you knew how to interpret every sound. You were forced to be so acutely aware of your surroundings that your sense of smell, of sight, of hearing, became almost superhuman. Not surprisingly, in the years to come, Coretta, Betty, and I became close friends. We knew, as no one else did, what our common pasts had done to us and to our families. ❧

The children and I remained in Jackson for a year after Medgar was killed. Mississippi was boiling over — the fever had broken shortly before Medgar was shot and erupted into a widespread epidemic of chaos after his assassination. He wasn't the first to lose his life in the battle, but he was nationally known, and his death upped the ante on both sides. During that year, and especially the following summer, the state was overrun with "outside agitators," as the locals liked to call the Freedom Riders and other northerners who joined us to wage the good fight. When I addressed the NAACP convention in June of 1964, shortly after Andrew Goodman and Michael Schwerner, two college students from New York, and James Chaney, a civil rights worker from Mississippi, had disappeared, I said, "We should have known this would happen again." I didn't hold out much hope for those young men. Their bodies were found a few weeks later.

I knew I needed to move my children and myself to a different environment. I couldn't purge my memory any more than I could scrub the blood from our concrete walkway or patch the bullet holes in my walls and my refrigerator. Signs of Medgar's life as well as his death were everywhere in the house. A plum tree in our yard bore fruit he didn't live long enough to taste — just as the movement was now bearing the fruit of his labors. The children and I had planted an oak tree in front of the house in his memory, and it was thriving. The question was, how would *we* four thrive?

The student at work at Claremont College.

3

WINGING IT

Survival and
the single parent

With Reena, Van, and Darrell in Claremont, before a portrait of
their father.

Forgiving is not forgetting; it's letting go of the hurt.

🕊 *Mary McLeod Bethune*

*L*eaving Mississippi in the summer of 1964 was one of the hardest moves I've ever had to make. I had vacillated about uprooting my family, feeling guilty, confused, and very angry. The day of our departure, the boxes were packed and a moving van waited in front of the house. Reena, not yet ten but already the little mother, was playing with four-year-old Van on the lawn. Darrell, who had just turned eleven, was at camp in the Poconos — a gift from NAACP supporters — and would be flown to California later. Althea Simmons, an attorney and western director of the NAACP, who had come south to help us, hovered nearby as I sat like a zombie on a windowsill, watching my life of twelve and a half years disappear.

Althea's voice echoed in the empty room, interrupting my reverie. "We're ready," she said cheerfully. "Everything's on the van."

I turned to face her, staring through her. "I'm not going," I said. "I cannot leave, I cannot leave." I repeated it over and over. "I can't leave Medgar. I'm being unfaithful to him. Who will carry on his work?"

Althea answered by taking my arm and leading me out the door. I was like a mule, pulling back, shouting, "No! I'm not leaving."

But leave I did, livid though I was at her urging. The four of us drove away in Medgar's light blue Oldsmobile, and in the rearview mirror Guynes Street disappeared, then Jackson, then Mississippi. I didn't speak to Althea until we arrived in Dallas, where we stopped at a hotel and stayed the night.

The next day, Althea took me to Neiman Marcus. In one of the display windows sat a huge crystal bowl that held different-colored cashmere sweaters, rolled into little balls to look like scoops of ice

cream — a rich man's sundae. On top sat the "cherry," a gold ring
with huge diamonds and rubies in it. I had never seen an image quite
like it, even in a magazine. For the moment at least, my amazement
melted away my anger and infused me with hope. In times of trouble,
I've always looked for signs from God. Was this one? *Myrlie*, I said to
myself, looking at the display and shaking my head in wonder, *there's
another world out there. Explore it.* ୧

In the wake of a crisis, whether it's a loved one's untimely death, the
shock of an unexpected divorce, or financial reversals, there are
always critical but painful decisions to be made. How do I carry on?
What do I want out of life? In what direction should I go? Such questions are the foundation of identity, the very core of one's being.
When you're forced, as I was, to make a monumental change, the
challenges feel most dramatic, but in actuality, the process of defining
one's self continues throughout life, in both obvious and subtle ways.

We grow, we move ahead, and we look back — ideally, not in
regret but to see and appreciate where we've come from. When
Medgar died, when Mississippi became no longer tolerable, I had to
face reality. Since then, whenever I've come upon other major and
minor crossroads in my life, I have had to do the same. No one could
make crucial decisions for me, no one could show me the way. I also
learned that life without risk is no life at all. In retrospect, it's quite
clear: I made my choices, finding solace in the support of friends, in
prayer, and in the knowledge that if, in fact, I did make a mistake, I'd
always be given another chance. With God's help, I've been down
many roads; with God's help, I'll see where the next one leads me.

In the months prior to our departure, Aunt Myrlie, eager to help,
had evicted one of her tenants and completely renovated the house
for us. She and Mama would take care of the children while I went
back to school. But I feared forever being viewed as nothing more
than Mrs. Beasley's granddaughter, Mrs. Polk's niece — the unfortu-
nate widow of Medgar Evers, retreating to the bosom of her family.
Worse, I knew I would have no control over my own life, let alone
my children's. Every decision I had to make would be subject to

discussion, debate, and, most likely, well-intentioned orders. After all, Mama and Auntie still thought I was their "baby."

I briefly considered New York, where the NAACP had been founded and still had its main headquarters, but California, a state Medgar often visited on behalf of the NAACP, seemed the better choice. Since 1940, hundreds of thousands of Negroes had migrated there from the South, nearly half of them settling in Los Angeles. The city's Black population had multiplied eightfold in twenty-odd years. Though racial discrimination was not as blatant as in the South, conditions in Los Angeles mirrored some of its worst problems, including poor schools, high unemployment, police harassment, and few opportunities for safe, clean housing. At the same time, the Black community had been able to make considerable inroads politically, forging mutually beneficial alliances with White liberals. By 1963 three Blacks had been elected to the city council, including Tom Bradley, who later became the city's first Black mayor. Clearly, while there was still room for improvement, Los Angeles had great potential for reform.

Prior to moving, I had made three trips to explore Los Angeles, and Althea Simmons, who knew the city well, acted as my guide. As she shuttled me in and around Los Angeles to see where the children and I might live, she gave me a crash course in local politics. The vast majority of the city's nearly 600,000 Negroes lived in Watts or in smaller Black communities. Gangs were becoming more prominent at the time. That wasn't how I imagined my children — Medgar's children — growing up. I wanted to expand our horizons.

Althea drove as far north as Santa Barbara and as far south as San Diego, but it was Claremont, to the east, that stole my heart. Forty minutes from Los Angeles and situated on the lower slopes of the San Gabriel Mountains, the city had tree-lined streets, plentiful parks, and well-maintained homes, all conveying a sense of safety and propriety. All over the country that year, juvenile delinquency was on the rise and racial tension was increasing, but Claremont, with its population of approximately 20,000, appeared to be untouched by the strife. It was clean — very little smog — and (thanks to its founding fathers) seemed more like a neat, self-contained New England town than a sprawling city.

Housing was certainly more reasonably priced than in comparable New York City suburbs, and the local schools were superb. Reading the variety of cultural events, courses, and extracurricular activities open to children and families, I was overwhelmed. The city was home to the six Oxford-inspired Claremont Colleges. The oldest of them, Pomona, had been cited in a recent copy of *Kiplinger's* as one of the nation's best small colleges. Even better, the article mentioned that the school was "looking for minority students." Still, the decision wasn't easy. I knew only one person in California, while I had dozens of connections in New York — people in the NAACP but also friends from college who had migrated there from Mississippi.

My grandmother and aunt believed that, in the end, I chose the West Coast because it was as far away from Mississippi as I could go without leaving the country. There's some truth to that, but mostly I opted for California because I thought Medgar would approve. For a long time after he died, I had his voice in my head, and I made decisions based on what I thought he'd want me to do. After months of wavering, one day I stood in my backyard, under the shade of Medgar's plum tree. "Well, Medgar," I said, looking up, "California is the only other place you ever considered. You said we'd move there if we ever left Mississippi. So . . . I guess California it is." ᴈ

It was only after I signed the contract of sale for our new home that I discovered that Claremont was lily-white. I had seen Black people on the streets when visiting there with Althea, but I didn't realize that during our drives through the area we had crossed the invisible line into the neighboring city of Pomona. Of course Althea knew, but the racial divide was not important to her, and she never mentioned it. Claremont's advantages and its benefits to the children and me were her only concern. However, members of the local NAACP were appalled and furious when they heard I had decided to live there. What was wrong with living in Pomona? Did I think I was better than they were? Was I trying to separate myself? The criticism stung, and I came close to forfeiting my down payment. But I loved Claremont and stood up for my right to choose where and how I wanted to live — another step toward independence.

Long after we moved, in fact, some Black friends continued to criticize me for bringing my children into a primarily White community. "Don't they feel out of place?" they asked. "How will they get to know their own people, their own culture?" My answer then is my answer today: I wanted the best for my children — the best schools, the best opportunities, and those things happened to be in Claremont.

I certainly did not want to *be* White and would not trade my blackness for anything in the world, nor would my children. But I left Mississippi because I wanted my Darrell, Reena, and Van to have a world of choice. We took frequent trips into Los Angeles to socialize with friends in the African-American community, to attend ethnic events and museums, and to eat in Mexican, Greek, French, and Italian restaurants (where, to my dismay, the children always wanted hamburgers!).

Prior to our moving to the house on Northwestern Drive, only one other Black family — a doctor, his wife, and their children — lived in Claremont, a city that viewed itself as very "liberal." But that family had little interaction with the locals; the children went to a private school and did most of their socializing in Los Angeles. Hearing news of our arrival, some Claremont residents were concerned that Blacks from Mississippi might overrun the place. Others were genuinely concerned about our well-being. Aware of the controversy, city officials held several town meetings to head off potential problems.

All but a few of the families on our street and in the immediate area welcomed us cordially. The people next door, who had tried to talk their neighbors out of selling their home to me, immediately put their house on the market. Another couple tried to prevent their children from playing with mine. Children being children, of course, all of them ultimately played with whomever they wanted. Over that first year, a few more of the intolerant left for whiter valleys, and the opposition quieted down.

Inside me, a war was raging as well. Although I knew that, regardless of race, there were good and bad people, I expected the worst from Whites. I believed that the White power structure in Mississippi had engineered my husband's murder and then allowed his assassin to go free. By the time we moved to Claremont, a year and a month after his death, I didn't just have a chip on my shoulder, I carried a log. In my emotional turmoil, I cast a blanket of blame over an entire race.

I didn't try to hide my anger. "Was Claremont as generous in its welcome of the other Black family?" I snidely asked one of my new neighbors. "How did you treat *them?*" On open-school night, I kept track of how much time the teacher spent with each set of parents and compared how long she spoke with me. At PTA meetings, I marched right up to the front of the room and took a seat in the first row, just to make sure everyone knew I was there. I was hypersensitive, defiant, ready for a fight. I had *attitude*. And guess what? No one cared. No one wanted to fight back.

In fact, most of the people in Claremont overextended themselves in welcoming us. So many brought casseroles the first month we were there, I never had to cook dinner. Many women dropped by to say hello or to see if there was anything the children and I needed. Several offered to take the kids on outings; Skip Meury, the Congregationalist minister's wife, and later a dear friend, even toted them off to Disneyland with her own brood.

Eventually, I began to see that most people in Claremont meant well. More important, I began to change *my* attitude, albeit slowly and painfully. Where I had once approached each new person or situation with skepticism, I tried to keep an open mind. It took decades for my anger to disappear completely, but at least it started to soften around the edges as I attempted to judge people as individuals. Medgar had taught me that meeting hate with hate and anger with anger only poisons your own being and has no effect on your enemies.

Situations arose to test me. For example, a few months after we arrived, I explored the churches in the area. At my visit to the Baptist church, which was predominantly White, everyone tendered a warm welcome to me except one woman, who literally recoiled when I extended my hand to her. "Ooh, I don't want to *touch* you," she said, as if my color would rub off on her. I stepped toward her, giving it a second try. Oh, the devil in me! She nearly fell into the shrubbery backing up to avoid me. I laughed at the sight of her. I had met enough wonderful people that day not to let a single unenlightened individual spoil it for me.

In the end, we joined the Congregational church in Claremont. Though I was born and bred a Baptist, I once again refused to let color be the determining factor in my choice. It is my belief that, wherever you reside, you have an obligation to become a part of that community. To not join a church in Claremont would have meant I wasn't wholeheartedly committed to living there. Besides, the members were friendly, the music was good, and the minister, Ed Meury, and his wife, Skip, couldn't have been warmer.

Every Sunday, weather permitting, after the service the minister held a reception on the neatly manicured grounds. At first I was nervous among all those strangers, but I knew it was a good way for us to meet people. The children had no trouble; in minutes, they were scampering about on the lawn with the other kids. Still very shy, I pushed myself to say hello to people and to look like I belonged too. Of course, I kept my antennae up as well.

We all have the gift of intuition — the ability to size people up — but rather than making snap judgments based on appearance, we have to pay attention to how we feel in others' presence. Indeed, when you've grown up in a society where you have been put down — and few among us haven't — you come to know if people are being sincere, nasty, or just unenlightened. *You can always tell.* If your conscious mind isn't tuned in, your body inevitably signals you — a rapid heartbeat, sweaty palms, shallow breathing — it's part of our survival instinct. In my case, the hairs on the back of my neck stand up when I sense someone's out to do me in. It then becomes a game, many times a silent one. Oftentimes, in fact, I just smile and allow insincere people to prattle on until they get caught in their own malevolent web; most certifiable bigots eventually do.

That first summer, I enrolled Van in a swimming class with other four-year-old children. Lessons were held at Claremont Men's College in an Olympic-size pool, the surrounding area beautifully landscaped. To avoid the midday sun, mothers sat on a shaded knoll overlooking the pool.

"We are so glad you are here," the other women reassured me the first day. Several began directing friendly questions my way:

"Are you settled in?"

"How do you like Claremont?"

"Have you met many people?"

I answered politely, watching Van out of the corner of my eye, remembering that if we had stayed in Mississippi we wouldn't even have been allowed in the pool. At one point, another mother turned to me with a warm smile on her face, nodded toward the children splashing about, and in all sincerity asked, "And which one is yours?"

I thought to myself, *Listen lady, mine is the only little black dot out there!* If I had felt that she had meant to insult me, I might have spoken my thoughts aloud or come back with some other sarcastic retort, like, "Oh, mine is the blue-eyed blond one over there." But I let it go, because I knew that the woman honestly didn't realize what a blunder she had made. Chances are, later that day she kicked herself. I have to say, though, that remembering that scene still brings a smile to my face.

Certainly there were incidents, most in the form of subtle, behind-the-back comments rather than the kind of in-your-face malice we had experienced in Mississippi. One that stands out happened shortly after the Watts riots in the summer of 1965. Reena and I were riding our bicycles around the neighborhood, enjoying the scenery, talking, having fun together. As we turned a corner, we heard laughing and saw the backs of a group of teenage boys as they ran behind some bushes. From there they shouted, "Nigger, nigger, nigger. Go back to Africa, go back to Africa!" I saw the look of horror on Reena's face; no one had ever been so overtly prejudiced in Claremont.

"Come on, Mom," Reena pleaded, as I stopped my bike and looked toward the bushes. "Let's just go home."

I ignored her. "Come out here," I demanded, knowing full well our harassers were still close enough to hear. Suddenly, I heard a noise on the other side of the street and realized that a man working in his garden had witnessed the entire incident and not said a word.

"Do you know who lives here?" I shouted angrily in his direction.

He admitted, rather sheepishly, that he did, but added, "There's no need to get upset. The parents of those boys are good, decent people. They wouldn't approve."

We rode home in silence. My heart was pounding; I'm sure Reena's was too. The minute I stepped into my house, I called Skip Meury and told her what had happened. "I want to find out who lives there," I insisted. "I intend to call the police and report the incident."

It didn't take long for the story to get around. In fact, the following Sunday, the boys' father stood up in church and apologized for his sons' behavior. That was a small admission for Claremont, but a big victory for us. I was grateful, too, that the incident gave Reena a dose of reality about California. Although there were no cross-burnings or lynchings in Claremont, it was important for her to know we weren't immune to bigotry and discrimination.

Medgar and I taught Darrell, Reena, and Van never to hate a person just because he was White, nor to automatically trust someone just because he was Black. Martin Luther King, Jr., also hoped his children would grow up in a world where people would be "judged by the content of one's character, not the color of one's skin." During our years in Claremont, racism came from both sides. Darrell remembers White boys driving past him, shouting, "Nigger." He dared them to come back and say it to his face, but they kept going, at which point he said to himself, *They're just a bunch of cowards.* And when he was a candidate for the all-league football team, Blacks from Pomona told him, "You're just a Tom — up there with all the White boys."

In any event, my advice was the same: Feel secure in yourself. If you know deep down inside that you're not bad or undesirable, no matter what others say about you, you can walk tall and with your head held high. After all, racial epithets speak volumes about the person uttering them, but nothing about you. 🦋

During our first fall in California, Darrell entered the sixth grade in the Claremont public schools and Reena the fifth, Van began day care, and I enrolled in Pomona College. I took only a small course load at first, both to give myself a chance to get acclimated and to allow time for my NAACP appearances. A decade later, older students going to school after a husband's death, a divorce, or finding themselves in an empty nest or a dead-end job, would be called "reentry women." But when I enrolled at Pomona, "reentry" still referred only to a returning space capsule.

I briefly considered a music major, sparked by my lingering desire to be a concert pianist. But I had three children, and such a career, assuming I could substantially polish my skills to get to a professional level, would mean constant traveling. (Little did I realize then that traveling would become a way of life for me anyway.)

Let's get real, I said to myself. *What is it you can* do? I considered psychology, but that meant studying statistics, and math was unequivocally my worst subject. (It would take another decade for me to discover that not all fears and incompetencies are a function of personal deficits. Women have been trained to avoid certain subjects — namely, the traditional "men's pursuits." In the late seventies, when a corporate employer sent me to the Simmons College middle-management program for women, which included a blitz course in finance, I was surprised to see that *most* of the women needed a refresher in basic math! In part because I realized I wasn't alone, and in part because that professor took the time to explain math properly and without making us feel dense, I broke through what was until then a lifelong fear.) Sociology seemed like the most practical choice, because it meant working with people and studying societal change. However, most of my credits from Alcorn College were not transferable, so I almost had to start my college career completely over.

I vividly remember orientation day, finding my way through a maze of ivy-covered buildings. With only around 1,500 students, Pomona itself was small, but it was set on a verdant 250-acre campus centered around a library and other facilities open to students at any of the six Claremont colleges. As I and some 300 to 400 other students streamed into the massive and imposing dining hall, I felt utterly conspicuous — Black and by comparison old, even though I was only thirty-one.

I averted my eyes to avoid students' stares. Some of them undoubtedly knew who I was; my picture had been in the *Los Angeles*

Times as well as in the local papers. But traditional students were there to study and have fun; the protests that marked the midsixties never seemed to affect this complacent campus. I looked around — some of the students were barefoot and in shorts — and thought to myself, *Good heavens! What am I doing here?* Oddly enough, though I felt grossly out of place and petrified, I was heady with hope. I felt as if I were in a dark hallway, groping my way into a new corridor of my life, but I could glimpse light beyond the doors, and education was the key.

A typical day meant getting the older children off to school, taking Van to day care, and making it to my own classes by nine. Every now and then I had to take Van with me, so I bicycled to campus with him in the child seat attached to the back and with my books in the red-and-green basket on my handlebars. At three o'clock, I picked up Darrell and Reena, came home, cleaned, cooked, helped them with their homework, supervised their bath-and-pajamas routine, prepared lunches for the next day, and went to bed when they did. I set my alarm clocks — actually, I had three, set ten minutes apart — for one or two o'clock in the morning, depending on the volume of homework I had to do. I studied through the night until the children's alarms went off. Then the routine started again.

One of the gifts my grandmother had given me as I was growing up was the discipline to study and to stay with it until the work was finished. She insisted that I sit in a straight-backed chair, with good lighting and with a dictionary at hand. But in the ten years since Alcorn, my study habits had faded. At first, I simply couldn't concentrate, couldn't seem to grasp the concepts. And on weekends, a time I might have used to catch up, I had three young children to care for.

I also felt as if the eyes of the world were upon me. People expected me to do well, and if I failed, I was failing not only myself and my children and Medgar, but the entire race. I was weighed down by insecurity that I had carried since childhood. Except for an occasional B, I had always gotten A's in school. Yet, Mama repeatedly asked why I hadn't done *better*. Although I had been salutatorian in both junior and senior high, I felt as if I had disappointed her. I was never Number One. How could I possibly succeed now? Mama's attitude was only confirmed by my father's comment in the middle of my first year at Pomona: "Why aren't you getting better grades?" asked Daddy. "You should be Phi Beta Kappa."

"Should be," indeed! My family's high standards always provided the basic training and the impetus I needed to survive the hard knocks of my life, but the constant prodding and criticism, however well intentioned, ate away at my self-esteem. I never challenged them or complained until I was close to graduating from Pomona and struggling with one of my last term papers. Aunt Myrlie had come to visit, and I told her, "You know, I never could satisfy Mama, you, or Daddy. I wish you had congratulated me on the A's instead of just questioning the B's. As a result," I explained, "I've been very hard on myself."

That was an understatement. I was brutal on myself and became my own worst enemy, always demanding perfection. Typically, when a question was posed in class, I mulled the material over in my mind and tried to formulate a response, carefully crafting my words. It had to be just so. By the time I was ready with my perfect answer, some bright young student would have already responded and the class had moved on to the next topic.

The daily pressure was overwhelming. My nerves were frayed, and I felt as if I were spinning out of control. A doctor I consulted prescribed Valium. Thereafter, I woke up to a little pink pill, took a second after rushing home from school, and a third before bed. At one point, even though I weighed only 130 pounds — an ideal weight for my frame — he also gave me a prescription for "diet pills" to boost my energy level; they made me feel as if I could go a thousand miles a day and accomplish *anything*. Then I needed something stronger at bedtime to calm me down, so he added a little red pill to my daily routine.

I took each pill according to the doctor's instructions, but the combination often made me feel weird, woozy and nauseated. Even though my druggist questioned the pharmaceutical mix as potentially dangerous, I continued to take the pills because a doctor had assured me that medication was the best way to manage my anxiety. This was long before Betty Ford inspired widespread awareness of addiction to prescription drugs and long before any woman would dare to challenge the authority of a male doctor. I would later learn that my situation was very common; drugs were typically overprescribed for women. Sadly, they still are today.

Eventually, my body rebelled on its own. One evening, after cleaning up the kitchen, I went into my bedroom, sat on the chair next to my bed, and washed down my red pill with a glass of stale water. A few minutes later, I had an out-of-body experience. I felt as if I were floating on the ceiling and could see myself sitting in that chair. I could even see through the walls, see my children in the kitchen, hear them talking. *Am I crazy, or is this real?* I wondered and panicked at the same time. Without thinking, I ran into the bathroom and poured the pinks, the diet pills, and the reds down the toilet. "No more!" I said out loud as I flushed. I knew I finally had to take control. Doctor's advice or not, I told myself, I had to look for better ways to cope. I had come too far — this was no time to self-destruct.

From then on, whenever I found myself with some time to spare between my schedule and the children's, I took my troubles to a secluded spot on nearby Mount Baldy, a peak among the San Gabriel Mountains some twenty minutes from my home. Seated on a cliff, I allowed myself to be lulled by the wonderfully serene sound of the water crashing down on the huge rocks below. I had so rarely given myself the freedom to just *be*. I've since discovered that many women are like me — human *doings*. We barely take time to breathe, much less reflect, and yet such time is essential. Even if it's only a fifteen-minute break — to sit quietly, read, take a walk, meditate, do nothing — such downtime recharges one's battery.

Relaxed and away from it all, I tried my best to assess my day and, equally important, to set realistic goals. *You don't have to be Phi Beta Kappa*, I told myself. *You don't have to succeed for anyone but yourself.* Tears were always close to the surface, but I fought them; if I started crying, I feared, I might not be able to stop. I was angry at my situation and unsure about my future but at the same time saying to myself, *You can do it. You can. You have to.*

On our living room wall hung a quote from Abraham Lincoln which Medgar had always found comforting. Now it spoke to me: "I have been driven many times to my knees by the overwhelming conviction that I had nowhere else to go. My own wisdom, and that of all about me, seemed insufficient for that day." So often, it was prayer that saw me through.

Nights, of course, were the worst, filled with memories of the past, fears for the future, and fragments of what I perceived as the day's failures — poorly done homework, being too slow to speak up in class, always feeling the shy outsider, never part of the flow. I looked around my bedroom, at my three alarm clocks — one on the nightstand next to my bed, a second one on the dresser across the room, which forced me to get out of bed if I didn't respond to the first, and a third on the floor under the bed, which literally brought me to my knees. Many a morning I stayed there, asking the Lord for nothing more than the strength to get through another day.

I frequently questioned God. What could he have in mind for me? Once, at around two in the afternoon, shortly before I was due to pick up my children, I was home alone, consumed by the feeling that I simply could not complete my degree. My classes were too much for me; I wanted to quit. I threw my pen across the room and hurled my books onto the floor in a rage. Papers flew, and I fell to my knees, looking up. "God," I cried. "Are you there? Do you really exist? I curse you for all you're putting me through!"

I beat the floor with coiled fists. Suddenly, I heard a voice within my head that touched my soul, patiently and with understanding: "It's all right, child. It's all right." I was stopped cold; it was the voice of my God. Then I heard Medgar: "Get up, girl, and stop feeling sorry for yourself. Do what you have to do." (When he was alive, Medgar called me "girl" to make me angry enough to motivate myself.) I knew I had to finish college.

Some days were better, some worse. I still wrestled with the twin demons of doubt and hope, the horrible mixture of fear and faith that so many women experience when they return to school. I can see clearly now that, as difficult as that time was, being the best student I could be also made me the best mother I could be. I was, unwittingly, a wonderful role model. Because my children saw me struggling with homework, it certainly enhanced my credibility when I told them to study or insisted that if they stayed with something long enough they'd succeed.

For a long time, I had no idea what I wanted from college or what I wanted to do afterward. Many reentry women faced similar dilemmas. Given the times, most of us took the traditional route of marriage and children and hadn't expected to find ourselves choosing what *we* wanted or exploring what we could do. We'd been raised to believe that being a wife and mother was all the fulfillment we'd ever need. Then life taught us otherwise. The best I could do was work hard and keep my eyes on the prize: personal freedom. I suppose my philosophy is best summed up by the shadow box fifteen-year-old Darrell gave me when I finally did graduate. The quote inside read, "If you can't impress them with your brilliance, dazzle them with your bullshit!" In other words, sometimes the best we can do is to pretend we can make it — and, then, somehow, we do.

Today I tell women in similar straits: "Think hard, act smart." And do whatever you can to make things easier for yourself. On many a night, I asked my sons and daughter to prepare their own meals. As a result, I got a break, and all three of them became great cooks. It's not only all right to ask your children to help, *it's good for them*. They often welcome the responsibility and appreciate the sense of contributing to the family. I asked friends and neighbors for assistance too, sometimes going so far as to check myself into a motel for the weekend so that I could complete a term paper or study for finals.

Another way to make the journey easier is to find other women in the same boat and row together. It helps to know that you're not alone and that others have gone through the same process and succeeded. The hardest part of going back to school is the fear and the uncertainty. You want to believe you're standing up for yourself, forging an identity, but most times you feel lost, eternally encountering the unfamiliar. You take two halting steps forward, one back, always hoping to find within yourself an untapped reservoir of confidence. "I knew I either had to change or die," one woman told me recently, relating her own experience of going back to college. "And for a while I thought dying would be easier!"

When I enrolled in Pomona, I was an oddity, one of three older female students on campus. My school life changed when I befriended one of the others — I'll call her Margaret — who had recently divorced and had children about the same ages as mine. After talking together for a few minutes, it was clear that we were both going through the same difficult adjustment. She felt slower than the young students. She felt lonely and out of place. And she was having a tough time finding her own identity. Quite by coincidence, we discovered that we even employed the same stress-busting tactic: chewing ice.

Margaret and I consoled each other mostly on the phone. We studied together too, but that was rare because of family demands. Most often, we simply bolstered each other's spirits and reminded each other that no matter how we *felt*, we were, in fact, doing okay — going to school, working, taking care of our children. We were surviving.

I have since talked to many women in these circumstances, for their numbers have greatly increased. In 1990 as many as one-third of all college students were over age twenty-five, a 75 percent rise since 1980. By the year 2000, some observers believe, mature women will constitute the majority of all students, if you include college classrooms, vocational school, and corporate and union-sponsored programs.

Shortly after I graduated, Pomona hired a staff person to create a center for "nontraditional" students. Educators know that returning women, while they typically make the best students, often require special services. Before using such services, my advice is, first figure out what *you* need — academic help, career advice, financial assistance. Bring your list with you when you see your adviser. Remember that you have a right to individual help; and most colleges today also offer some facilities that provide counseling and even day care. A center that provides such services may help you find a mentor; if not, seek one on your own. It may be a professor who encourages you, a person in the field you're hoping to enter, or even an upperclassman whose work you admire. A good mentor helps you devise a plan of action and track your progress and, by example, shows you what success looks like.

Unexpectedly, my last semester was the hardest. For one thing, it coincided with my father's long, painful death from lung cancer. Visiting him in his final days caused me to miss classes and fall behind in my assignments. I was barely recuperating from his loss when a medical condition I had been trying to ignore flared up. I was in such agony I walked bent over, my arms hugging my abdomen. I could barely make it to class, let alone concentrate. My doctor prescribed medication, but it was obvious that I needed surgery — which I desperately did not want. I was so fearful of not being able to finish school, I kept saying to everyone, "I'll crawl if I have to."

But Claremont is small; word got around. People at church encouraged me: Have the operation, we'll help out. I finally agreed. Dr. Schiff, my adviser, who had wisely convinced me during the first year to persevere and had supported me all along, couldn't have been more helpful. After the surgery, my professors reviewed their lectures for me and allowed me to make up what I had missed. I mended slowly, managed to get my work done, and, when finals came around, filled in those dreadful blue books. Appropriately, I was finally able to stand up straight by June, when I proudly took my place among the graduates of the Class of 1968. When my name was called to receive my diploma, the huge audience stood and applauded. I had cleared one hurdle and was ready to take on whatever the world had to offer. ℀

Being a good parent was perhaps the easiest of all the challenges that faced me in those years. Even when Medgar was alive, I could have qualified as a single parent. He adored the children and was wonderful with them, but his work kept him away from home, sometimes for weeks at a time. I didn't have very definite ideas about child-rearing. Everything I did was based on the way I had been brought up by my grandmother: Give them all the love you can possibly give but also let the child know who's in charge. I find that to be sound advice even today.

Like Mama, I wanted my children to know how much they were cherished and, at the same time, wanted them to grow up honest, with a sense of responsibility, and respectful of their elders. For all the nature/nurture debates I've heard and had, I've reached the conclusion that children come into this world with very definite and distinct personalities. You can certainly build on their strengths and teach them how to compensate for their weaknesses, but you have to work with what you've got!

Luckily, I was blessed with sensitive, loving children who instinctively knew that despite my obligations, they came first. In turn, I needed their cooperation. When I was enrolled at Pomona College, I continued to make appearances on behalf of the NAACP and do the lecture circuit, for speaking was my only source of income. I brought them with me whenever I could, but when I left them at home, they knew what was expected of them.

Each child had chores, a practice I can't recommend heartily enough. When Van was old enough to pull weeds, he was expected to help Darrell with the yard work. All three learned to cook, clean, do their own laundry, and iron. When I had to travel, I arranged for Mrs. Porter, an older woman, to stay at our house, but they were responsible for their chores nonetheless. They laugh now, recalling the mad scramble to clean up when I was on my way home from a trip.

I did depart from my grandmother's practices in several important ways. I didn't — and don't — believe that children should be seen and not heard. I wanted to be more open with them — among other topics, about sex. I also vowed to deal with my own children differently when it came to schoolwork; I urged them to give it their all and tried to help them develop good study habits, but did not apply the undue pressure my grandmother exerted. Besides, I didn't have the luxury of time that Mama had had, nor did I believe in coercing children, as she had done with my piano lessons.

Above all, I was determined to have fun with Darrell, Reena, and Van. When I was growing up, mine was not a particularly playful household. In contrast, I laughed with my children, made silly faces, climbed fences, rode bikes, took trips to museums and amusement parks, had picnics, played dress-up, and always left them little love notes. One rule I did enforce — no dancing on Sundays — was a carryover from Mama, who wouldn't so much as cook on the Sabbath. But other times, how we four loved to dance! I'd put a Motown record on the living room stereo, turn up the volume, knock on one of the kids' doors, and peek in, smiling. They knew the cue. I'd start moving, they'd start moving, and before you knew it, we had our own little spontaneous *Soul Train* going, dancing to the sounds of James Brown or Marvin Gaye or Smokey Robinson. We'd bop and boogie from room to room, creating some of our favorite family moments.

Make no mistake, though. As in all families, we had good times and hard times. My children were children, but they typically hid their insolence from me, rebelling behind closed doors rather than challenging me head-on. Darrell and Reena both had record players, from which they blasted competing Beatles music throughout the sixties, driving me mad in the bargain. All three fought with one another, which, as an only child, I didn't realize was normal. Suffice to say, I faced the typical perils of parenting, learning to deal with each child's manifestion of his or her individuality.

I always tried to be fair with my children. At night I made the rounds, going to each child's room, mentally noting how many minutes I spent there. I never wanted one child to feel I had favored another — even though they each accused me of doing so. We had family meetings to discuss chores, curfews, and money issues. I listened and encouraged their feedback but, like Mama, I was the boss.

My children didn't need much discipline, but if they did, I wasn't above using the switch, though never my open palm. In Claremont, I used corporal punishment only rarely, although my children have a different memory on that account! Quiet anger, I found, was an even more effective method, silence the worst punishment. The children knew they were in trouble when my voice dropped, I called them by their full names, and I employed "the hiss," as they called it — a slow, deliberate manner of speaking that let them know I was not pleased.

Because I traveled often, my children ate more Swanson TV dinners than I'd like to admit and had far less time with me than we all would have wished. They already had lost a father; and my being away so much aggravated their feelings of loss, especially because I often made the same kinds of speeches as Medgar had. Though we lived in California, not Mississippi, they feared for my life all the same. "Mom, I thought we were going to lose you too," Darrell later admitted, referring to my NAACP work. "Then we would have no parents."

I did the best I could to compensate. I called every night and went over their homework. (While I was at it, I should have bought stock in the telephone company!) I sent them cards from the road. When they had trouble in a particular subject, I hired college students to tutor them. And I always tried to make it home by Saturday, so that we could at least go to church together on Sunday and have a big dinner afterward, a feast of roast chicken, dressing, vegetables, Parker House rolls, some kind of special dessert, and sweet tea — southern-style iced tea, sweetened when it's still hot.

Coming from a long line of Black women who held their families together and nurtured their children with food (a value portrayed so accurately in the film *Soul Food*), I knew those Sundays together, sharing prayer and a good meal, provided the glue my family needed. I encourage working mothers today, even though time is scarce, to find little ways of being with their children — a walk, a game, a surprise ice cream cone after school, a few minutes watching a TV program that you both can enjoy. Schedule family rituals just as you would a business meeting or social date. It will make a difference and, not so incidentally, build wonderful memories. ⅋

The daily ups and downs of life were shaped by our loss. Though Medgar's murder caused us incomprehensible pain, it also brought us closer together. We were a *team*. "We all knew we had a responsibility to make it work," Van told me recently. "We had too hard a life and too painful a tragedy for us not to feel like we were in it together. It wasn't just you who kept it going," he reminded me. "We felt like we had to keep it together *with* you."

Knowing that my children had witnessed their father's death was by far the most difficult reality I faced in raising them. That awful night, after President Kennedy's civil rights address ended, they continued to watch TV, while I drifted into a light sleep. The moment they heard the shots outside, the two older children understood what had happened. Following Medgar's orders to take cover, they pulled Van off the bed, fell to the floor, and crawled toward the bathroom. But when they heard my piercing screams, they were torn between their father's training and their fear. They rushed to the front door and came outside to see their hysterical mother kneeling over their father, who was lying facedown in a crimson river, blood and bits of flesh everywhere. Darrell went into shock and stood motionless, looking at his father. This was the moment for which Medgar had tried to prepare him. Reena, who had been clutching little Van's hand, got down on her knees too, and screamed, "Daddy, get up! Get up!" Her nightgown was soon stained with blood. She reached for Medgar, trying to turn his face toward her. Watching her, Van froze. He was three years old, unable to really comprehend but aware that something horrible had happened to his daddy.

I ran inside to call for help, having no choice but to leave the children alone with their terror. Within minutes, sirens blared and police lights illuminated the lawn. People were everywhere, it seemed, screaming, crying, shouting orders and suggestions. Reena's mattress was pulled out of the house to serve as a stretcher. The entire scene had played out in no more than ten minutes, ending when Houston Wells drove away with Medgar's body in the back of his station wagon. But for me it was in slow motion — the duration of a lifetime — and I knew that my children would never be the same.

Someone took Darrell, Reena, and Van across the street to my good friend Johnnie Pearl Young's house, where they stayed the night. The next day, when they came home, the house and neighborhood were teeming with friends, reporters, curiosity-seekers. At one point, Darrell got on his bicycle and started pedaling down the street. Someone tried to tell him to stop, implying that his behavior was disrespectful to Medgar. None of us realized that riding his bicycle brought his father closer to Darrell; it reminded him of their races, Darrell on bike, Medgar on foot, always winning.

After Medgar's body was prepared for burial, I took the older two with me for a private viewing of their father in his casket. Though I feared it would be hard, I didn't want their last remembrance to be of his bloodied body. A day later, at the funeral, which was held at the Masonic Temple — the same building that housed the Jackson NAACP office — Van was at home with a neighbor, but Darrell and Reena were at my side. Four thousand people streamed into the auditorium in 103-degree heat. Mama and Auntie; Big Mama; my mother's half-sister, Frances; Medgar's brother, Charles, and his wife, Nan, were there, as were hundreds of people who had worked with us throughout the years, including many celebrities and prominent civil rights figures such as Martin Luther King, Jr. But mostly the room was filled with strangers, among them many reporters with noisy cameras and bright lights. I resented their intrusive presence and wondered what was going through my children's young minds. I winced as they stared at the casket, now closed, and heard Roy Wilkins, then executive director of the NAACP, say of their father, "If he could live in Mississippi and not hate, so shall we, though we will ever stoutly contend for the kind of life his children and others must enjoy in this rich land."

Although I tried to reassure the three of them that we would be all right, I worried endlessly in the days that followed. How would such a horrifying event affect their lives? What would it mean for them to go through life without their father? At first I tried to be mother *and* father to them, but I soon realized that I couldn't play both roles. Over the years, various neighborhood men extended themselves to Darrell and Van, especially in Claremont; both excellent athletes, the boys found father figures in numerous coaches as well. But it wasn't the same. For Darrell, who had begun taking fishing trips and developing a special bond with his dad, there was no way I or anyone else could be a substitute for Medgar. I remember standing on the sideline at a high school football tryout when Darrell made his first touchdown. I was at once filled with pride and profound sadness. It seemed like yesterday that Medgar had placed his hand on my bulging middle and boasted, "That's my little football player." Other mothers noticed my tears, reached out, and before I realized it, they were crying with me. I surely felt Medgar's presence then and on many other occasions, but there was scant consolation for our children.

Darrell internalized his emotions. Always a deeply spiritual child, he told me years later that, on the night of the assassination, he suddenly felt Medgar as "a soul" and finally "in a place where no bullet or anything could touch him." Medgar was Darrell's hero, and though he missed the man beyond words, what was most difficult for him was dealing with *my* reaction to our circumstances. He saw both my vulnerability and my rage. Fortunately, Darrell's physical activity — running, riding his bike up Mount Baldy, his competitive spirit on the football field — provided a healthy release for feelings he could not easily share.

Reena, Medgar's baby girl, had her own special way of mourning. Always one to express her emotions freely, Reena cried often and had terrible nightmares. She soothed herself by comforting and nurturing others. I can still picture my precocious pigtailed daughter in the days following Medgar's murder, putting her arms around me as I sat weeping at the dining room table. "Mommy, don't cry so much," she said in a caring voice. "Daddy was so tired. Now he can rest." For years to come, though, she made one wish on her birthday candles: "Bring my daddy back."

It was Reena who objected most when, three years after Medgar's death, I slowly began to have a social life. My dates were few and far between, but every man had to bear Reena's scrutiny. I'd usher him into the living room, where my three lined up like little soldiers, waiting to be introduced. Darrell, very observant, sat quietly or retreated to his room, with Van on his trail. I didn't see him again until I returned home later that night, where I invariably found him waiting up for me.

Reena, however, planted herself on a chair opposite my suitor, staring at him as he tried to make polite conversation with me. If I excused myself for any reason, she seized the moment, ran to her room, and in seconds reappeared, cradling Medgar's picture in her lap.

"Is that your daddy?" one poor man asked innocently.

"Yes," she answered in as surly a tone as any preteen girl could muster. I couldn't help but notice that she lingered on the "s," drawing it out like a hiss, the way I did when I was angry. Then she just sat there holding the picture and continued to stare him down.

If I happened to date the same man more than once, Reena really swung into high gear, not only clutching Medgar's photo but weeping. She'd run out of the room, boohooing loudly. If any man thought he was going to replace *her* daddy, he had another think coming.

I talked about Medgar often, and the older children had their own recollections. Sadly, Van was too young to really know his father.

Whenever Darrell and Reena reminisced, he could recall only vague images of Medgar. It wasn't until he was twenty-three that the memories finally came rushing back and, then, they were about the murder, not the man. "I remember the screams, I remember the blood," he kept repeating after watching a rough cut of the two-hour docudrama based on my earlier book, *For Us, the Living.* "I remember the screams, I remember the blood." The 1983 movie, which starred Irene Cara as me and Harold Rollins, Jr., as Medgar, was somewhat inaccurate; nevertheless, it graphically depicted the horrors of the South, as well as the terrible events in our family. During the assassination scene, which was particularly gory, Van left the room. After a few minutes, I went to look for him and found him in the hallway, his eyes red and filled with tears. I asked, "What's wrong?" and he collapsed in my arms. It was the first time (that I knew of) that he had actually cried for his father. The next few days, he spent hours in our garage, going through trunks in which I had stored Medgar's papers. He seemed desperate to recover a sense of his father.

Unfortunately, too many of the memories and experiences we shared centered on danger we faced as a family, danger that continued to find its way to our front door and follow me around the country as I spoke out for the cause. The children knew they had to be careful. "I'd have to check every room — the doors, the windows — to make sure nothing was disturbed, and no one was there," recalls Van, who, after his older siblings were on their own, often came home to an empty house. "The threat still lives with me."

My mood swings were also hard on the children. Not wanting to burden them further, I tried to cry only in the privacy of my bedroom, but every so often one of them would find me in tears. It bothered them; to see me crying meant that their lives and all around them were unstable. They also noticed the pill bottles lined up on my dresser. Now it is clear to all of us that I had been going through a depression — a word not in common use then — but then I assumed they weren't aware of it. I was wrong.

The important lesson here is to never underestimate your children. When you're troubled, they *know* it, and they want to help.

However, we parents must walk a fine line, sharing feelings honestly with children but not burdening them with adult concerns. My children would respond by standing near me in quiet support, retreating to their rooms, or telling me not to cry and reassuring me that everything would be all right. Reena told me recently that whenever they heard me playing "Amazing Grace" or "Just a Closer Walk with Thee" on our Hammond organ, all three knew I was grasping for strength I didn't think I had. Oftentimes, we got down on our knees and prayed together.

I regret that I leaned on my little girl more often than I should have, perhaps because we were both females and showed our feelings more easily. Particularly after a partner's death or following a divorce, it's tempting for a single parent to seek solace from a child, especially the one who freely responds to others' needs, as Reena did. But allowing a child to "parent" is neither fair nor beneficial. We must turn to adult confidants, and let our children be children.

My fears and misgivings about my ability to carry on without Medgar, coupled with very real threats of further violence that never let up, prompted my being overinvolved in their lives. When they didn't want my help with homework, I insisted. Shades of Mama! When one of them came home earlier than curfew, I asked, "What's wrong? Didn't you have a good time?" Because I remembered Mama's disregard for my privacy, though, I never went into their rooms uninvited. However, seeing a closed door upset me. "Are you all right?" I asked as I knocked. "Do you need anything? Is there anything you want to talk about?"

"No, Mom, I'm fine," groaned whichever child I had zeroed in on. The tone was unmistakable: *Not again.* Without a doubt, I sometimes drove my children mad, worrying, watching, especially when the older two became teenagers. They simply wanted to pull back, like teenagers do, and I was afraid to let them.

Looking at my children today — admittedly, through biased eyes — I can't help thinking I must have done *something* right. They are incredibly loving and loyal; and their seasoning has made them wise beyond their years. Their sense of unity is born out of a need to

survive and to protect, often causing them to distrust or fear outsiders,
but their pride in our family is boundless. They have found many reasons to be grateful, despite the pain and anger of their past.

I often prayed for guidance: *Dear God, tell me what I have to
do to break through. Tell me how I can protect them.* The truth is, I
couldn't. We parents may want guarantees that we are doing the right
thing and that our children are going to be fine, but that's not possible. We just have to put one foot in front of the other, keep doing the
best we can to let them know we're there, and trust that a force greater
and wiser is looking out for them.

4

FLYING SOLO

Making a way out of no way

Taking care of business.

*Concern should drive us into action and not
into depression.*

                  ≈ *Karen Horney*

I may not have been mother *and* father to my children, but I was
surely their sole provider. In that regard my struggle is familiar to
most single mothers, who all too often find themselves knee-deep in
bills, floundering in a morass of financial instability. What do we pay
first? Where do we turn next? We need to make money; we need to save
it; we need to get credit in our own names; we need to be savvy about
investing; and we want the advantages that money affords. Many families face some of the same problems, but when a woman is widowed,
divorced, or abandoned, the buck quite literally begins and stops at her
door. Today, many feel they are losing the battle. Of families below the
federal poverty line, 46 percent are headed by Black single mothers and
nearly 25 percent by White single mothers.

When I look back, I'm grateful I did not become part of that statis-
tic. I'm also amazed at the breadth of my journey, from small-town
Mississippi to the urban sprawl of Los Angeles, from menial jobs to
corporate power, from suffering understandable fears to enjoying
solid confidence in my ability to support my family. How did I manage to put a roof over our heads and Sunday dinner on the table,
much less afford the extras that I wanted for my children and me? I set
goals for myself, I was willing to work hard to attain them, and I always
tried to remember what was truly important. I never allowed money
to rule my life or compromise my values. *If you're not careful,* I
reminded myself along the way, *you can gain the world but lose your
soul.* Still, I wanted the best life possible, which included a good education for my children and travel to expand their horizons. I wanted

my children to have the kinds of opportunities I didn't have, and *that* required money. ⅋

Early on, Mama taught me the importance of stretching a dollar. Buy only what you can afford, she advised; be willing to sacrifice for someone you love; and always, always save for the future. I must have been no more than four or five years old when Mama walked me down the hill to our dilapidated general store — to buy a penny piece of peppermint candy. It was no more than an inch long and shaped like a pillow, which made it difficult to break, but when we got home, she wrapped the candy in a clean blue-and-white-checked dish towel and, using the handle of a large table knife, whacked the candy in two. She gave me one half and wrapped the other in waxed paper, explaining, "That's for tomorrow." A few sweet, crunchy crumbs were left on the dish towel. Those were for Mama.

Mama's father, James McCain, was her role model, and she in turn was mine. James's father was a plantation owner, his mother, a slave who worked in the Big House. His mixed heritage gave him special privileges, and with his sharp mind, my great-grandfather James learned to read, write, do arithmetic, and, from a comfortable distance, observe the ways of White people. Mama, born in 1883, after James had been freed, grew up watching her father use his education to get ahead. James instilled in his daughter, Annie, the importance of learning, working hard, and being independent. She saw firsthand how arduously he toiled to acquire a small plot of land, farm it, and eventually amass enough money to purchase more. For generations to come, the words "education" and "ownership" were linked with freedom and, as such, meant everything to our family. That was how you got ahead. That was how you pulled yourself up. That was how you fed your children without anyone's help. These principles are no less relevant today.

Mama taught me that there were only two things I could count on: God, who would carry me through the darkest days, and myself. I had to have faith that God would guide me, but *I* had to do the footwork. "God helps those who help themselves, Baby," she would say.

And if I could provide for myself, she told me, I'd never have to worry about being dependent or, worse, being "put out into the cold." She was stern about money, but thinking back, I wonder if more parents today might not profit from her example. Sadly, I observe many young people who seem to believe that they are the center of the universe. They expect their parents — and, later, the world — to provide for them. Some behave with an air of entitlement if not downright defiance. They resent having to get jobs or save money; many seem to live for immediate gratification.

At the same time, I have been impressed by some fine young people who work hard, take after-school jobs, and contribute part of their income to their households. They complete their schooling and then help their younger brothers and sisters do the same. Although I have no statistics to back me up, I've observed, particularly in the South and in smaller communities elsewhere, that the more economically deprived the family, the more apparent the team effort to help children stay on steady footing.

I held my first job at twelve, giving piano lessons to younger children. I squirreled away just about every penny I made, proudly depositing my earnings, such as they were, into the Christmas savings account Aunt Myrlie had helped me open. When I finally saved twenty-five dollars, which took an entire year, I marched into the bank and demanded my check. I remember how exalted I felt carrying my own money into the Valley that day, albeit through the side door. I had just enough to buy the gray wool princess-style coat I had had my eye on for months. Purchasing that coat was one of the proudest moments of my young life, and it taught me a lesson I never forgot: Keep your eye on your goal, and work hard to achieve it. When you do, there is nothing quite like the "I can" feeling of self-confidence.

When I speak with young women today, whether single or married, widowed or divorced, rich or poor, I stress one basic theme: *Don't play the innocent when it comes to finances.* In other words, *never* put yourself completely into someone else's hands — not a father, a husband, or even an ace accountant. Earn your own money, learn how to manage it, *and* learn how to invest it. Whether you pool your salary with a mate or depend on his income, you have a right and responsibility to know what's in the bank. And even if you add only a dollar a day, open your own savings account.

Granted, some married women do not want to work in paying jobs. Their husbands earn enough to allow them to stay home with the children, managing the household and, perhaps, doing volunteer work at local schools or community centers. In any event women must not underestimate their value, nor should they take a backseat to their husbands regarding finances. I suggest making a list of home duties and putting a dollar figure next to each responsibility, as if you were paying someone else to do the work. Add it up, and you will see that, although your worth is not quantified, your contributions help the partnership function.

I learned all of this the hard way. When we first married, I depended completely on Medgar to make all our financial decisions; he had a degree in business administration, and I, only two years of college. Because we deposited our paychecks into a joint checking account, I at least felt that it was "our" money in the bank. When I stopped bringing home a salary, though, everything changed. It suddenly became Medgar's money. We agreed on an amount for household expenses, but like a child, I had to ask Medgar for every cent of my own spending money, which was demeaning and infuriating. After I finally put my foot down, I began not only to write checks and keep the books but also to manage our household finances. Secretly, I also began to set aside a contingency fund in case of emergency.

Not that we had much to set aside. We barely had enough money for necessities, never mind frivolous extras. Every payday Medgar would say to me, "Pinch those pennies until they scream, baby." And did I! Medgar reminded me of my earlier thriftiness at college, when I lived on the monthly five-dollar allowance my grandmother doled out and still managed to save fifty cents or a dollar, whereas coeds who received three or four times that amount found themselves broke at the end of the month.

By observing Medgar, I also learned "money sense." He had been frugal since childhood, when he hoarded pennies in a jar beneath his bed; and by the time we met at Alcorn College, he had become a full-fledged entrepreneur. One of his more creative ventures was a portable snack bar. We students were not allowed to cook in our rooms, but some dared to break the rules, because there was no other way to eat on campus after 8:30 P.M. Hard-boiled eggs and sardines were a favorite combination, and when the hot plates came out of hiding, you couldn't miss those sulfurous fumes wafting through the corridors. Seeing this demand for after-hours snacks, Medgar purchased bread, cold cuts, mustard, mayonnaise, pickles, and waxed paper, and enlisted a bevy of his admirers (all girls, of course) to make sandwiches and distribute them to the various dorms. He "paid" his staff a sandwich per girl!

Medgar also taxied students to and from the bus station. He made arrangements with the local dry cleaner to pick up and deliver clothes at the dorms. And he often loaned money to students who ran short at the end of the week — and he charged them interest! He advised me about my own meager savings: "If you have a little extra, Myrlie, keep it. Pretty soon, they'll come to you. Then you can charge interest or barter something in return."

After a few years in Jackson, Medgar was earning $6,100 a year — his top salary from the NAACP. It was a stretch to pay the mortgage, feed a family of five, buy clothes, and pay tuition for the two older children to attend a Catholic school. But I had come from a long line of astute money managers who taught me how to stretch the little you have, to shop wisely for food, to let seams out and hems down to accommodate growing children, to wait for sales, and to always look for bargains.

I saved by purchasing meat from farmer friends and by buying produce from truck stands along Mississippi roads, just as I had seen my grandmother and aunt do. I had also learned from them to select inexpensive but meaty neck bones and cook them in mustard or collard greens for seasoning. I'd remove the bones (a little meat always remained), put them in homemade barbecue sauce, and bake them in the oven. Ah, the wonderful smell, the delicious taste, the sense that you had more than you did. There were times when I took three sad, small frankfurters, sliced them paper-thin, combined several ingredients from my pantry to make a "special" sauce, and served the combination over rice. Our children were never hungry.

A year or two before his death, Medgar got a good deal on an upright freezer. Buying in bulk meant always having a supply of food on hand and we also saved hundreds of dollars a year. As it turned out, the meat and frozen foods Medgar had stocked in that freezer a few months before he was killed sustained us for the year until we moved to California. Indeed, that cache of food was one of the few tangible assets Medgar left behind.

During the last few weeks of his life, Medgar and I had many soul-gripping talks. I would later realize that he had been aware of the latest, most serious threats to assassinate him, but at that point, he only hinted that his days were numbered. It was too frightening to discuss outright, but in his own way, Medgar was trying to prepare me for life without him. Among other things, we talked a great deal about our finances.

"Honey, I know you can make it without me," he said.

"I know I have to," I answered. "I know I can." But I didn't believe it, and Medgar saw through me.

"You have lived such a sheltered life," he reminded me, as if I could have forgotten. "But you must remember to measure your options, Myrlie." Wisely, he was reminding me that there are always choices in life, and that I must keep my eyes open to all possibilities.

After he was killed, I pondered his advice often, especially when I went to the spot in our backyard where I "talked" to him. He had left the children a marvelous legacy of courage and integrity, and endowed me with the unshakable knowledge that I had been loved and cherished. But sometimes, shaking an angry fist in the air, I raged. I was furious at him for having left us, for having put himself on the front lines as he did, for having abandoned me, thereby forcing me to cope with everything on my own. Other times, seized with terror and emptiness, I wept openly. How would I manage to pay the mortgage, the medical bills, the utilities, and to buy new school clothes?

I was $6,000 in debt, plus the mortgage, and had more questions than answers. With only two years of college, what kind of job could I get in Mississippi? Would Medgar's Social Security payments and GI benefits cover our expenses? Should I, as some friends suggested, go on welfare? Ironically, Medgar, who had once sold life insurance, had none himself. Our mortgage insurance at least would have paid for our house, but a week before he was killed, the policy had expired because we were unable to pay the premium. Medgar also died without a will, which presented another set of problems. The house was in both of our names, but under Mississippi estate law, I owned only a quarter of his half and the children three-quarters; I couldn't sell it without incurring considerable legal fees. As with most couples of that time, the title to our car was in his name — another legal hassle. (As it turned out, it took me more than two years to get clear title to it.) Faced with such complex difficulties, I tried to determine what to do and to whom I could turn.

I quickly learned that I couldn't count on family for financial support. A month or so after Medgar's death, I was sitting at Nan Evers's kitchen table when Charles walked in and immediately launched into a litany of complaints about how many groups wanted him for speaking engagements. "Call them and tell these people I can't make it," he ordered Nan, handing her a stack of messages.

Charles had moved himself front and center in the wake of Medgar's murder. Hours afterward, he had announced that he would return to Mississippi from Chicago to take over Medgar's position as field secretary. This came as a great surprise to Executive Director Roy Wilkins and others in the New York office, whom he had not bothered to consult. Charles also began accepting paid speaking engagements. "I have two families to take care of now, mine and my brother's," he repeatedly told audiences. "I need your help." (Later he would tell me and others how gullible people were.)

Listening now to Charles complain about the barrage of speaking requests, I saw an opportunity. "Hey, Charlie, I need extra cash to make ends meet," I said. "Bills have to be paid. My babies need clothes. Why not recommend *me* as a substitute?"

He just looked at me. There was never much love between Charles and me. In his own book, he wrote that I "took Medgar away" from him, and for years he seemed to have harbored resentment toward me. "You don't need it," he answered coldly.

I hadn't asked him for money, only the opportunity to make it on my own. I stood up slowly and looked Charles straight in the eye. "From now on, if I ever hear you say to anyone, any audience, any reporter, that you are taking care of your brother's family, I am going to call a press conference and denounce you publicly." Charles just glared at me; no one else said a word. "And," I continued, "if you don't believe it, just try me."

Realizing that I had no one but myself to depend on, I tried to believe what Medgar had always told me: "Myrlie, you are stronger than you think. Everyone sees you as so shy, so timid. I know better. I live with you every day!" Whenever I sank to my lowest, I thought of Medgar's love for me and the devilish expression that played on his face whenever he challenged me or pushed me. Knowing that he had confidence in my ability gave me strength even after he was gone. I was determined to make it on my own, as Medgar believed I would. I'd stumble or crawl to my goal if need be. "One push out of the nest," as Medgar would say, "and, girl, watch you fly!" ❧

In the months following Medgar's death, I was comforted by the bags of mail that were deposited on my Guynes Street doorstep, bringing sympathy and support from every corner of America. While most were letters of condolence addressed to me, many also contained checks and money orders of varying denominations payable to the NAACP, indicating that they were for the Evers family. A few were even made out to me personally; but, thinking that they were intended as donations, I sent them on to the national office. I was afraid to do anything improper. All the same, I would be less than forthright if I didn't now admit to having had mixed feelings about forwarding all of them. Thousands of dollars flowed into the NAACP, while I, personally, was desperate for money. Who would know if I kept some of the checks with my name on them?

I was still more than a little upset with Executive Director Roy Wilkins for not having protected Medgar and then for being so proprietary toward the children and me when several national groups, including the Negro Baptist Convention, announced to the media that they would work together to set up a fund for the Evers family.

Wilkins had responded dismissively: "We don't need your help. The NAACP takes care of its own. We will set up a scholarship for the children." Hearing this I thought, *How can he say that?* The fund he was referring to was earmarked for future needs — what about *now?* I felt this was political grandstanding, and I resented anyone using our tragedy for the NAACP's gain. (I later realized and appreciated Roy Wilkins's view that Medgar's family belonged to the NAACP; he was only trying to nurture and protect us.)

In the end, I did what I felt was the right thing and forwarded each and every check that came to me. During those first few months alone, I must have sent thousands of dollars to the New York City headquarters. As the old saying goes, "It is better to gauge your wealth not by the things you have, but by the things you have for which you would not take money." I had my pride, my good name. I had my memories. And I knew all too well that no amount of money would bring my husband back.

I also remembered Medgar's words: *Measure your options.*

In times of stress, it's so easy to get lost in the confusion of your own emotions. You concentrate only on the one tree that's blocking your view, forgetting that if you change your perspective, you'll see a whole beautiful forest in front of you. In this case, Roy Wilkins's turning down outside help allowed me to grasp the bigger picture: Medgar's death had given the NAACP an opportunity to reestablish itself as the preeminent civil rights organization. There had been other violent deaths in the movement, but Medgar's was the first of national interest. Once the media gave the public a glimpse of his thirty-year-old widow at the podium a mere twenty-four hours after his death, people wanted *more.*

In short, the children and I became a powerful public relations tool, which was just what the NAACP needed. The organization reprinted a photograph taken at Medgar's funeral, a close-up of my face, showing a tear running down my cheek. It appeared in train stations and bus terminals throughout the country. Calls and letters poured into the New York office, requesting my appearance at branch offices, at membership drives, and at functions held by all sorts of other organizations and corporations that supported the cause. After I spoke, people would literally empty their wallets with tears in their eyes, desperate to offer a monetary token of support along with their comforting words.

I was moved by this outpouring, although I had no direct financial benefit from it; whatever money was collected went to the NAACP. At first I saw my appearances only as a means to keep Medgar's memory alive (I knew how quickly the public could forget); then I realized it could be a way for me to support myself and the children without feeling as if I were getting a handout. I had watched Wilkins seize the moment for the NAACP, and I had watched Charles carve a new career for himself; I knew it was now time for me to make *my* move.

"Mr. Wilkins, as you know, I have no income right now, only bills," I told him. "If you wish me to leave my children during this critical time to attend fund-raisers for the NAACP, it would be nice if . . ." I paused at this point, making sure I was being as deferential as possible, reminding myself that I would catch more flies with honey than vinegar. I took a breath and went on. "It would be nice if the NAACP would continue to pay Medgar's salary to me and the children."

Wilkins quickly agreed: He would send me Medgar's paycheck; I, in turn, would continue speaking and fund-raising. It was, in fact, mutually beneficial. The income, though meager, helped me go back to school and start a new life. And during that period, contributions to the NAACP reached the highest levels in history and membership rolls increased dramatically.

Sometimes I wonder what I would have done had I been an anonymous widow, or a woman whose man had abandoned her and her children. Would I have survived if my husband hadn't been murdered — and martyred? Would I have made it without the NAACP's help? I believe I would have, because I would have had to. I see many women succeeding against formidable, and often overwhelming, odds. Some use their volunteer experiences to create an impressive résumé. A woman who has been president of the PTA, for example, knows a great deal about organizational management and conflict resolution. And as we women know, homemaking skills, such as long- and short-term planning and completing several tasks simultaneously, translate directly to the workplace. Writing a good résumé involves recognizing such talents as a way of repackaging oneself.

Some women ask relatives for help, take out loans, or even go on welfare until they get back on their feet. There's no harm in accepting a handout, so long as you have a recovery plan. Others have no choice but to take menial jobs or jobs they don't like, just as long as the pay at least chips away at the bills. They may start by doing work they're already good at — like cleaning or cooking — with an eye toward moving into work they'll enjoy. (For some lucky women, the two can merge. I heard of one woman who *loved* domestic chores and hired herself out as a "wife" to busy working couples. Talk about creative marketing!)

I would have scrubbed floors if there had been nothing else in the offing. I wasn't going to give up; I knew there had to be a way. I had been brought up by two powerful women, Mama and Aunt Myrlie, and their voices were in my head, saying, "Stand tall. Brace yourself. Go ahead and do what you have to do." And that, I think, is the key. Millions of women out there who have had to fend for themselves are living proof that if you look long and hard enough, there is always some honorable option that will allow you to move to the next step. ₹

When I settled in California with the children, we set ourselves up as a kind of corporation. We had regular monthly meetings to assess our situation. In concrete terms, I explained how much money I made and how much we needed to live, running down the list of our expenses. The three of them surprised me sometimes, coming up with clever ways to cut back. Although I was the family CEO, they all knew what our finances were and had a real hand in determining what was needed.

I'd recommend this to all families. I don't believe in burdening children, or making them fearful, but I think it's important to be realistic. It's never too early to teach a child that there's no such thing as a free lunch. Their allowances were tied to their performing chores to my satisfaction, and I evaluated them as objectively as any employer. Because they were aware of the state of our budget, Darrell, Reena, and Van knew they couldn't have everything they asked for; at the same time, they understood that if you wanted something badly enough, you strived for it. Given our highly competitive society, young people need to learn to approach challenges with a can-do attitude that says, "I will work vigorously and handle whatever comes my way."

All three of my children found jobs by the time they were sixteen; they *wanted* to work, to make it on their own. I also encouraged each one to open a checking and savings account. The boys disliked bookkeeping and did it reluctantly, but Reena happily stepped into the role of a little manager, a carbon copy of Mom. It's important for older children to learn how to write checks, balance a checkbook, and read a bank statement, skills needed to survive in the world. I'd even suggest paying teenagers' allowances by check, forcing them to deal with banking. To encourage savings, start when the child is young. You might even offer to match what your child is willing to put away, dollar for dollar if you can afford it.

My children might not have spent wisely all the time, but they usually were quite levelheaded about finances and certainly light-years ahead of peers whose parents didn't entrust them with such responsibilities. And because I never tried to hide our financial strains from my children, and because I made them part of the solution, they understood early on that sometimes sacrifice is necessary. For example, our not having time together, because my work required frequent traveling, was a trade-off that enabled me to pay our bills. As they grew up, they began to appreciate the extent of our financial struggle. With each step they saw me gain confidence in myself as a breadwinner. I daresay, my rising self-esteem bolstered theirs; watching me slowly climb the ladder of success inspired them to make their own ascents. We were always there for one another with words of encouragement: "You can do it — we support you." ⁊

By 1968, when I earned my baccalaureate degree from Pomona College, I was far from being a mogul, but the future was looking brighter than I ever could have anticipated. I had published my first book, *For Us, the Living,* in which I told the dual tales of Medgar and the civil rights struggle. More and more organizations began to seek me out as a speaker, and *Ladies' Home Journal* invited me to serve as a contributing editor. Although only part-time, the position allowed me not only to write articles about issues that mattered to me but also to have some voice in policy. One of my proudest moments was prodding the *Journal* to use its first Black models.

That same year, I was also hired for a full-time job. Prior to graduation, I had been approached by Professor William Rucker, who had been asked to establish the Center for Educational Opportunity, which would administer programs to attract bright minority students to Pomona. The college already had funds earmarked for the project. Might I be interested in coming on board?

I didn't have to think long or hard about this invitation. I had already decided that I didn't want to become a teacher; had I stayed in Mississippi, that would have been about the only profession open to me. I had moved to California precisely because I wanted to spread my wings, and the position Rucker described seemed ideal. I could work with people, which I loved, and do a job that truly mattered: helping Black, Hispanic, and Asian students attain the kind of education that only an institution like Pomona could provide. I had just experienced the difference a quality education could make. Magnolia High and Alcorn College had provided the best they could, given their meager resources, but the education I received at Pomona went far beyond anything a segregated institution could offer at that time.

I knew that I had qualities the college valued. I was a hard worker, organized, and, perhaps most important, a perfect liaison to minority communities. I was relatively well known and had been quite involved with many organizations in Los Angeles. Both the college and I understood that while parents and teachers in Watts or other minority communities might be suspicious of a predominantly White college's recruiting their brightest students, they would welcome me.

During the interview process — a series of Sunday teas with faculty members — I enjoyed the exchange of ideas and the quiet bartering of power. I knew the faculty was observing me, listening to my ideas, seeing whether I could think fast on my feet. It was exhilarating to be a player and to meet the challenge. I was sufficiently self-possessed to know I didn't have to have all the answers, I just had to know where to find them.

Those informal gatherings led to a bona fide job offer in June. I was beyond proud of myself, remembering how I once had been so shy that Medgar had had to secure a secretarial job *for* me at Magnolia Mutual. This position was purely mine, and it meant I would finally have a steady income to support my children and myself while continuing my speaking engagements and writing for *Ladies' Home Journal.*

I did not earn a huge salary, and although my new post was technically a forty-hour-a-week commitment, I usually put in many more hours. I learned an important lesson, however. The job was worth more, both financially and emotionally, than the dollars it brought in. It offered benefits, including insurance, and, most important, a feeling of utter joy in my own abilities. I was being paid for my hard-won expertise. Indeed, I always tell women — young or old — when you contemplate a prospective position, don't just count the money you'll earn (or imagine spending it!). Consider both the practical benefits, such as health insurance, pension plans, college courses paid by the institution, and the intangibles — the stature, the new experiences, the heightened self-esteem. Think about the longer-term opportunities for training and advancement and ask yourself where this job can take you in five years. Is there room for personal growth as well as economic advancement? And what do you bring to the position that will enhance both your role and the company's position?

I was positively radiant when I was employed at Pomona, managing several programs simultaneously. I raised funds from private citizens, local businesses, and government agencies and visited schools to describe the program to parents and students. Before long, I was given a raise and a new title: assistant director of planning and development for the six Claremont Colleges. I couldn't help but imagine Medgar smiling down on me. ⅔

New beginnings notwithstanding, some old financial problems lingered. The children were getting older, their needs more expensive. In my new job, and with my increasing visibility, I needed a business wardrobe. At every turn, there seemed to be another bill staring at me. I had no choice but to persevere and to believe that I could get out of debt on my own.

What helped me through this time? First, the realization that all I could do was take a small bite out of my debt and that I must focus only on immediately pressing financial concerns rather than allow the enormity of my overall problem to engulf me. When I said to myself, *Myrlie, all you really have to deal with is today,* I felt less fearful. Instead of worrying, I talked to God and prayed for guidance. Instead of obsessing over what I wanted or didn't have, I became grateful for all I did have — my children, my health, the support of my friends, a rather nice roof over my head, food on the table — more than little Myrlie Louise Beasley ever could have dreamed of.

I also learned various strategies as I went along. I found, for example, that if you owe money, it's best to deal with creditors head-on. Call and let them know you intend to pay it back. Even if you can only scrape together ten or twenty dollars a month, most creditors will applaud you for your directness and cooperation and will appreciate not having to chase after you. And they will probably be willing to negotiate additional time for you to pay off the debt.

Never put off confronting your money problems, whether they involve monthly bills or yearly taxes. Some of us become paralyzed and feel as if we cannot act at all, so that even the thought of handling finances becomes daunting. But it's better if you at least take a stab at addressing your problem. Think in terms of slowly whittling away your stack of bills — the important thing is to get started. If you don't, your anxiety will only build, late penalties and other unforeseen charges can accrue, and your problems will escalate.

Also, don't be too proud to ask for help — advice, time, labor, even money. I'll never forget my sister-in-law Nan Evers for her kindness when she pilfered a "loan" from Charles's back pocket. She knew how much I hated "begging" and that I never asked for help unless I really needed it. There were times when I had no choice but to take out a loan. Whether the source was family, friends, the NAACP, or a bank, I paid back every cent. How wonderful that felt! It also gave me a good credit history, so that if I needed to borrow again, I could.

After I moved to Claremont, I applied for a credit card from the Bank of America. My paltry checking account was there, and I assumed that it would therefore qualify me for a card. But most banks at the time were less than eager to advance funds to a woman. When I met with the credit manager, the look on his face said this one was no different.

"Mrs. Evers," he said solemnly, "we cannot issue a credit card in your name. You don't qualify." Accustomed as I was to prejudice and exclusion, for an instant I thought that race was the reason. But the manager explained otherwise: "You can only qualify as *Mrs. Medgar* Evers, not as *Myrlie* Evers." That seemed ridiculous, and I protested — but not too loudly. I needed that card. It would be another two years before I could obtain a credit card in my own name.

If you've never had your own credit card, get one, even if you have to deposit an advance amount before obtaining approval. When you use a credit card, it's like taking out a loan; by faithfully repaying the amounts you charge, you establish a credit history, a track record that shows you make good on your debts. However, beware of overextending yourself. If you need cash, borrowing on a credit card is rarely a good idea, because the interest rates are so high. For every hundred dollars you borrow in principal, you're paying an *additional* thirteen to twenty dollars a year in interest. Ideally, credit cards should be used only for convenience and the balances paid within thirty days to avoid interest charges. At the very least, pay the minimum required every month, and add whatever you can above the minimum so that the principal balance is paid as quickly as possible.

I had always had mixed feelings about buying *anything* on credit. In my family, the philosophy was to purchase everything outright. If you did have to take out a loan, you paid it off as quickly as possible. To Mama, good money management meant being debt free and saving money — therefore, never having to worry. Even in the most dire times, if I only made a dollar, I tried to put away a dime. This bears repeating: Save, save, save. If you don't think you make enough money to save, think again. Better yet, think of Osceola McCarty, the Hattiesburg, Mississippi, laundress who made national headlines in 1997. The money she began to save from the few dollars she earned washing and ironing other people's clothes grew over the years and enabled her to donate $150,000 to the University of Mississippi to establish a scholarship fund for young Black women.

Clearly, I didn't always live by Mama's no-debt credo. Among other reasons, the cost of homes and cars made it impossible for me (and most people, for that matter) to buy such big-ticket items outright. I had a mortgage, I took out a loan to buy the car of my dreams, and I sometimes carried small balances on my credit cards. I heard Mama's voice in my head, saying, "Be careful, Baby Sister, you never know . . . ," but her words were often drowned out by another voice that said, "You go, girl!"

Of course, in order to make intelligent financial decisions, you must educate yourself; money matters are far less menacing when you fully comprehend what you're doing. Help yourself, by reading books and articles, enrolling in a financial seminar, getting together with a group of other women who want to learn, or consulting a financial adviser. Today, banks and brokerage houses try to educate their consumers, especially women. This is due in part to the growing number of women who are making their own decisions, as well as to the presence of more women in management positions at financial institutions who realize the importance of catering to female depositors and investors. The Internet is a great resource for financial information, but remember that many web sites are geared to selling products — mutual funds, brokerage services, financial newsletters. The best way to protect yourself is not to depend on any one source. Gather as much information as you can and then make responsible, *informed* decisions.

Know your options and understand what degree of risk each type of investment involves. The investment that offers the highest rate of return is also usually the riskiest. For example, if you put $1,000 in a stock market fund that averaged 30 percent growth annually (which many funds did between 1995 and 1998), it would take only two and a half years to turn $1,000 into $2,000. But stocks can be erratic, and there's always the chance you could lose your thousand or see it greatly diminished. On the other hand, if you put that same $1,000 in a money market account — a conservative investment, returning around 4 percent per year during the same period — the chances of losing money would be virtually nil, but at that rate it would take eighteen years to double your money.

Some of us have more tolerance for risk than others. And some people, because they are younger and/or more affluent, can afford more risk. If a thirty-year-old corporate executive loses money on a stock, she is in a better position to recoup the loss than a forty-five-year-old divorced woman who has been out of the job market for twenty years. Moreover, each woman has to decide for herself what's best for *her*. Start small and careful until you gain confidence, and never risk more than you can afford to lose. That way, even if you make a few mistakes with your money — we all do — you'll have given yourself a margin for error. And be sure to heed one piece of Mama's advice: Whatever type of investment you choose and however much money you risk, make sure you can sleep at night. *

Money is both a tool of survival and a symbol of power. As I struggled with finances, I faced moments of doubt and despair; but there were also times when I clapped my hands and danced around the living room because I felt so good about my financial self. My joy wasn't entirely the result of having money in the bank. It was equally a function of my growing independence and a recognition of the strides I was making. My pride was a reflection of how I felt inside about where my life was taking me.

By the time I left my position at the Claremont Colleges, in March of 1970, I had matured tremendously and had several options to consider. I signed with a speaker's bureau, and over the next few years was commanding larger fees than when I first began to travel the lecture circuit. I also became involved in California politics. More than anything, though, I still wanted to test my mettle in corporate America, which I had encountered through my work for the colleges and which seemed to offer more exciting possibilities. God must have been listening, because an opportunity literally fell into my lap in 1973, when my hairdresser (of all people!) told me that Seligman & Latz, a New York firm that owned beauty salons and numerous

upscale boutiques in Saks department stores, was looking for someone
to handle advertising and public relations. This was a stretch for me,
although I saw how my Claremont job could be redefined as a relevant asset for the new position. I had done a great deal of writing and
fund-raising, which are certainly public relations skills, and had
proven myself to be an effective spokesperson.

When I met the principals of the company in New York, I became
even more intrigued. There were only two woman executives in the
organization, one being Adrienne Arpel, who was a partner in the
firm. I would be the only Black — the showpiece. A few of the inter-
viewers were more than curious to see if I had the skills to compete
and if I had something to offer other than mere public recognition.

Coupled with a considerable salary increase and the title of vice
president, the position was the proverbial offer too good to refuse. The
biggest drawback was that, although Los Angeles would be my home
base, the work involved a great deal of traveling. Darrell and Reena,
then twenty and nineteen, were out of the house (Reena, in fact, was
attending school in New York), so fourteen-year-old Van was my
major concern. However, he was a responsible and independent
young man by then. What is more, there were several families in our
neighborhood who had adopted Van, and I trusted that they would
look in on him regularly.

Indeed, I did travel constantly, paying calls on the CEOs of Saks,
Bergdorf Goodman, and Neiman Marcus, the store whose window
displays once dazzled me. I wrote radio ads, placed them in target
markets, and served as the voice of the company. I found the work
demanding but thoroughly enjoyable. Immersed in a world far different from any I had known, I educated myself about art and food, visited galleries, and read a variety of business-related books. I made a
practice of always asking questions whenever I saw something new. I
became more familiar with the feel of good cloth and the artfulness of
design. Naturally, I wanted to own some of the beautiful things I saw
and wanted my children to have them as well.

Women, especially African-American women in corporate America, will understand when I say that I also believed I needed to look

the part. If I looked successful, I reasoned, I'd seem successful, and everyone values a winner. Particularly when it comes to appearance, we women have to be careful about what our attire says about us. If we dress too sexily, too boldly, too casually, or too cheaply, we're apt to be criticized, or have comments whispered behind our backs. It infuriates me that women are judged by their clothing in a way that men rarely are. As Brenda Ross, a coworker at Atlantic Richfield Company (ARCO), where I worked for nearly twelve years, observed, "They don't care how many degrees you have, you need to *look* a certain way."

I took my own small stand against the double standard, first at Seligman & Latz and later at ARCO, wearing bright-colored business dresses or suits, often with coordinated turbans, rather than the stereotypical corporate female uniform — the blue or black suit, the silk blouse with a bow at the neck. I knew I had to present a good appearance, and I did, but on my own terms. From the first day in 1976 when I walked into the Twin Towers — the sleek, fifty-two-story, charcoal-gray glass-and-granite building that Atlantic Richfield called home — I *looked* like the executive I would become by the time I left the company twelve years later.

How did I manage on such a limited budget? Following Aunt Myrlie's example, I hunted for sales and made friends with salespeople, just as she had. And thankfully, a young coworker at ARCO introduced me to Loehmann's. I had never seen a cut label until then, but once I discovered the joys of discount shopping, I made weekly pilgrimages. I became a pro at sorting through the bargains, able to scan a sale rack in seconds, just by feeling the fabric. I also read *Vogue*, *Essence*, and *Harper's Bazaar* to become familiar with the season's styles. I'd go to upscale department stores to see the latest fashions and then return to Loehmann's, where I invariably found the same items at a much lower price. The thrill of the hunt was but another aspect of the game.

The danger of discount shopping is spending more time shopping than you should and buying things you don't need. I advise *planned* shopping excursions, being aware of what you already have in your wardrobe, so that you only fill real needs. To that end, I keep my closet neat and well organized; I rotate my clothes, recycle, and mix and match, so that, year after year, I can use many of the same items in a new way. Moreover, my clothes are arranged according to season and occasion, a throwback to the days when Mama encouraged order. If I have to travel, I can easily and quickly choose a week's wardrobe.

We all favor certain textures and colors; go directly to those when you shop, and coordinate whatever you buy with what you have. Choose classic lines and stay away from radical styles that might look foolish the next year. And if you're tired of wearing the same old thing, simply edit and update parts of your wardrobe. Buy a new blouse for an old suit, a new pin for the lapel, a new belt for the skirt. A smart shopper can always find a good bargain, especially if she looks for quality — good fabrics, secure stitching, ample seams — more than for labels; and the benefit of buying well-made clothes is that they *do* last longer. ℘

Though I sometimes quaked in my boots when I found myself in intimidating business or political settings, I kept my insecurity hidden and never looked like an outsider. Once, for example, at a political luncheon at the Beverly Hilton Hotel, I was making polite chitchat with a group of wealthy women when the conversation turned to the problems of "the help" — cooks who stole, gardeners who were lazy, cleaning ladies who didn't clean well, live-in maids who had boyfriends that dropped by. One of the women, perhaps noticing my silence, finally turned to me and said, "What about you, Myrlie? Do you have these problems too?"

"Oh no," I said, without missing a beat. "My cleaning lady has been with me for years. She does everything, even windows!"

Were they impressed! "You're so lucky, Myrlie. You don't know how blessed you are."

"Oh yes I do." I smiled. Later, back in Claremont, I took off the suit I'd worn to the luncheon, put on my jeans, and said out loud, "Come on, maid, get busy." I then proceeded to clean my house. Did I feel duplicitous? Not a bit! True, I had conned those women, but it was my private joke. In a way, though, I felt somewhat superior, because I knew that even without the trappings of the good life, I was coping — and *surviving*.

No matter how high I climbed, I never allowed myself to forget who I was or from whence I had come. This was in part a result of my grandmother's constant reminders that there were other girls out there more attractive and smarter than I was. She never allowed me to become conceited. I also kept a check on my ego, because I saw around me examples of what I didn't want to become. Traveling in the fast lane I met many women — White and Black — who were, as we used to say, "seditty" — snooty, putting on airs. Many had come from equally humble backgrounds, but had married wealthy husbands. A few had made it on their own too, pulling themselves out of poverty through education and sheer will. But either way, I knew their origins, however much they might try to forget them. I'm often tempted to say to such a woman, "Come on, girl, get real. It hasn't always been this way for you." But, of course, I never do.

I have no problem with someone's trying to reach for a better standard of living than she was born into — I did it, and I'm proud of all that I accomplished and all that I could offer my children. But no one should ever forget her roots, nor delude herself into thinking that the one with the most toys is, in the end, the better individual. In God's eyes, the person with material riches is no more or less than the person without.

Move on up that ladder; go for it. Acquire possessions, and have a big bank balance. But always keep a running account of your inner self. And when you want to determine how wealthy you really are, look into your heart and your soul. The only ledger that matters in the end is the one between you and God. Make sure you've relegated money to its proper place — as a tool to make your life easier perhaps, but never as an end unto itself. Give to those in need as readily as you take for yourself. And when you give, give time as well as money, and never make the person you're helping feel "less than."

Through Mama and Aunt Myrlie's example, I learned very young the importance of service and community and sharing with one's own. No one we knew went hungry when I was growing up, and no one went begging. We didn't wait for someone to say, "I need," or "I don't have any food." Through informal visits and quilting parties, information was transmitted organically; no one specifically asked or offered, you simply cooked a pan of cornbread, say, and took it over. When you baked pies, you baked two; if you could only bake one, you took half of it to your neighbor. Likewise, you handed down clothing and shoes.

It was a value system I never forgot. Over the years, whenever I've encountered a single mother who is struggling and striving to make something of herself, I have tried to help. For example, in 1970 I got a call from Norma Johnson, a twenty-four-year-old single mother with two children, then living in Nickerson Gardens, a crime-infested, low-income housing project in Watts. After reading *For Us, the Living*, she felt compelled to contact me. She remembered Medgar, of course, and was inspired by his example, but she also was moved by my story. To her surprise, I agreed to meet her for lunch.

Our friendship blossomed quickly, and ranged from our having long heart-to-heart talks on the phone to meeting for coffee. To an outsider, perhaps, it was an unlikely association: I had a job, and she was on welfare; I was trying to explore new territory in corporate America, and she was attempting to enter junior college, battling the system all the way. But as Norma recalls, "It was a bonding experience. We talked girl talk."

I knew Norma's plight too well; I'd been there. And I could also see past her circumstances. She was tough — a real fighter — as well as insightful, intelligent, and a loyal friend. We were equals as women and each capable of giving the other emotional support. We shared stories about raising children alone and commiserated on the difficulty of returning to school. Over the coming years, we talked about men, friendships, life in general. I told her about my corporate struggles and my new love, Walter Williams, when he and I began dating.

Norma never asked me for anything — not money, not contacts. She was proud. She had skills, and she never sought anyone's help without giving something in return. At the same time, I understood her needs. When she was in school, I helped her purchase textbooks. Once, when Walter had gone fishing and caught enough for the entire neighborhood, I called Norma, who was between jobs, and asked, "Hey, Sis. Want some mackerel?"

Today, Norma holds a master's degree and is completing her doctorate in criminal justice. She owns her own home and heads the Victim's Assistance Program in the Los Angeles Police Department. And she remains my "little sis." When Walt and I wed, Norma was my maid of honor.

Women like Norma represent the struggle and the hope. They keep it fresh for me and remind me of my own efforts to survive. Certainly, the challenge of "making it" has been intoxicating, but I have always kept at least one foot on the ground. I've never let money, in and of itself, be a deciding factor in anything I do, any job I take, or any friendship I make. I relished the chase and the challenges, and I have basked in my triumphs, but I also never let myself forget what was really important: my children and family, my friends, my devotion to God and good works. From those things have grown the successes of which I am most proud.

5

MASTERING THE GAME, MEASURING THE GAIN

Reflections on the
Black glass ceiling

ARCO's director of consumer affairs in
Prudhoe Bay, Alaska, 1976.

Signing papers as Los Angeles's commissioner of public works, 1988.

Don't find fault, find a remedy.

➴ Henry Ford

Neither my grandmother nor my aunt could have fathomed the notion of a glass ceiling, or more specifically, a Black glass ceiling. Mama and Aunt Myrlie were certainly accomplished in their world. Both were college-educated, both became teachers and pillars of the community, and both saw to it that their "baby" went off to college too. To them, teaching was a fine career from which a cultured Negro woman might rise, at best, to the position of school principal.

Mama certainly never envisioned my becoming a woman of the world. That was a far too risky venture. If you put yourself out there, you opened yourself up to criticism, disappointment, even danger. Besides, in her eyes, Vicksburg *was* the world. She knew her place in both Black and White society and, accordingly, she taught me mine. She could never have imagined any woman, let alone a Negro, finding a place in the halls of power.

In contrast, when I ask female college students today, "What do you aspire to be?" they don't hesitate. They want to be lawyers, doctors, engineers, vice presidents, president of the United States. When I ask, "Where do you see yourselves in five years?" they see themselves managing entire companies or starting their own businesses — in short, charting what once would have been considered unlikely territory for women. Many even wonder if there is, or ever was, such a thing as a glass ceiling. And if they concede that one does exist, they believe that there are plenty of cracks in it.

They're right. But those who have found a foothold and are pushing themselves through the ceiling stand on the shoulders of the women of my generation. We didn't have MBAs; in fact, we barely had dreams. Many of us needed to find menial jobs before realizing that we also might want, let alone have, careers. We grabbed what we could; we scrapped and scraped our knees and learned about power as we went. We kept climbing even when we had no idea where we were going. And as we reached each new rung on the ladder, we hung on for dear life, afraid that whoever stood above — usually a man — might try to kick us back. ℞

When I graduated from college, I had no plans to secure a corporate position — and limited training to do so. Serving as assistant director of planning and development at the Claremont Colleges suited me just fine. In the same way, I didn't apply for the job at Seligman & Latz with any specific long-term goals in mind. It simply seemed like a good opportunity, and I seized it. But after two years with the firm and dozens of trips to New York and other cities, I was beginning to feel physically drained and wanted to find work closer to home, a job that would give me more time with my children while enabling me to continue to grow professionally. So for the first time in my life, I actively began looking for a new position.

My job at the colleges involved analyzing businesses that might underwrite our various education programs, and I had learned that one of the best ways to research a corporation is to read its annual report. Not only does it offer you an overview of the firm's financial stability and salaries at the executive level, but it also provides insight into its history and current goals as well as the degree of its commitment to social responsibility. Most annual reports feature photographs of department heads as well, which help give you a sense of managers' ages and the company's ethnic makeup. And so, as I put out feelers, I also requested reports from a number of Southern California–based companies.

ARCO especially piqued my interest. It recently had moved its corporate headquarters from the East Coast to Los Angeles, and I was aware that the company was actively engaged in recruiting women and minorities. However, I did have certain reservations. As a member of the advisory board of Friends of the Earth and other environmental groups, I had learned about the questionable practices of the petroleum industry and had more than a few misgivings about its politics. Still, ARCO was then ranked fifteenth in the Fortune 500 and, of the oil companies, was known as "the best of the bad ones."

Although I had a contact in the legal department at ARCO, an attorney who happened to be both Black and female, none of my initial overtures panned out. Once again, however, God seemed to put me in the right place at the right time. I had agreed to serve as emcee at a major NAACP fund-raiser in Los Angeles, and who should be sitting next to me at dinner that night but John Gendron, senior vice president of government and public affairs at ARCO! I was more than a bit pleased, knowing that a social event such as this was a great opportunity to make new contacts and talk business. Gendron and I chatted amiably, but I made my position on the industry quite clear: Oil companies were not only polluting the environment, they were gouging the consumer. On his way out, Gendron invited me to visit him at ARCO headquarters. He wanted other vice presidents to meet me and hear my views; I would, in effect, be a one-woman focus group.

A few weeks later, I was ushered into a large, wood-paneled office on one of the top floors of the Twin Towers, its windows overlooking all of Los Angeles. Sitting in a plush upholstered chair opposite four or five high-level managers, I smiled confidently and thought to myself, *Okay, Myrlie, here you are. Let's see what this challenge is going to be about and how you're going to handle it.* I felt that the "game" was getting even more exciting at this point — bigger risks, higher stakes — and I knew that I was being watched carefully, so I made sure I gave them my best. I held my own at that first ARCO meeting, performing well and enjoying every minute of it. After we said our good-byes, Gendron took me aside and asked if I was interested in working for the company. "Let me know what you have in mind," I answered. "I might be able to help you."

I hadn't been officially offered a job — it was clear that this had been a look-me-over meeting — but I left feeling almost invincible. In the months that followed, I was interviewed by several ARCO executives. I informed each one that I was no yes-woman. If they hired me, they would get *me*, not only my expertise but my opinions as well. I knew that I was viewed as someone with good contacts in the community as well as in government, someone who might further improve the company's image and, in the process, its bottom line.

Eventually the matter was placed before the board of directors, a practice unheard of for a position at my level, and I was offered the newly created post of director of community affairs. The reason the process took so long was that although certain people in the company championed my joining ARCO, others wanted the position filled from within. The decision was not welcomed by the employees who had been passed over. Having had some experience in company politics, I knew I had to win my coworkers' respect; one must be a team player to succeed in a large company. Initially, though, I had to prove myself worthy of the job. ⅋

I remember well my first day at ARCO, walking through the stark but beautifully decorated office suite, my feet sinking into the deep carpet, all the while thinking, *I made it*. My new title was impressive. But whatever notions I had of stepping into a bona fide executive position were cut down to size when my immediate supervisor, Steve Giovanisci, operations manager of the public relations division, showed me to a tiny cubicle in the middle of a maze of other tiny cubicles. My "office" looked like a box without a top and was constructed of wood partitions covered in a gray sound-deadening fabric. I had a desk, a filing cabinet, a phone — and a crushed ego.

"Uh . . . there must be some mistake," I said, trying to muster as much dignity as I could.

"No," he said, "this is your office." I had already accepted the job; I knew that the benefits and chances for advancement were good. How did I weigh all that against the minuscule space? What did this office say about my position? How could I ever ask anyone to meet me here?

It wasn't hard for Steve to gauge the expression on my face. "That's the way it is, Evers," he said. "I just got *my* corner office, and I've been with this company sixteen years." The system at ARCO, he explained, was strictly by the numbers. I was hired at a "grade fourteen" level, and anyone below grade fifteen was relegated to a cubicle. "Miss It" would have to work her way up the corporate ladder.

That day was a rude awakening for me. I discovered that money and advancement don't necessarily go hand in hand with prestige. At that point, thirteen years after Medgar's death, I had met with U.S. presidents, been a guest at the White House, dined with representatives of Congress, and appeared on top television shows. I had moved up quickly, seizing opportunities as they presented themselves, maneuvering and soaring, earning respect. But life can play funny tricks, especially in the pursuit of the American dream. Just when you think you have it made, someone or something lets you know you're just part of the flock.

I offer the following career advice not out of pessimism, but out of realism. Be humble, but not too humble, lest your humility be mistaken for weakness. Expect anything, and be prepared to roll with it. Even if you're hired with a large salary, you may end up low person on the totem pole. Keep striving to ascend, but in the meantime make the best of your position and take advantage of the opportunities it offers. View every negative as a positive, a chance to stretch and grow. But try not to stay at the bottom a minute longer than you have to.

My first assignment was to solidify community relationships and to develop projects focusing on women and minorities that ARCO would then fund. The task involved meeting with community representatives, as well as with boards of directors of other corporations and foundations. That, at least, was a role with which I was familiar. Given my puny office, I had to become creative. More often than not, I conducted meetings elsewhere. I made friends with secretaries from various departments who booked conference rooms, so that when a visitor came, I could easily usher him or her into an elegant wood-paneled area and act "as if." That's still a strategy I use whenever I'm faced with a situation I can't change, or circumstances that make me feel vulnerable. I take a deep breath, summon up my inner reserves, picture things the way I want them to be, and then swing into action. Believe it or not, when you visualize your goals, you're more likely to achieve them.

However, working in that cubicle had another drawback: I felt totally exposed. My phone calls were easily overheard, and people could peek in at any time to see what I was doing. As someone who had lived life looking over her shoulder, I found the lack of privacy very unsettling. I knew enough about the corporate world to realize that this was no time to stop watching my back. And at my very first staff meeting, I found out how right I was to be cautious.

In preparation, I had written a detailed review of various community groups in Los Angeles, with recommendations on possible ways ARCO could enhance its image by providing program funds. I proposed that community groups — not only in California but throughout the country — could seek funding directly from my office, or, alternatively, that I could identify specific needs and offer financing for worthwhile projects. I was quite proud of how thoroughly I had compiled the information and showed up bright and early, eager to strut my stuff.

Eight of us, including one other woman, took our places around a big conference table. The meeting was led by Steve Giovanisci, and one by one, each person offered his or her input about the various items on the agenda. I hadn't yet refined my strategy of being the first to speak, so I just sat, listening, nodding politely as my colleagues spoke. As one of the men — I'll call him Fred — began to talk, I saw red. Item by item, he offered the very recommendations I was making in my report — the report I had naively left on my desk the night before, never dreaming that anyone would actually "borrow" my proposals.

When I finally found my voice, I said, "Interestingly, I have exactly the same ideas, Fred." I then reiterated his presentation, finishing with, "I have been working on this proposal for some time now." Then, with a smile aimed directly at Fred, I added, "Perhaps I should not have left my report on my desk last night."

From then on, I kept my work under wraps and made certain that, whenever meeting procedures allowed, I led off the discussion. I came to work on Saturday mornings, if it gave me an advantage over my competition. And I began to pay careful attention to how alliances were formed, how people conducted themselves, and who jockeyed for the seat directly to the right of the highest manager — the seat of power.

Interestingly, I saw something then that I still see today in mixed-gender meetings, both in corporate settings and other large organizations, like the NAACP. As a rule, men seem to have no trouble protecting their turf. They speak up without hesitation, and they literally take up more space than most women — in the ways they position their bodies and in the forcefulness of their gestures. We have been taught to be "ladies" and are often polite to a fault. We hesitate to interrupt and then wonder why men seem to get the jump on us. My ARCO experience taught me to be civil but aggressive, to forge ahead. Remember, no one is going to clear a path for you but yourself. Aggressiveness, even more than assertiveness, is a skill all women need, regardless of whether they're working with male colleagues in the professional trenches or dealing with male administrators at their children's school.

Information is a source of power anywhere, but especially at a large company. Know what's going on, know more than your own little domain, and seek out knowledge wherever you can find it. I kept my eyes and ears open at all times. To that end, I didn't hesitate to go out to lunch with my secretary and other support staff. They were privy to office history and rumors — they knew where all the skeletons were buried — and I found it helpful to consider their opinions. In addition, I believed in treating everyone equally. At ARCO, my philosophy was shared by Thornton Bradshaw, then the president, who was a democratic manager. "You're as good as the people who surround you," he once told me, "and those people can make or break you." Many years later, at a commencement address, I would hear Bill Cosby echo that sentiment: "Get to know the janitors where you work," he advised the fresh-faced graduates. When they snickered at his suggestion, Cosby explained: "They know everything that's going on."

Indeed, getting friendly with the support staff at ARCO unlocked more than just the doors to conference rooms. I was well liked and respected and had proven that I could be trusted. My people skills, always my strongest asset, served me well. Colleagues recognized that I cared about them — sometimes to the chagrin of my supervisor. He, like most managers, believed that the bottom line was the *only* measure of success. ⁊

Probably the most humbling lesson at ARCO during my first year was my first experience with a zero-base budget. Math had never been my strong suit, so imagine my dismay when Steve Giovanisci told me to prepare a financial plan for the following year. Wanting to do a good job but feeling somewhat at a loss, I asked my secretary to locate the previous year's plan to use as a guideline. I worked and I sweated; I wrote and I calculated. When my deadline finally arrived, Steve called me into his office and said, "Let's see what you've got."

I proceeded to explain each item. When I finished, he looked at me and said, "Myrlie, this is all very worthwhile, I'm sure. I can see you have good intentions. But we're just starting this department, and we have to crawl before we can walk. I can't justify such large increases over last year."

"But Steve," I pleaded, "I came here midyear and did not spend all the allocated funds. I need this size budget to meet our goals for next year."

Unswayed, he took a pen and began slashing items right and left. Later, I learned that although my budget was in reality larger than most, he made comparable cuts in everyone's numbers. After all, that was his job as manager. But I took his actions personally; all I felt was his disapproval.

"You have no faith in my judgment," I said, with as much conviction as I could muster (though I felt myself about to cry). "You said I would be running the show here, and you're not giving consideration to the things I need."

"Look, Myrlie," he responded, "you're not the only one in my department. I respect what you're trying to do, but I have others to worry about."

With that, large, shiny, wet tears began rolling down my face. Crying in the office was unforgivable, and the look of uneasiness on

Steve's face told me I had crossed a line. "Myrlie, I can see you're upset," he said, "but you have to understand. This is not a personal issue. It's not a reflection on your judgment. This is standard operating procedure."

With increasing skill, I learned to adjust to life in a corporate structure. I also learned not to take company politics as a critique of my performance. But there were other incidents during that first year in which Steve guided me through the rigors of company life. For one thing, my lifelong perfectionism put me at a clear disadvantage at a large company. I sometimes worked and reworked projects to excess, figuring every angle, polishing the prose, making everything just so.

"I need it *now*, Myrlie," Steve would insist. "It doesn't have to be perfect." Or, if I was to make a presentation to top management, I always wanted it to be more elaborate or to take more time than was allotted. Steve would look at me and sigh: "We don't have the money *or* the time for that, Evers."

Eventually, I learned how to save time, honing both my written and oral presentations to highlight only the most critical points and anticipating the needs and questions of management. As I got to know my colleagues, found some allies, and accumulated a few successes, I gained a more realistic perspective. I even accepted the fact that I might make mistakes. In any case, I learned that when something didn't go my way, I had to move on.

There were times, though, that I used my perceived naïveté to my advantage. For example, on one occasion representatives of a local YWCA came to me requesting funding for an outreach program they hoped to implement which targeted girls in junior and senior high school. A survey they had conducted, called "The Cinderella Story," indicated that these young women defined their dreams in terms of marriage, 2.5 children, and being taken care of by a Prince Charming. The project's goal was to move the girls beyond such traditional thinking and encourage them to stay in school and prepare for careers. Female volunteers from ARCO would go into the schools and talk to the students, thus serving as real-life role models. This was in 1976, as the consciousness of women's issues was seeping into the mainstream.

I couldn't have been more sympathetic to the proposal. The YWCA needed $12,000 to launch the program, but our money was doled out in $3,000, $6,000, or $10,000 grants. I had no authority to approve anything higher. All the same, I did.

A few weeks later, Steve called me in to review my report of grants that had been dispensed that quarter. "What is this?" he asked, pointing to the YWCA allocation. "You didn't get approval for this amount."

I had the good sense to remain quiet while he spoke. It's always best to let people have their say before responding to them; you can then gauge, thoroughly and intelligently, where they're coming from. Before hastily defending your position, sit back and contemplate your options. In this instance, I didn't have to defend myself at all; Steve did it for me.

"Well, I guess you're still new, and you didn't realize what you were doing," he declared with a sigh. "We can overlook it this time."

Sometimes when you confront hurdles that seem too high, you may find that you have to crawl beneath them. I knew I had no right to approve that $12,000, but I also knew that the program was one of the best and most ambitious to come across my desk. I was convinced that our involvement would benefit the students and the ARCO volunteers, as well as enhance the company's image. Neither could have happened if I had followed standard operating procedures. However, one must be very cautious about bypassing rules; weigh the benefits against the possible disadvantages. Is your job at stake? Your reputation? In my case, had the same incident occurred a year or two later, Steve probably would have considered it an act of insubordination, and my bending the rules might have compromised my career at ARCO. ⚮

I was promoted in a relatively short time to director of consumer affairs, a position that carried influence beyond my initial domain of "community relations." As such, I had to become knowledgeable about various aspects of ARCO's business that had impact on the public. One of the most critical issues was the monumental — and controversial — construction of the eight-hundred-mile Trans-Alaska Pipeline.

I made my first trip to Alaska in 1976, with Maureen Kindel, then the wife of a prominent Los Angeles lawyer, and a mover and shaker in her own right. She had no official capacity on this trip, but I was happy for her company and support. When we landed in Anchorage, a sea of African-American faces — members of the Anchorage NAACP — greeted me with a huge bouquet of long-stemmed roses. Many of Alaska's Black families had originally come some sixty years before, to build the Seward-to-Fairbanks railroad, and had stayed on. Their children, now adults, hoped to find work on the pipeline, which would employ about twenty thousand workers during peak construction months.

While it was gratifying to be welcomed in Alaska by my own people, my primary mission was to learn about ARCO's operations and to deal with the slew of consumer issues that were arising now that construction had begun. I was the troubleshooter, a role that suited me perfectly. It was an aspect of the job I liked best and did best: bringing disparate groups together, facilitating consensus through open dialogue and earned trust. I am nothing if not a good, empathic listener.

The Red Dog Saloon in Juneau, where many a deal was struck, was the hottest spot in town — beer by the pitcher and all the roasted peanuts you could eat. On countless cold, gray afternoons, I sat there in a rickety wooden chair, the floor covered with broken peanut shells, and listened to the grievances of everyone affected by the pipeline. I met with native Alaskans and environmentalists who worried about the destruction of wildlife, locals who objected to our presence, and workers who had a vast array of complaints to air.

Construction of the pipeline, which commenced in 1974, was a herculean task that involved laying some 100,000 pieces of pipe, forty feet long and four feet in diameter, a distance equivalent to that from Chicago to Denver. The pipeline extended from Prudhoe Bay in the north, through arctic desert and over the high mountain ranges in the central region of the state, ending at Valdez in the south. The project would take ten years to complete and cost over $6 billion. The expected ten-billion-barrel output of oil would nearly equal the combined reserves of Louisiana, Oklahoma, Kansas, and half of Texas. Understandably, community leaders and elected officials, who saw the tremendous profit potential for the oil companies, wanted the residents to be paid well for their troubles. (Their negotiations bore fruit; today, every Alaskan who meets the residency requirement receives a minimum of $1,000 a year from the pipeline.)

One of the most memorable aspects of that first visit was our jaunt north, in a tiny prop plane, to Prudhoe Bay, where construction on the pipeline had begun. Talk about being a long way from Mississippi! The average winter temperature on the North Slope is twenty-seven below zero, and the wind-chill factor makes it feel even colder. Fair-skinned Maureen and I made quite a pair — "salt and pepper in the snow," as she called it. No matter how warmly we were dressed, we could stand outside for no more than five minutes at a time.

I also visited the drilling sites on the Kenai Peninsula in the south where, for the first time in oil industry history, women worked side by side in the field with men. Recently passed labor laws, which guaranteed equal employment opportunities for everyone, meant that women could not be legally prevented from working as roustabouts, as these laborers were called. In Los Angeles I had fought hard for support to research and publish *Women at ARCO*, the first corporate booklet in the industry to deal with the issues of women in nontraditional jobs; other companies would later follow our example. But producing a booklet about equal opportunity was one thing; actually having women on the oil rigs was the acid test.

Interestingly, neither of the first two young women hired to work on the platform considered herself a feminist. However, both were aware that they were beneficiaries of the women's movement, which had paved the way for them to do the dangerous and demanding work while earning the same $2,000 a week (roughly equivalent to $4,000 today) as their male counterparts. The female roustabouts had expected criticism from male workers but believed that, in time, their job performance would dispel the men's concerns. But they were hurt and insulted — and somewhat surprised — by the opposition they encountered from their coworkers' wives, who claimed to be worried that the women might not have the necessary skills or strength, especially to handle emergencies.

Against the advice of my colleagues, I organized a town meeting which both groups of women attended. Hearing my plan, one of the female roustabouts said she trusted me to do the right thing: "You know what it's like to be pushed off into a corner, not only because you're a woman, but because you're Black." The wives, too, admitted having more faith in me than in the male executives, because as a woman I could identify with their concerns. Getting the women together exposed the real problem. It was not safety; the wives were worried about their marriages! Life in that remote region was hard enough. *Women* working on the platform and living in such close quarters with their husbands was the last straw, and it gave the wives an issue toward which they could direct their anger. However, once the two groups talked with each other, the women realized that, in fact, they had a lot in common. The wives understood that, like them, the female roustabouts had husbands and children at home, and that they had taken these dangerous jobs to put bread on their tables.

On five or six subsequent trips to Alaska, I successfully dealt with similar matters. I brought together parties who otherwise would not enter the same room, encouraged them to air their complaints, and facilitated a détente. One colleague criticized me for "spending too much time with people." I tried to share with him my grandmother's wisdom — there's always more than one way to solve a problem. I sensed, too, that he was so focused on protecting the company's bottom line he forgot that *people* made ARCO a success, and that people might also stand in its way.

Ultimately, I was able to convince the male executives that my work did benefit ARCO financially, but the impact was not always demonstrated by conventional balance-sheet measures. For example, the goodwill my diplomacy generated earned the respect of consumer groups and lessened legislative opposition. Local, state, and federal representatives opened their offices to us and eased up on the usual hard-line approach. We generated extensive press about the pipeline, most of it positive. At one point, I even prepared a spreadsheet showing how much it would have cost us to purchase comparable print space and airtime. I have to admit, though, that my greatest personal reward was the recognition by managers who had doubted the pragmatism of my approach. ⮞

I faced one of the most severe tests in my career some five years into my stint at ARCO in the form of a colleague I'll call Clark, a southerner who was transferred to the Los Angeles headquarters during a companywide reorganization. On his first day, he immediately put me on notice: "You think you have the upper hand, because of who you are. But when this is over, only one of us will be left here."

He was referring to the restructuring that was then under way. Such massive reorganization always brings out fierce competition, if not downright dirty tactics, among anxious employees who are determined to retain position and prominence. By then, Clark and I were at approximately the same grade level, but our respective bosses — both vice presidents — were vying for power. By a strange quirk of the restructuring, Clark had gained a certain degree of authority over my staff, even though he wasn't my boss. Such are the tangled machinations of company politics.

Like many other fields in the seventies and early eighties, the oil business was a male-dominated culture. Women were barely tolerated, particularly those of us who had ideas about getting ahead, and in the entire industry, only two women had attained the level of vice president. Clark, though, was another matter entirely and, I'm sad to report, emblematic of a certain corporate type who is intimidated by women and, therefore, determined to keep them down. That I was also Black and had a fair degree of visibility outside the company while enjoying respect within it made me that much more threatening. In one sense, his fears were not unfounded. Because we had to put forth extra effort to prove ourselves, women who made inroads into the corporate world during this period routinely kept longer hours and were more dedicated than men in similar positions. We often *were* better because we *had* to be. And this applied doubly to Black women.

Clark did whatever he could to undermine me. When I called a meeting, he strutted into the conference room — big and bad — and told my staff what *he* wanted them to do. On many mornings, when I walked into my office, he stood in his doorway and tapped on his watch, as if to say, "You're late." On one such occasion he remarked, "You know I'm keeping a file on you."

"A file?"

"A record that you come in late, and —"

I didn't let him finish. "You're being very unprofessional by constantly overriding my authority, " I said with fire in my eyes. "I will not tolerate it!"

His blue eyes were icy. "Oh really? Well, I'll tell you one thing," he threatened, "you're just going to be another notch on my belt by the time you leave here. I don't allow any woman, especially a Black woman, to talk to me like that."

I had tried my best to appeal to his decency, but he was obviously having none of it. I always take the high road first, but with some people you have to be prepared to get down in the mud. A few days later, sitting in my office, I overheard a commotion next door. Clark was shouting at one of the women who reported to me, demanding an explanation about a report that hadn't been finished. I walked over and stood determinedly in the doorway.

"Why isn't this report done?" he shouted when he saw me.

"Excuse me? No one, and I mean *nooo one*," I said, drawing out the words slowly and deliberately, "yells at me and gets away with it." I turned on my heel, returned to my own office, and promptly began typing a memorandum to his vice president and to Steve, the vice president to whom I reported. Then I called Steve and told him I refused to stand for this treatment. I intended to file charges with employee relations. Clark had gone beyond hardball; he had, in effect, declared war. Yet his belligerence played right into my hands. I have always been able to deal more easily with people when they are in my face than with those who attack from the rear.

Not so incidentally, this event occurred when many women in corporate America were filing lawsuits, complaining of harassment, unfair work policies, inequities in pay and promotions. ARCO, I knew, would not want its name sullied. Within an hour, several people, colleagues and superiors, had called, some offering support, some trying to calm me.

It didn't take long for word to trickle up to Mo Benson, the executive vice president responsible for the restructuring. He came to my office to speak to me in person. As he made his way down the corridor, low-level whispers followed him. What was Mr. Benson doing here? Normally a man in his position invited staff to *his* office.

He sat in a chair facing my desk, looking worried, as I explained in great detail everything that had happened, how Clark had undermined me, how he had even threatened to have me fired. What choice did I have? Benson reassured me: "Myrlie, I've always been here for you, and I've always steered you in the right direction, haven't I? If you just bide your time, hang in a little longer, I promise I'll take care of things."

In addition to Steve Giovanisci, who had taught me so much about corporate life, Mo Benson had indeed been a primary mentor at ARCO, my guardian angel. He also had real power. I thanked him for his concern and promised not to pursue my complaint.

Two weeks later, Benson announced that he would host a reception for me in the executive dining room. The company was abuzz. Is Evers retiring? Is something else happening to her? To her job? I knew the truth: Benson was making a deliberate and very public statement of support.

"Invite anyone you wish, Myrlie, " he had told me. "Not just from the company, but outside as well." My mentor was well aware that I had developed a strong following in the community. He knew that a large number of people turning up to honor me would send a message to the company: Myrlie Evers is a valued commodity. That is precisely what happened, which is why I stress the need to build support externally as well as internally. The perception of outside support — from the community, from other organizations — makes a tremendous difference in your treatment by those within a company.

As Clark had predicted, we hadn't seen the last head roll. Shortly after my reception, another "cut" list was circulated; it bore Clark's name, not mine. He hadn't envisioned *that* scenario. ๖

Women often ask me about those years in the business world, "What was worse, the sexism or the racism?" I always answer that, frankly, it depended on the day. Sometimes my being a woman made me a target, sometimes it was being an African-American. Even now, as many Blacks achieve prominence in politics, show business, sports, and the corporate world, none is truly exempt from bigotry. I know, for example, that no matter how well dressed or "respectable" my sons may look, they are likely to be interrogated by doormen and stopped by the police, simply because they have dark skin. Nor are Black women immune to such hasty judgments and discrimination. Congress-woman Maxine Waters once told an *Ebony* writer that she is routinely questioned when she attempts to hang her bag in the first-class compartment of an airplane — flight attendants assume she's in the wrong place. I know the feeling: No matter what city I'm in, taxicab drivers tend to pass me by, for fear that I might ask to be taken to the Black part of town or that I'm dangerous or simply unable to pay the fare.

On balance, however, I would have to say that the intolerance, suspicion, and resentment I experienced in corporate America were more frequently a result of my gender rather than my race. I was never allowed to forget I was a woman. If I was aggressive, I was considered bossy. If I complained, I was a troublemaker. If I accompanied men on business trips, they asked, "Are you sure you can manage the pace?" Did I need special treatment, being of the "delicate" (weaker) sex? I never experienced sexual harassment per se, but on business trips I learned quickly enough to decline an invitation for a nightcap, and to say no when asked, "Are you lonely tonight?" For some men, a woman's saying yes to anything is considered carte blanche for further advances. And I learned to turn a deaf ear to compliments about my appearance, lest one comment lead to more intimate talk and, ulti-mately, to a proposition.

In the old days, women believed they had to suffer workplace innuendos, even out-and-out sexual remarks. Today we no longer have to endure this treatment, because women talk openly about these issues and know that they are safeguarded by laws that not only prevent discrimination but also forbid harassment on the job. However, *attitude* cannot be legislated. Although many men are genuinely eager to work with women and exhibit a sincere sensitivity to sexism, there are still some who live in the past, preferring women in the bedroom not the boardroom. We must address sexism wherever we see it and continue our efforts to make those dinosaurs extinct. Never, never let "innocent" slurs slide by. And, most important, always carry yourself in a way that commands respect.

It's encouraging to see that the picture is changing: A greater number of opportunities are open to women today, and those entering the workplace are, on the whole, better prepared for their jobs. They're more savvy about corporate life and, as a result of our experience, have been warned about the land mines. Support groups and seminars addressing issues like sexism are plentiful. Today women can be proactive and actually plan their careers; and they are no longer afraid to seek power.

I don't mean the kind of abusive power Clark exercised. That's "power over" — power that attempts to crush competition, which, in my view, is born of insecurity, not confidence. I tried to explain this to a vice president who once took me aside. "I don't understand you, Myrlie," he said, shaking his head. "You have so much power, yet you don't use it."

He explained what he meant: "People inside the company like and respect you and your work. Community leaders ask only for you. I would have thought you'd be more . . . ruthless."

I just smiled, realizing that in one sense, he was correct in his assumption. I did have power. But he didn't understand my attitude. I didn't need to prove my power by walking over people or by flaunting it. Power comes from within — knowing you have it and using it for positive gains, not to make people feel small. I prefer to convince colleagues to cooperate by asking, not ordering, by acknowledging their abilities, by encouraging their progress, and by lifting *them* up, not elevating myself. In the end, everybody wins. My management style also incorporates firmness and decisiveness. I'm no pushover. When necessary, I am thoroughly capable of making tough choices and carrying them out, as much of my experience with the NAACP demonstrates. But when I do take a strong position, it's out of a deep belief in my purpose, not to flex my muscles.

I learned a great deal about management from observing ARCO's president, Thornton Bradshaw, who treated people with respect. He was firm — there was no question about what he expected. Under his regime, performance was scrutinized very carefully, both in regular meetings with one's superiors and in written annual reviews. Bradshaw also encouraged his employees to be creative, which meant either that one had enough rope to hang himself or the vision to get a job done in a better way. In the latter case, Bradshaw always gave credit where it was due. As a result, he was loved and his staff would do anything he asked.

Though I grew tremendously at ARCO, it was always clear to me that I had limited potential for growth within the company. I couldn't advance beyond public affairs, because I lacked a background in science, engineering, and finance. A more serious obstacle, though, was the new order that was ushered in when Bradshaw resigned. (He later became CEO of Westinghouse.) My feud with Clark was emblematic of the changing tone in the firm. Although I won out over Clark, ARCO no longer felt like family. The new management team seemed distant and unsympathetic to employees' needs. Heads rolled; expectations were dashed. As colleagues were terminated — and given "golden parachute" packages as severance — those of us who retained our jobs felt both sad for those who had been dismissed and apprehensive about management's next move.

Making matters worse, I had hit my ceiling. I knew my job inside and out; the thrill of accomplishment was gone, and it felt as if I were going nowhere. I was anxious and restless, suffering through months of turmoil. Ultimately, it was my body that betrayed my real feelings about the newly toxic environment at ARCO. Headaches plagued me; I found myself crying on the Los Angeles freeways to and from work. Part of my indecision was a reluctance to lose my salary and the benefits. Walt, whom I had married shortly after joining ARCO, assured me that he'd "take care of us," but I had grown accustomed to the lifestyle and, I'm sad to say, the stress. It was hard to leave it all. But it was time to fly again. ⁊

In 1987 I took a political leave of absence from ARCO to run for the Tenth District city council seat in LA. When I lost the election, I returned to ARCO, still feeling burned out and not having a Plan B. In retrospect, that was a mistake. But few women of my generation had a professional game plan; many of us rarely planned more than a year in advance. Certainly, we had talent and skill, but, starting our careers late in life as so many of us did, we didn't have the mindset. How different it is for young women today. Hence, my advice is to do as I say, not as I did. Always have a backup plan. Whether an ideal job turns sour, a respected supervisor leaves, or the raise or promotion you've been counting on doesn't materialize, when you can't negotiate a better deal, you must be ready to walk. That might sound impractical, even cavalier, but you always have options. The key is to evaluate your situation regularly (so that nothing takes you by surprise), keep your résumé current, and maintain good relationships in your industry. That way, you're dealing from a position of strength. With the right education or training, a solid network of business contacts, and confidence in yourself, you can always find a better job, or even open your own business.

In fact, according to the National Foundation for Women Business Owners, the number of women-owned businesses has increased by 78 percent in the past decade. What is even more heartening is that only 16 percent cite the glass ceiling as the reason for choosing self-employment. According to *Working Woman* magazine, which published the findings, more than 40 percent say they felt "bored and stifled by the corporate milieu." It's not that the women in the study weren't making money. They simply opted for the freedom to do what they wanted to do.

However, being in that uncomfortable place — unable to move ahead, not wanting to remain — can be a wrenching experience, and it's important to gently prod yourself. Start by sorting out the pros and cons of your current situation. Decide whether it is better to renegotiate or to leave altogether. Come to a decision in whatever way works best for you, by talking to friends, writing your thoughts in a journal, praying. Then, take some step, however small, however symbolic, so that you don't become paralyzed. Make phone calls. Meet with a career counselor. Go to the library and research other companies. Have lunch with someone in your field or in a field you'd like to enter, so that you know what's available. At some point, the dread of staying put will be worse than the fear of the unknown — and that's usually when most of us are ready to make a change.

After listening to my dilemma, a friend who advised me about ARCO said, "Myrlie, you have a choice, you know. You can stay and just go through the motions and collect a fat paycheck. Or you can step out into the unknown." He was right, but some tough decisions are like hard-to-open jars. You keep trying; you hand it to others, and everyone takes a crack at it. Then, suddenly, someone comes along and — pop! — the jar opens. For me, that someone was Los Angeles mayor Tom Bradley.

Late one night, I was sitting in my kitchen, surrounded by piles of papers and memorabilia left over from my campaign. Walt and I were having a cup of tea when the phone rang. "Myrlie?" questioned the voice on the other end of the receiver. "Tom Bradley here. Where have you been? I've been trying to reach you."

I was taken aback. For various political reasons, Tom hadn't supported my bid for public office. On a personal level, though, we were friends; he and Walt were lifelong buddies. "I'm here now, Tom. What's up?"

"I have a position open on the Board of Public Works. Are you interested?" Tom had never minced words.

"Of course I am," I answered quickly, my heart beating with excitement and disbelief. What an opportunity! "I'm still at ARCO, as you know, but I haven't gone back on a permanent basis. Technically, I'm on political leave."

"Good," he said.

"So when can I meet with you?"

"Oh, we don't have the time for that. I have to make the announcement tomorrow. You've got the job if you want it."

"Tomorrow?" I was speechless, marveling that my prayers had been answered. "I'm saying yes to you, Tom, but I can't leave ARCO that quickly. When does the position actually become vacant?"

He told me June, which was a month away. My mind raced, as I thought out loud of all the people I would have to contact. "Do it tonight," Tom commanded. "I'm making the announcement at a press conference tomorrow morning at nine."

And so I embarked on a new direction. I'd never suggest that women leave their careers to fate as I did. But I would say that career planning incorporates flexibility. Always keep your eyes open for unexpected opportunities.

Luckily, because I had been on leave, I wasn't in the middle of any important projects. Steve Giovanisci and my other superiors at ARCO understood my decision — the new job meant a significant pay cut, but a tremendous leap in responsibility and stature. They all gave me their blessing.

It is no small irony that I was sworn in as Commissioner of Public Works for the City of Los Angeles on June 12, 1988 — the twenty-fifth anniversary of Medgar's death. I was only the second woman to hold the post and the first African-American woman. My responsibilities were far greater than those I'd handled at ARCO. Among other city business, I would be overseeing new construction projects, sewer maintenance, garbage disposal, street lighting, and the scheduling of movie shoots. The job brought with it a spacious office suite, a car, and a host of other perks. Equally important to me as a lifelong learner was the fact that I would be mastering so many new areas of expertise.

In my new domain, I was head of the second largest public works department in the country (New York being first), and I loved it. All the managers and most of the seven thousand employees I oversaw were men. At first I wondered how my staff would feel taking orders from a woman, but I was determined to utilize the same balance of nurturing and nudging that had worked at ARCO. I was fortunate that my reputation preceded me, so that I had respect even as I began.

Moreover, the men clearly admired my spirit, particularly the fact that I relished the field visits. Wearing a hard hat and leather gloves, I rode the garbage trucks. I flew to construction sites and potential landfill locations in helicopters without doors — in spite of my terror of heights. I frequently dropped in on managers to assess their needs and hear their ideas. After a few months on the job, many of the workers told me that no one in my position had ever sought their input before. Nothing could have gratified me more than when they affectionately began to call me "Commish."

Naturally my new job was not without problems; no job is. I worked extremely long hours — longer than at ARCO, because I had the last word. And, I had *the badge*, which, I have to admit, I enjoyed. I never abused my privilege, but whenever I was on city business, that commissioner's badge got me into special parking places and past police barriers.

I found that the badge even worked on foreign soil! Once I took a delegation to Germany to observe some new waste disposal plants. The Germans had discovered a safe method of refining sludge for fertilizer. We packed several samples to bring home. At the airport in Frankfurt, a German customs officer, inspecting my staffers' bags, began to question them relentlessly, so I stepped forward.

"What is the problem, sir?" I knew he spoke English and understood my question.

"And who are you?" he demanded. "Are you with them?"

"Yes, I am."

"Are you also carrying this . . . this . . ." He hesitated, not knowing what to call it. ". . . dirt?"

"No, I am not, but I am their supervisor." With that I opened my leather wallet and flashed my badge. The seal of the City of Los Angeles left no doubt that I was an important official and, after briefly conferring with his colleagues, he let us all pass through.

One of my men patted me on the shoulder. "Thanks, Commish."

I was called at all hours to resolve disputes. One night, the phone rang at around eleven o'clock. One of the Hollywood studios had been filming in Studio City, a quiet residential area, and the homeowners were up in arms about the disruption at so late an hour. City policy dictated that filming was prohibited after ten to avoid such problems. I got out of bed and drove to the location.

"You're almost two hours over the limit," I told the producer. "We've had complaints from the neighbors about the lights, the noise. You're going to have to shut down."

He looked at me as if to say, "Who do you think you are?" then said very curtly, "I can't."

"You will," I responded. "Or I will summon the police and have them do it for you. And if I do, you will have great difficulty getting another permit to film in Los Angeles."

He knew I meant what I said. I had the power of the badge behind me — I spoke for the City of Los Angeles. All the same, I knew I walked a fine line. During the eighties, the city was losing a lot of film location business to Vancouver and San Diego, where there wasn't as much red tape. We wanted to encourage filmmakers to utilize locations in Los Angeles, but at the same time, public interests needed to come first. After I was sure that the crew was closing down the set, I knocked on doors of residents who had complained and spoke briefly with them. People appreciate that kind of personal attention. They realize that someone really cares, that it's not just a job.

In the rare quiet moments during my tenure as Commish, I often caught myself smiling thoughtfully. *If Medgar could only see me now.* In retrospect, those reflections were really more about me than about Medgar; imagining his response was an indirect, and safe, way of congratulating myself — something I still had great difficulty doing. It seemed that whenever I took a stride forward, the old insecurities came back. For instance, when a friend congratulated me on my appointment and remarked on how far I had come, I remember demurring, "I haven't done *that* much."

Luckily I heard my response and had a serious talk with myself. *Can't you accept a compliment? Look where you've been. Why do you always feel you have to do more?* It's one thing to feel that way in one's twenties; but I was then in my midfifties. I had pondered my insecurities before. How long would I continue to criticize myself for not getting all A's? I also realized that the "why" was less important than "how" — how could I stop the self-demeaning chatter in my head?

I gave myself an assignment, which I'd recommend to any women in the throes of self-doubt: Write down your achievements — work experience and life experience, paying jobs and volunteer work, committees you've served on and events you've helped organize, the family you manage as well as the staff you oversee. Think of every accomplishment, no matter how minor, and add it to your list. You'll be amazed. We women tend to minimize our successes. In doing so, we remove ourselves from the roll call of achievement.

Instead of dismissing your accomplishments, savor them, and be proud. Many of us mistake pride for vanity. It's not. The next time anyone compliments you, instead of saying something like, "That was no big deal," simply say, "Thank you." And then take a moment by yourself, look into the mirror, and say, "Good job!"

Today I have no trouble acknowledging how much I grew in my stint as commissioner. Having a nine-hundred-million-dollar budget, I lost my fear of number-crunching. Managing a predominantly male staff honed my ability to be in control without being overbearing. And because I had to deal with sensitive issues, most notably the common practice of constructing incinerating facilities in poor and minority neighborhoods — a problem that continues to cause controversy in major cities today — my skills as a mediator were greatly enhanced.

Regardless of whether you have a staff of thousands or just one employee, it's important to be strong, be tough, be fair, and always be a careful listener. Be friendly but firm. Especially with male employees, trying to placate or seeming to condescend will not earn respect. You must believe in yourself and in your ability to make good decisions, for if you act in a way that reveals self-doubt, you will be eaten alive.

As commissioner, I had to be decisive. But during our thrice-weekly public meetings when other city officials asked questions, I wasn't afraid to say, "I don't know." When I didn't have answers, I made sure I got them. There was never a question in anyone's mind that I was in control, but I was never afraid to ask for help. Getting assistance is not a sign of vulnerability nor an indication of incompetence. In fact, when you surround yourself with good people — who may not know more but who have different perspectives — it makes you better.

If you're really fortunate, you'll also have people like that waiting for you at home. When I first began my upward climb, the children and my good friends were a comfort, but there were times when I ached for an adult who could truly share the burden with me, times when I wished a handsome gentleman would come along and help to make my life easier. The irony was that when he finally appeared, I barely recognized him.

6

TWICE BLESSED

Secrets of a successful relationship

At home with Walt after our wedding, July 1976.

> At the simplest level, "being a self" means we
> can be pretty much who we are in relationships
> rather than what others wish, need, and expect
> us to be. It also means that we can allow others
> to do the same.
>
> — Harriet Lerner,
> The Dance of Intimacy

*I*n 1968, when I first met Walter Edward Williams, I was hardly in the market for a man, much less a husband. Even if I had been, he surely wouldn't have been in the running. For one thing, his pants were too short. When he walked into my office at the Claremont Colleges, all I could see was the white socks, blinding against the dark blue material of his trousers. Although he was unquestionably a good-looking man — tall, with a richly handsome face — his appearance said "country." This bashful man, who talked slowly and softly, wasn't my idea of a guy who'd set the world on fire.

Opening a portfolio of drawings onto my desk, he began to explain the idea he had come to pitch — a deck of playing cards featuring the likenesses of civil rights leaders. He wanted my permission to use a picture of Medgar.

"These are very nice," I said politely, leafing through his drawings of Martin Luther King, Jr., Sojourner Truth, Rosa Parks, and my late husband. As I examined his work, Walter explained that although he had demonstrated considerable talent as a young man, his teachers discouraged him, insisting that a career in art was sheer folly for a Black man born in 1918. Hence, he became a longshoreman and union organizer instead, but he had always resented those educators' foreclosing his options and regretted that he had taken their warnings to heart. Now, in his spare time, he was developing this project, utilizing his gift to educate our young people about the great leaders who paved the way. I certainly applauded his intentions.

We talked at length about Medgar and his work. Walter told me how devastated he had been by the assassination. A year or so before Medgar was killed, he had heard him speak at an NAACP meeting in Los Angeles. Inspired, he organized a group of longshoremen to take up a collection which, he hoped, Medgar would distribute to people who needed it. He recalled, "I told friends, 'This man is good, and he's honest, but he's not going to last long.'"

Walter discussed his own civil rights work too. During the forties in Los Angeles, he was a member of the Victory Committee — an early ad hoc group that attracted men like bandleader Count Basie, boxer Joe Louis, and Tom Bradley. Long before most of the nation was aware of a civil rights movement, its members picketed and boycotted businesses. They challenged Woolworth's hiring practices, investigated injustices, formed a co-op of Black merchants, and sent angry telegrams to President Truman, detailing the conditions under which Negroes were forced to live in California.

After a spell of amiable conversation, I pointed to Walt's drawing of Medgar. "Please feel free to use this on your cards," I said earnestly and smiled. "You've really captured his essence."

"Oh no," he protested, "you don't have to decide now. Let me leave these with you so you can really think about it."

He had left the door open for a second meeting, but after he returned a few weeks later to pick up his artwork, I didn't give the man a second thought. ⋇

Being receptive to any man still seemed out of the question. Nudged by well-meaning friends, I had dated sporadically but rarely enjoyed any part of the process — and my children certainly didn't. In my mind, I compared each suitor to Medgar, and each fell short by a mile. I knew I'd never find another Medgar.

Aunt Myrlie, who had never married after Uncle John died, worried about my attitude. Once I had settled in California, she called like clockwork every Saturday morning. The first question she asked was, "How are you and the children?" The second was, "Baby, have you found a man yet?"

"No, Auntie," I'd say wearily. "I'm not looking."

"Well, you'd better hurry up and find one," she said, chuckling, "because you're getting older and uglier every day!"

I laughed at her wit and understood her concern, but as often as she warned me about how "lonely" life could be without a partner, I invariably concluded that I would be sufficiently fulfilled by my children and my career. However, as I swirled my way through a long and sometimes jolting courtship dance with Walter, I learned what it meant to care deeply for someone and began to consciously contemplate what kind of man I wanted in my life. In short, I learned some of the secrets of a successful relationship.

Some women get this education from magazines or books — God knows, there is more than enough written about how to choose the right partner, marry for keeps, have good sex, and, when all else fails, how to have a good divorce. But I was schooled in life. On-the-job training taught me that no relationship is without its problems and its "learning moments," so to speak.

Many a woman, myself included, starts out believing that a man will make her "whole," that he'll make life easier. As I discovered, a partner can't make you anything you're not — not happy, not successful, not secure, not even rich. (When all is said and done, if it's his money, it's always *his* money, which is why I said earlier that it's smart to have your own.) Only *you* can make yourself who you are. *You* make your life what it is, and if you're lucky, you find someone to share it with.

It has been said that every relationship is "an assignment from God," an exercise that enables you to grasp important points about yourself and how you act with another human being. Each partner is, in effect, a teacher, and from your union, you grow and you learn new skills. I have, indeed, been twice blessed, finding not one but two terrific men in my lifetime from whom I gained valuable insights.

When I look back on my two husbands, I see two vastly different men; but more important, I see two vastly different Myrlies in the mirror of each relationship. A sheltered girl from a conservative family, at eighteen I loved Medgar instantly and more than life itself. I looked to him to mold me and, certainly in the beginning of our marriage, to direct me. Through the relationship, I saw my self-confidence blossom; I learned how to stand up for what I needed and wanted. In contrast, I was forty-three and very much an adult when I married Walter — self-assured at home and in the world. My attitude was, "Move over world . . . Myrlie's coming." I had had more than a modicum of success as a public figure and speaker. I didn't need a man to define or support me. In fact, I had promised myself I'd never love again: I couldn't live through that kind of hurt a second time.

When I met Walter, I didn't rush into his arms. I didn't hear bells and whistles. I didn't fantasize that he'd carry me off to a better world. And as a grown woman, I didn't worship him as I had Medgar. However, I did come to care deeply about Walt, first as a friend, then as so much more. Ultimately, I felt free to love him, because by then I not only loved myself, I *liked* me. And in our relationship, there was no doubt that I was his equal. ℛ

Walter later confessed that his visit to my office was a ruse. His playing card project was real, but his primary purpose was to meet me. A friend of his, whose daughter was enrolled at Pomona, had mentioned that I was now working on campus. Walt admitted that he had fallen in love with me years before — when he saw me on television after Medgar's assassination, being interviewed by Dan Rather, who was then a rookie newscaster. "I wanted to scoop you and the children into my arms, protect you, and take care of you forever," Walt told me. "You looked so helpless and just devastated."

Five years passed before Walter came back into my life. By 1973 I was working for Seligman & Latz and increasingly involved in Los Angeles politics. Tom Bradley, newly elected as mayor, had asked me to join a task force that would meet with gang members and others to address street violence. This was the first time a Los Angeles mayor had tried to bring representatives of various gangs together in hopes of achieving peace.

Bradley had also invited his old friend Walter Williams to the community meeting, which was held at a high school in Watts. Walt and Tom were the same age, both from families that were carried by the tide of Black migration to California during the twenties and thirties. When his parents arrived from Atlanta, Georgia, in 1920, Walt was two years old; Tom, whose family came from Texas in 1924, moved into the same racially mixed neighborhood. The boys grew up together, played on the same streets, double-dated, and stood side by side with their Mexican friends when Whites harassed them. Bradley, an outstanding athlete, attended UCLA on scholarship, completed law school, and secured a job with the Los Angeles Police Department. Walter went to Los Angeles Community College and then became a longshoreman and union organizer. He and Tom had followed separate career paths but always remained close friends, each challenging and changing the system in his own way.

Walter later told me that he'd known in advance I would be there. The other panelists and I sat at the front of the room in a semicircular arrangement of chairs, facing the audience. At some point, I noticed a good-looking man across the room who seemed to be staring in my direction, but I couldn't quite place him. After the meeting, members of the audience milled about, talking with panelists. Quite a few of us expressed the fear that we might exit the building to the sound of gunfire — retribution from gang members who thought we should mind our own business. In the middle of one such conversation, Walter approached me, reintroduced himself, and refreshed my memory about our first meeting. I remembered the short pants.

He asked, "Are you here with anyone?"

"No." I answered somewhat curtly — polite, but certainly not encouraging. After a brief exchange, I walked away, but everywhere I went, it seemed, Walter followed, asking if he could take me to dinner. He raised the question three or four times, and each time I skirted the issue or found some pretext to excuse myself. Finally, just to get him to stop asking, I gave him my home number — something I never did — and said, "Call."

"Well, I'll walk you to your car," he offered, without asking my permission. "This is kind of dangerous territory."

After he escorted me to the parking lot, he repeated his promise to call me. I thought, *This man is persistent. He just won't stop.*

A few weeks later, I finally agreed to meet Walter at a restaurant in Los Angeles. I always insisted on driving my own car on dates, an act of independence that provided a quick getaway, just in case. Years afterward, we had a good laugh reminiscing about our first rendezvous. He couldn't have missed me, he said, as I strode across the room in a long-sleeved leopard-print dress with a flared skirt and a tight bodice, my hair in an Afro, looking "like a Nubian queen." I remember feeling his intense gaze as I approached his table. He later admitted, "It was difficult to keep from devouring you with my eyes!"

By the end of that first date my initial impressions of Walt had vaporized. Walter Edward Williams, I realized, was a man to be reckoned with. He told me about himself — that he grew up in the Depression, living with his mother and his brother, George, who was two years his senior — and about his father's leaving home when the boys were very young. His mother, who worked as a maid, had no choice but to leave her two young sons alone. She would tell the boys to stay close, never separate, and take care of each other. Every morning, after she put a few cents under the Bible for milk, she knelt down to pray: "God, I have no one to take care of my babies. Please watch them for me until I get home."

Because he grew so tall and muscular, Walter was able to lie about his age and, as a result, got his first job unloading produce at age ten; he was driving a truck by the time he was eleven. During the Depression, when some 300,000 people in Los Angeles were out of work, a Black boy with a job was an easy target. On more than one occasion, Walter and George — smaller in stature but an excellent boxer — fought their way out of angry encounters with resentful coworkers. Walter moved on to various factory jobs and finally found his niche operating giant cranes on the docks.

In 1940, when Walt was twenty-two, Blacks constituted more than 30 percent of all the longshoremen in the United States, because most Whites viewed work on the docks as undesirable. For a long time, though, dock workers did not have the protection of a union. To begin with, Southern California had been notoriously antiunion; from 1890 to 1934, it was known as the "last citadel of the open shop." Both legal measures and outright violence were used to squelch efforts to organize workers of any color. In addition, the International Longshoremen's Association, an affiliate of the American Federation of Labor (AFL), was historically all White. The organization justified its Jim Crow policy on the ground that "discrimination was practiced before the Federation's birth" (in 1897) and that "human nature was unalterable." In 1935 the Congress of Industrial Organizations (CIO) was founded with the express purpose of unionizing the millions of unskilled and semiskilled workers the AFL had rejected. Its West Coast affiliate, the International Longshoremen's and Warehousemen's Union/Pacific Maritime Associates (ILWU/PMA), allowed Blacks to join, but the union often provided separate (and very unequal) facilities for non-Whites.

It was into this tense climate that Walter stepped when he began working on the docks. He and other courageous Black organizers worked tirelessly to change hiring practices and to bring about reform in the union itself. Listening to him talk about his work, I had great respect for Walter; he and Medgar obviously shared many values and strengths.

Equally important, though, I respected the nurturing qualities that Walter exhibited, even in our first meetings. My grandmother used to tell me, "If you want to know what a man is going to be like as a husband, look at how he treats his mother." Walter had dropped out of college to care for his mother. His brother was married by then, and Walt said he didn't want George to be burdened with two families. Here was a man, I could tell, who knew how to take care of the people he loved.

In the weeks that followed that first date, we frolicked at the beach, each stealing furtive glances at the other's body; we took walks together; we went out dining and dancing. My children immediately loved him, and it was easy to see why. He was intelligent and perceptive, both interesting and interested in others. He had no false pretenses. His steady and dependable Taurus was a perfect foil for my erratic Pisces. Conversation just flowed between us. We not only shared the same values and deep religious convictions, but we also had much else in common — our activism, the ways we cared about our children (Walt had five by previous marriages), the same sense of humor, and a true love for music and sports. Walter was passionate about baseball, basketball, horseback riding, and boxing; I loved soccer; and we both enjoyed football. Walt had a penchant for bike-riding, and I for long walks, and we often joined each other in both activities.

Best of all was our intense mutual attraction. When we finally kissed, I was amazed. It had been ten years since Medgar had been killed and, for the first time, another man's lips felt right. There was sheer electricity between us, which lasted throughout and strengthened our marriage. In fact, long after we were married, we still stared at each other crossing a room and felt our hearts flutter. He was a strapping man — six foot four and 230 pounds of pure muscle — yet he was incredibly graceful and light on his feet. I found it thrilling to see him run, his long legs loping, his biceps rippling, with the elegance of a Watusi warrior racing through the bush. He was a remarkable dancer too, and whenever we hit the floor I felt at home and deliciously safe in his arms. To paraphrase the Beatles' "Something," a song that invariably reminds me of Walt, something in the way he moved attracted me like no other lover.

Walter was my soulmate. He helped me appreciate fun, fantasy, and freedom. We never felt threatened by each other. And, oh, could we laugh! Humor is, I believe, critically important to a good relationship — in my view, close to the top of the list of "secrets" of success. Laughter is a wonderful method of bonding and of relieving stress. In fact, that ability to lapse into hysterical laughter was one of the most precious things Walt and I shared.

Another bond was our friendship. In many relationships, when the initial high-energy, physical phase fizzles, there's nothing left. I gave myself the time to really get to know Walt, allowing my trust to grow. In part, I was motivated by wisdom, in part by fear. I had grown suspicious over the years. Whenever any man showed interest in me, I fretted to myself: *Is it because of my name, my contacts, or the mistaken opinion that I have money?* During our courtship, I pushed Walter away at times, testing to see if he loved me enough to persist. But I also recognized that he offered me more than I'd ever expected. He was good to my children, a caring listener, a supportive ally. And he loved me purely for who I was, which in my book is the hallmark of a true friend and the basis for a solid relationship. ✾

With all of his virtues, and as much as I adored being with Walt, we had many differences to reconcile too — differences that became even more pronounced as he began to entertain thoughts of marriage. I say "he" because I was perfectly content to let our situation remain as it was. The longer we dated, the more I saw that the two of us had conflicting notions about relationships. For one thing, he was fifteen years older, and we naturally had dissimilar professional goals. I was determined to set the world on fire, just as he was slowing down. He had simple tastes, and I had become accustomed to an upwardly mobile lifestyle. My first marriage had been about taking care of a husband; now, embarking on my career at ARCO, it was I who needed a "wife."

Walt definitely wanted a woman who would "be there" for him when he came home, an expectation I certainly didn't meet. When we started dating, I was still traveling a great deal. While we made the most of our time together, we spent much of our time apart. Consequently, our early relationship was characterized by long absences and passionate homecomings. We often met in Los Angeles, at my apartment at Bunker Towers, which I had begun renting during my ARCO tenure, to alleviate the need to commute daily to Claremont.

During one of our discussions about relationships, Walt declared that a man who was actively pursuing a woman should have the right to monitor her activities if he felt the need. A few weeks later, I found out exactly what that meant.

"I was on my way here to see you last night, and your drapes were open," he informed me one evening as we sat in my apartment. "I could see a man in your living room."

It was bad enough that Walter might draw the wrong conclusion about my entertaining another man. (For the record, my guest and I had been talking, waiting for others to join us for a work session.) I was fiercely protective of my reputation and didn't want to give anyone an opportunity to question it. I was also very conscious of my responsibility to serve as a role model for my children. However, it was what Walt said next that was even more infuriating.

"I decided not to come up because you were obviously busy, so I pulled over to the curb and observed for a while."

I lost it; his deliberate spying was simply unforgivable. "Might I remind you, Mr. Williams, that we are just *dating,* and you have no right whatsoever to monitor what I do or with whom I spend my time. I am a free woman. Do that again, and you lose me."

He was dumbfounded. "That's what a man does when he cares about a woman," he offered in his own defense.

"Not this woman," I said.

Defining the boundaries beyond which you will not let anyone pass is probably *the* most vital secret of a successful relationship. Deepening intimacy can be confusing, because you become entwined in each other's lives. You start to share friends, stories, even secrets. But merging is never healthy. Just because you invite a person into your world and reveal your inner self, that doesn't mean you turn over your will, become dependent, or leave yourself defenseless. I knew that if I weren't emphatic with Walter — stating in no uncertain terms that it was *not* all right for him to think of me as his property or as someone he needed to watch over — we would be heading down the slippery slope of dashed expectations. I would have come to resent his behavior and, one day, ended the relationship.

Of course, you can't expect a partner to be a mind reader; as so many articles and books advise us, you must express your needs and feelings. Obviously, a relationship is headed for trouble (or is there already) if the partners talk *at* each other, with neither one listening to the other, or if one talks down to the other, assuming that one's point of view is superior. But good communication is even more than that. You each must be able to share candidly who you really are. Even if you fear that your partner has other ideas regarding something you feel strongly about, be true to yourself, and lead with your best shot. Otherwise, you will be subsumed by his or her life and standards, and you will lose yourself in the bargain.

Another difficult issue Walt and I faced was our different social positions. Some supposedly well-intentioned acquaintances questioned our relationship; they saw him as less educated and accomplished than I, an improbable partner. When they worried out loud whether Walt was a "suitable" mate for me, I knew what they were implying. They unfortunately restricted their view to Walt's career, not his character. I would not be honest, though, if I didn't admit to having my own reservations. Would our differences lead to conflicts? I was looking for higher mountains to climb. Were our life goals too dissimilar? Though I recognized that I no longer *needed* a man to take care of me financially, what if I *wanted* one to?

Many African-American couples today face a similar challenge: The wife may make more money or have the better, or at least more socially acceptable, job. Or maybe she's not yet earning a higher salary but is clearly more ambitious. Such divisions lead many sisters to shy away from certain relationships, fearing there's no way to equalize or compromise; and they lead many Black men to either complain endlessly or leave altogether. I'm pleased that neither Walter nor I ran from our differences; rather, we acknowledged them.

People can change or accommodate one another's needs, but many a woman labors under the illusion that she can change her man into the person she wants him to be. That's foolhardy; down the line, she's almost sure to come up against the very traits that annoyed her in the first place. Differences between two people, whether they emanate from personality or life circumstances, don't magically disappear. I had to really examine my concerns about our dissimilarities. I didn't expect to change for Walter, and I couldn't expect him to change for me. However, we had to work out ways to accommodate each other when it was important.

We also tried to determine where one's strength could complement the other. Instead of viewing his laid-back attitude as a liability, for example, I came to accept his pace as a good balance to my own

driven nature. What little rest I took, I have to admit, was because of
Walt. Even today, when I'm pushing too hard, I hear his voice saying,
"Honey, you've got to slow down."

My point: Every woman has to determine what she wants in a
man and from her man. She may not find exactly what she wants —
there are no perfect packages — but at least she has to articulate to
herself what's important to her, look at his assets and his drawbacks,
and do a little math. Does the good outweigh the bad? Can you live
with the shortcomings? Can you bear in mind that you have shortcomings too, and that he has to live with yours? Remember that dis-
agreements are bound to come up — whether over finances, in-laws,
exes, sex, religion, or the way you plan to raise children — and you
need to talk about them. Put it all out there, because whatever you
keep inside builds up and eventually spills out. ♪

Even though I knew in my heart that Walt had the characteristics I
wanted in a man, for a long time during our courtship, I was reluctant
to even discuss the subject of marriage, because I feared that becoming "Mrs. Williams" would compromise my independence. Whenever Walt brought up the subject, I steered the conversation in
another direction, often by saying, "You're such a good friend — I
can't bear the thought of ruining our relationship. I just don't want to
take that chance."

"But don't you *love* me?" he'd ask.

"Yes, of course I love you, and I respect and admire you. But I can
marry anyone. To have a real, true friend — now, that's *special*."

One day, though, Walt wouldn't allow me to engage in my usual
dodging. We were standing in my kitchen in Claremont, having just
returned from Vicksburg, where he had met Aunt Myrlie for the first
time. She adored Walt instantly and made no secret of her feelings.
He knew her approval was important to me.

"Look, Myrlie, you know I love you," he said firmly, "but this relationship doesn't seem to be moving anywhere, not forward, not backward. I want to know, where do *you* think we're going? Do you want to
marry me or not?"

I reiterated my speech about our friendship, adding, with what I thought was an air of finality, "I'm satisfied with where our relationship is."

"Well, that's not good enough," he responded in a tone of sternness I'd never heard from him before.

"Too bad," I answered flippantly, calling his bluff. "That's the way I want it, and that's the way it's going to be."

"No it's not," said Walter, giving me one of his long, reproving looks. "I want to know if we're ever going forward."

I stuck to my guns. "No, Walt, I've told you. I don't want to get married. I'm happy with my life as it is."

Then, to my surprise, he simply said, "Okay. Are you sure that's your answer? If so, I'm not staying around. I'm not going to be used."

"Yes, I'm sure," I said, not believing him.

"Well, I guess I can say it was nice while it lasted. I'm gone."

He quietly walked out the door and got into his car. One, two, three, four days passed with no word from Walter. Everyone was pressuring me not to let him go — my aunt, my children, my best friends. Here was a man who embraced me, embraced my children without trying to replace their father, and was secure enough to make room in our relationship for Medgar's ghost. Darrell, who was going on twenty-three at the time, was angry that I pushed Walter away. "This man really loves you — don't hurt him," he insisted. "He's just what you need — someone you can't walk over."

Five, six days, a week passed, and still no word. I waited by the phone in disbelief. I was too stubborn to call, but the waiting finally got the better of me. I phoned to tell Walt I wanted to meet him. "I have something important to discuss with you," I said cryptically.

"No," answered the cold, disembodied voice. "I told you I have nothing else to say to you. There's no need for us to see each other." I was crushed and astonished. In his own quiet way, Walter was stronger than I had realized; if there was ever a time when he exhibited his fortitude, this was it.

Two or three more days passed, and I called again. "I need your advice on something," I lied.

He reluctantly agreed to meet me for lunch the next day. When he appeared at the restaurant, he was downright icy. After a few minutes of small talk, he said gruffly, "I thought you had some business to discuss with me. What is it?"

I smiled coyly. "You know why I'm here."

"No I don't." His somber expression didn't change, nor his tone. "Tell me."

"C'mon, Walter," I said, beginning to lose my patience. "Cut the bullshit. You do so know why I'm here."

"No I don't," he repeated. "And if you don't tell me what this is about, I'm leaving."

He had me. I said to myself, *Myrlie, you have an opportunity for true happiness here. Don't be a fool and waste it.* I took a breath and warmly looked into his eyes, desperate to get through to him. "I don't want us to end. I don't want this to be over. I'd like to move forward, if it's not too late."

Walt sat straight and tall in his chair, and his eyes narrowed as he met my glance. "I love your children, and I loved you," he responded, making sure to emphasize the past tense in his description of his feelings for me. He wanted me to squirm. He was clearly tired of tolerating my indecision, and rather than riding out the ups and downs, he was finally taking a stand. After nearly four years of pursuing me, he was letting me know that I was going to have to chase *him* to get him back.

"Give me another chance," I pleaded. "I just wasn't sure I could give you the kind of love you deserved. Just give me a little time."

With that, Walter finally melted. He reached across the table and gently held my hand. "That's okay, baby," he reassured. "Haven't I always told you I love you enough for both of us?"

I looked at him and I *knew*. Not only was this man too good to let go, but he understood me. "I love you, Walt. You know that, don't you?" I paused and swallowed hard. He waited for me to continue, which I finally did: "And I'd be honored to marry you."

Things between us changed. Up to that point, we had had almost the opposite dynamic of that which existed between Medgar and me — Walt catered to my every whim, and I seemed to have the upper hand. But thanks to his refusal to maintain the status quo just because *I* wanted to, the scales tipped, and we achieved a better balance. He still brought flowers and little presents for me, but not as many as in the past. I, in turn, became a bit more solicitous than I had been; I didn't want to lose him.

No relationship remains static, with a fifty-fifty balance. One partner loves a little more than the other, one has a slight upper hand. The trick, I believe, is to make sure that you work toward a reasonable equilibrium so that you don't get stuck in a rut. There will be some areas in which one person has a greater degree of authority, although not necessarily dominance. If you're lucky, you can reach a point where you both give and take — as Walt and I did — and you will no longer need to measure. Walt may have *appeared* to be in the submissive role in our relationship, but when it counted, he proved to me just how tough he could be. I needed that show of strength from him, and that provocation.

As we began to make plans for our wedding, Walt and I set some ground rules. When a couple even begins contemplating marriage, it's vital to understand each other's expectations and cover as much as possible *in advance*. How do we combine our money? Is it yours? Mine? Ours? Who's responsible for the household, for children? This latter issue is a particularly relevant one for young career women who come home and, even today, are expected to do the drudgery. When they try to reapportion responsibilities, their men are often shocked. The most some husbands concede is a promise to "help out."

In my first marriage, I had scrubbed and shined enough hardwood floors and washed enough windows and cleaned enough bathrooms to last a lifetime. I made it clear — and only half-jokingly — that I wouldn't get married unless Walt agreed that either he'd help with the heavy chores or we'd hire someone to do them. We also put our money issues down on paper, each making a list of expenditures and income. (Walt confided that he had never shared this information with anyone before, so it was extremely difficult for him.) What was his was his, we agreed, and what was mine was mine. What we would build together, regardless of who paid for it, would be *ours*. I didn't expect him to provide for my children — and vice versa.

I can't overstress the importance of this kind of rigorous sharing of needs and information. Although Walt and I didn't draw up a formal premarital agreement, it's often a good idea to do so. Preparing such a contract might seem to take the romance out of your relationship momentarily, but in the long run, it might just keep the passion alive. Too many young couples go into marriage believing that love alone will see them through the rough spots. When the honeymoon is over, though, and there are bills to be paid, a house to take care of, illnesses, and children to deal with, you need more. You need trust, communication, and maturity.

Ideally, each partner ends up doing what he or she does best and enjoys — say, you love to do yard work, and your mate finds it comforting to fold warm laundry. But you need to be able to negotiate with each other the things that don't fall into place quite so neatly. Remember, too, that the typical arguments between wife and husband are never really about who cooks, who does the dishes, or who takes Johnny to his music lessons. They're about reciprocal respect and power. Walt's and my relationship thrived because we accepted each other, faults and all, and had tremendous respect for each other's strengths. When it came to making small or big decisions, we listened to the other's point of view and measured it against our own. Even if more of my actual dollars or his went toward purchasing some item, it didn't matter, because we had equal input and equal power in the relationship. And we didn't try to make each other over. ⅊

This may sound odd, but the day I married Walter, I was still not in love with him — or at least I didn't think I was. Truth be told, right up to the ceremony itself, I continued to worry about whether I was doing the right thing. I didn't even want a formal wedding. My original idea was to get married in jeans, high atop Mount Baldy, and have a picnic afterward. Walt and his daughter Donetta started an annual tradition, which my children and I had joined. We all — children, grandchildren, and great-grandchildren included — reserved an area in the park, where we barbecued, sang songs, and played softball and other games. Walt's and my turn to host the event was coming up and, we thought, why not combine the two events and put the money we'd have spent on a wedding toward painting the house in Claremont?

When informed of our plan, Reena shook her head in disbelief. "Mom, you're never going to do this again," she said pointedly. "Do it right." And ultimately we did. But at precisely five o'clock on July 31, 1976, when the wedding party proceeded down the aisle of Little Bridges Chapel, on the Claremont College campus, I was frightened to death. Van and Darrell stood on either side of me. Just as we three were given the nod to start the march to the altar, I whispered to them, "I can't go through with it."

I laugh now when I look at my wedding album, because one of the pictures captures that moment perfectly. There I am in my long, peach-colored wedding gown, while on either side of me are my sons, in light blue tuxedos, like matching footmen, arms linked in mine as they escort me through the church doorway. The expression on both young men's faces is clear: "Forget it, Mom, we're not going to let you off the hook!"

A psychiatrist in Beverly Hills, whom I'd seen for a few sessions, told me that I was still holding on to Medgar, and he may have been right. My defenses were so strongly honed that I probably had convinced myself that I could never love Walter in the deep, earth-shattering way I had loved Medgar. I do know that when I finally reached the altar — Reena, my matron of honor, on one side, Walt on the other — I could almost see Medgar's smile and hear his sigh of relief, as if he were blessing our union. I imagined him saying, "Whew! I don't have to worry about you anymore. This is the right man for you."

I have friends who tease me now, recalling the many conversations I had had about marrying Walter, even after I accepted his proposal. Should I? Shouldn't I? Those talks enabled me to look at who I was and really say out loud what I was afraid of. This is crucial. Whatever has happened in your past, it's vitally important to review where you've come from and what kind of relationship you've been in, and to examine the particular "baggage" you've been carrying around. Do so, if you can, by talking to good friends who have the ability to be impartial, or by consulting a professional.

I'm grateful that Walt forced my hand. He obviously practiced Medgar's favorite tactic: Tell Myrlie she can't have something, and she'll do whatever she has to to get it! I finally understood that Walter loved me fiercely and that he cherished my children. And I knew he was genuinely in love with *me*, not my image. Conversely, he never tried to impress me. He was always himself.

After our marriage, though, Walt was pigeonholed into a role not unlike that of an entertainer's spouse: relegated to the sidelines while I stood in the limelight. As a result, there were some difficult times for him. Having been Medgar's supporting player for so long, I understood and identified with his situation. I made sure I took his arm whenever we were in a crowd of people who knew me; I stayed directly at his side and let the world know, *this man is my husband.*

The first formal affair we attended after our wedding was the Urban League's annual Whitney Young Dinner in Los Angeles — *the* social event for the African-American community. Walter looked dashing in his tuxedo, yet several people spoke only to me as they met us, snubbing him with obvious disdain. With each slight, I could feel his hand tighten in mine and imagined steam emanating from his nose and ears. One man — let's say his name was Carl — chose to look right past him, even though he knew who Walt was. Disgusted, Walt started to walk away, but I squeezed his hand and said to Carl, who was being as warm to me as he was cold to Walt, "Carl, you do remember my husband, Walter Williams, don't you?" Embarrassed, Carl gave a perfunctory nod — he had no choice at that point — but I knew Walt wanted to take him out. We walked away abruptly, leaving Carl standing there, his mouth agape.

After a year of such treatment, Walter finally reached a point where he said to me, "I just won't go to those affairs."

I pleaded with him, "Don't pull back now. Come with me." He did — but only because he knew how much it meant to me to have him at my side.

The challenge for both of us was to continue to do our own work and, when we could, bring our two worlds together. We also scheduled time that was specifically *ours*. In the last several years of our marriage, Walt always traveled with me; whenever I was scheduled to deliver a speech or make an appearance, I demanded airfare and accommodations for him in my contract. In all honesty, it was one of the few ways we could carve out time together. On those jaunts, we always set aside a private day to do whatever we wanted, even if it was just to walk around the city holding hands. Our relationship withstood whatever philosophical and economic differences we had, because we both knew that the personal was more important than the political.

Also, both of us were secure within ourselves. I had come a long way from Vicksburg, and I had no doubts about my ability to stand on my own two feet — which is precisely why I was able to let down my guard and lean on Walter as much as I eventually did. He was a strong man, large in every sense of the word, self-possessed and steady. I always described him as "my rock of Gibraltar." The snubs rankled us, to be sure. But he knew he was just as good as the next man — better, I always told him, *better.*

Long before meeting me, Walt had spent years associating with politicians and corporate executives. In his own world, among activists, among organizers, he had a following, too, and was highly respected. There were times when I accompanied him to one of his meetings and I was ignored. At other times, I purposely took a backseat, allowing him to bask in the recognition he so deserved. I was proud of him.

More often than not, though, it was he who stepped aside for me. Bette Midler's song "The Wind Beneath My Wings" says it all about Walter: He never felt diminished in my shadow. Whenever he traveled with me, younger men gravitated to him and inevitably asked, "How do you do it?" They wanted to know how his male ego withstood being "the husband of," and how he not only lived with a prominent woman but also with a persistent and revered ghost. The key — the answer he repeatedly gave to those who questioned him — was his secure sense of self and his belief in my love.

Perhaps the most tangible evidence of Walt's self-confidence was his suggestion that I keep the Evers name. "I have watched you work so hard to be your own person," he said on the day of our wedding. "I want you to continue to use Evers professionally." I was speechless, and my heart melted. We had never discussed whether I would change my name; truthfully, I had no intention of doing so. But I thought to myself, *How wonderful that he thought of this on his own.*

"I love you, and I know you love me," he added. "But I also know you have a public face. It's enough for me that you will be Mrs. Walter Williams at home."

Walt's resolve was tested when I was at ARCO. One of the vice presidents had said to me after Walt and I had married, "You are no longer Evers. Your name is Williams." I didn't respond, refusing to dignify his small-mindedness. But I thought to myself: *Poor man, I'm not going to start anything here that I might be sorry for.* A few months later, the same VP hosted a staff party at his home, and Walt was there with me. Damn if that man didn't approach Walt and say in all seriousness, "I don't know how you put up with this woman. She has not changed her name yet."

Walter smiled politely, looked him in the eye, and said, "I hope you don't have a problem with it, because I don't. I know who I am, she knows who she is, and we agree. She's Myrlie Evers professionally. She is Mrs. Walter Williams in her personal life."

And I was. ℟

Of course, Walt and I continued to have our differences; every couple does. One part of my own personality could be — and has been described as — demanding. Especially when I'm under stress, and deadlines are piling up, I want what I want when I want it, and I expect everyone to fall in line. There were times when my grown children, who adored Walt, reprimanded me for treating him too brusquely. "Mom, you are not giving directions to your staff," Reena told me on more than one occasion. Of all my children, Van was probably the most protective of Pops, as he called the man who came into his life when he was thirteen. Walt, after all, was the only father he'd known.

What my children didn't see was that Walter was not only extremely capable of taking care of himself, but that he knew exactly how to deal with me when I was at my worst. He tolerated my outbreaks, my bossiness, my insistence about doing things *my* way — but only to a point. Then, with a look that could paralyze, he'd very quietly say, "Myrlie. . . ." When he spoke my name that way, it was my cue to retreat. "That's it!" he'd warn me.

I backed off every time. Although I knew Walt loved me tremendously, I also knew I could push him only so far. He carried himself in a way that commanded respect, including mine.

Sometimes we tested each other's limits, on occasion having rather loud, intense debates. Still, we always honored the primary rule of fair fighting: Never let an argument reach the point where you say something for which you'll later be sorry. We were both genuinely grounded and sensitive. We knew that it doesn't matter how repeatedly or sincerely you apologize for speaking cruelly, or how satisfying it feels afterward to kiss and make up; hurtful words always remain in the recesses of the mind.

Our previous marriages taught us lasting lessons about dealing with conflict. In my marriage to Medgar, I had rarely expressed anger and could hold grudges for months. In his earlier relationships, Walt had learned how important it was to communicate feelings immediately — as long as no one got carried away. Whenever we found ourselves nearing that limit, we claimed space for ourselves. I might call a halt to an argument by heading for the door, explaining, "I'm going for a walk," "I'm going downstairs," or "I'll be in the kitchen . . . if you need me," emphasizing the "need me." Walt, who loved to drive his burgundy Buick, would say, "I'm leaving. I'll be back shortly," and I knew never to ask, "Where are you going?"

I had carried over one very important practice from my marriage to Medgar. We never knew whether a bomb would go off in the middle of the night, or whether we'd ever see each other again when Medgar left the house. Therefore, we made it a rule neither to go to bed nor to depart from each other in anger. Every night and every morning, we embraced and said, "I love you," and if we were angry at each other, we added, "but I don't like you right now." I did the same thing with Walter and with my children, who, later on, maintained the practice with their own loves.

Through it all, Walter and I allowed each other to grow and learn — to learn from each other and from our mistakes. We followed

Kahlil Gibran's advice about marriage, "Stand together but not too near together. For the pillars of the temple stand apart, and the oak tree and the cypress grow not in each other's shadow." Partners need to work together *and* apart, play together *and* apart — have their own friends and activities enjoyed outside the relationship. Walter and I experienced life together, but we also had our separate interests. We expanded our minds constantly and later shared what we had learned. Ultimately, we became bigger together than the sum of our separate personalities, while never losing our individuality.

Regrettably, Walt and I seldom had a normal life together. I worked during the day; he worked at night; after officially retiring, he continued to do volunteer work with the longshoreman's union. I traveled; he took time with his ailing mother. We never had the luxury of spending a week or a month together without my having to be someplace other than home. Moreover, for the greater part of our nineteen-year marriage, I was locked into high gear where my career was concerned. The pace I kept was a source of worry to both of us. A letter Walt wrote to me in 1978, when ARCO sent me to a ten-week management course for women at Simmons College, in Boston, says it all:

> Please get as much rest as you can. I guess this is almost selfishly motivated, because I know I don't want to lose you. Neither do I want to see you ill or suffering. Please ease up if the strain is too much, even though you are close to finishing up. You don't have anything to prove to me. I loved you before ARCO. I will love you eternally.
>
> Your husband, Walter

In 1987, when the restructuring at ARCO was continuing to weigh me down, Walt looked at me and said, "Quit, baby. I can take care of you. Allow me to do that." And when I — quite understandably — worried about not having my own salary, he urged. "Come on, honey. You always said you could pinch a penny until it screamed. Prove it." Though I did leave ARCO, I immediately dove into even greater political and managerial challenges. Walter still tried to get me to slow down, while doing his best to take care of me.

Among other positive life changes, Walt was responsible for my finally leaving the rat race of Los Angeles. He often said, "The only way I will get you out of this madness is to move you away from the center of it." We had frequent discussions about leaving, but for me it was just talk. When I sustained a back injury on the job, though, I was forced to take a medical leave from my position as commissioner of public works, and Walt seized the moment.

Through his work, he had become familiar with the Pacific Northwest and had fallen in love with the area. He wanted to look for a home in Portland or Seattle, where he had many friends and, because these cities were seaports, he had union contacts as well. He had already started an oral history of his years on the docks and was involved in another project whereby the union would underwrite scholarships for young people studying maritime law. Both undertakings would have been easier to work on in port cities. However, we knew a couple who had moved from Los Angeles to Bend, Oregon, a town of some ten thousand residents in the high-desert interior of the state, 120 miles southeast of Portland. Because our friends had raved about the area, we decided to pay it a visit.

I was initially less than enthusiastic about making any move. When my back injury had kept me at home, it was the first time Walt and I lived together twenty-four hours a day, seven days a week, leaving us to wonder: *Could we really be with each other all the time? Would our marriage hold up? Could I slow down?* With those questions in mind, we made the sixteen-hour drive to Bend one glorious July weekend and, once there, stumbled upon a house that we both loved. It was a modern split-level, redwood structure, with lots of windows and an expansive deck facing the Cascade Mountains. It was set on two and a half acres of Oregon desert — a vast space punctuated by juniper trees and sagebrush.

Surveying the property from the back deck, Walt asked, "Do you think you can live here?" In the distance, we could see the crests of Mount Bachelor and the Three Sisters, an astonishingly beautiful vista. To my surprise, my mouth opened and "Yes" came out. The small-town feeling and the physical qualities of Bend were compelling — the sparkling air, the fresh smell of pine trees, the rippling Deschutes River, the mountain views and, at night, stars so bright you felt you could touch them. My body and my soul were crying out for this kind of retreat from the smog, crime, and bustle of Los Angeles. Though I continued to commute every week after we first moved to Oregon, when I resigned as commissioner of public works in 1990, Walter finally had achieved his victory.

In Bend, we reveled in the small pleasures of life, having breakfast together, watching the squirrels chitter-chattering, the deer peeking out from the brush, and the birds feasting on the feeder Walt had hung outside the window. He rode horses, went hunting, and was happier than I'd ever seen him. After all the years of running and being "Miss Thang," I came to enjoy our peaceful solitude, too. I puttered in the kitchen because I *wanted* to. I cooked elaborate meals, cared for my rose garden, had friends over, went swimming. Some days, I even slept late. And best of all, I took long, thoughtful walks with the husband I loved more than life.

Walter was a loyal, passionate, and giving man. I lay next to him at night, feeling his warmth. He heard me and held me, respected me, and gave me the precious intangibles that money couldn't buy — love, peace of mind, and security. I often chuckled at the irony of it all, remembering my days as a struggling single mother, when I fantasized that some Prince Charming would carry me off to his kingdom and pamper me with riches galore in a palace all my own. I had found my prince, and I was in heaven.

7

THE *MISSION*
AND THE *MOVIE*

Staying the course

Arriving at the courtroom for the De La Beckwith trial with Darrell, Reena, and security.

*Those who cannot remember the past are
condemned to repeat it.*

೭ *George Santayana*

Along with raising my children and advancing my career, one of
the three dominant themes of my life has been to find meaning in
Medgar's death. I would not and could not forget him. His presence
was constant; I heard his voice in my mind and saw his reflection in my
children's eyes. And I felt his spirit in the changes that transformed
America in the sixties and seventies.

The day after Medgar was assassinated, my grandmother had tried
to comfort me by saying, "Baby, a lot of good will come from his
death." Though I resented what I felt was the insensitivity of her words
in that moment, time proved her to be correct: Medgar's death did
indeed galvanize the civil rights movement, inspiring more people
than ever to join the struggle. The coming years brought legislative
gains nationally — among them, passage of the Civil Rights Act of
1964 and the Voting Rights Act of 1965 — as well as significant
reforms in Mississippi itself. It was nothing short of astounding that by
1965 a handful of Negro policemen, firemen, and school crossing
guards — albeit restricted to Black neighborhoods — were on the
Jackson city payroll. I often thought to myself: *My husband paved the
way for this.*

By the midsixties, nonviolent protests gave way to riots in Watts,
Detroit, and other cities, and African-American leaders were divided
over the rising tide of Black nationalism. Medgar had become interested in our African roots early in his life and had always stressed
racial pride. He would have embraced many of the principles of Black
Power, but he was not a separatist. He believed in working toward economic gains for our people and felt that the most productive strategy

would be to achieve political solidarity, with organizations making a concerted joint effort to reform the system, not to live outside it. It upset Medgar to see various leaders battle over their respective courses of action and jockey for prominence. He perceived the big picture, and viewed personal agendas as self-limiting barriers to achieving justice.

That the groups continued to compete with one another after his death would certainly have troubled my husband. Even more distressing, had he lived to see it, would have been witnessing the Nixon administration's policy of "benign neglect," which, though not labeled as such, was carried out more insidiously through the Reagan years and beyond. True, growing numbers of African-Americans were elected to public office, achieved prominence in a variety of fields, became professors at formerly all-White universities, were invited to discuss policy with the president, and were openly courted by the Republican Party, but the vast majority of our people became even more disenfranchised. For them, a combination of forces — racism, substandard education, a lack of job opportunities and good housing, and the belief that their vote didn't make a difference anyway — translated into virtually no political or economic power. Speaking out on these issues, as I did frequently during this time, I would caution the audience, "We have made gains, but we must fight just as hard or perhaps harder to hold on to them." Then I'd quote Medgar's exhortation: "Freedom is not free; you cannot ever let up on your quest. Be vigilant always."

I kept his words in my heart as I made my way through the decades, for I was on a personal mission as well. Younger generations of African-Americans had little idea who Medgar was and scant appreciation of his role in the movement. I often thought to myself, *Medgar was too early.* Even more disturbing to me was the fact that his murderer had been identified and tried but never convicted. However much change had occurred in Mississippi, which by 1990 had more Black elected officials than any other state, in my mind, justice had not been served. Byron De La Beckwith was technically still under indictment for murder, but he was allowed to return to his hometown, Greenwood, Mississippi, to work, to continue to spew his racist venom, even to run for lieutenant governor in a state primary election. In short, he was *free*. "Tried twice without being convicted," I wrote of Beckwith in my 1967 book, *For Us, the Living*, "he is unlikely to be tried again unless there is new evidence of his guilt." I was determined to get that evidence

I learned perseverance at my grandmother's knee, and I learned from Medgar's example as well: Stay the course. Even when the outlook is bleak, even when the prize seems out of reach, you must keep going. Thus, for thirty years, I kept my sights on my dual missions: to secure a rightful place in history for Medgar, and to see his murderer convicted. ❧

After I moved to California, I made a point of returning to Mississippi at least three times a year with the express purpose of keeping tabs on Delay, as Beckwith's sidekicks called him. The Magnolia State was still home; in a sense, it always will be. I had made a good life for myself in the West, but Mississippi never stopped calling out to me. My experiences there are forever embedded in my senses: the feel of the dark Delta dirt under my feet — dusty in summer, "gumbo mud" in the winter — the smells of pine trees and magnolia blossoms, the sights of kudzu trailing down a hillside and farmers selling produce from the back of their trucks, the sounds of birds and crows, mingling with the mournful strains of a blues guitar off in the distance. Medgar, too, loved Mississippi and always said, "Once Mississippi changes, it will be the best place in the world to live."

Though the state had undergone tremendous change, to my family and me his assassin's freedom was the embodiment of everything Medgar fought so hard against. From the day of the first hung jury, when Beckwith departed from the courthouse and stood on the steps flaunting his invincibility and racist views, I knew that someday, somewhere, this man was going to brag about his role in Medgar's death. And I was determined to be there when he did, or at least to be certain that his acknowledgment of guilt would be recorded. With no funds to hire an investigator, I launched a plan of action, identifying resources and using them to achieve my goal. I subscribed to Mississippi papers, searched for a scrap of information here, a tidbit of gossip there — anything that might be used to convince the state to reopen the case.

I also depended on news that was relayed through my network of sympathetic friends. This means of communication dates back to the time of slavery, when the so-called house niggers, who toiled in the Big House, unobtrusively listened to the masters' conversations. Whatever they overheard while serving meals, cleaning rooms, doing laundry, or taking care of the children, was passed down to the field niggers. My own contacts were people who worked in judges' homes and kitchens, for legislators on the Sovereignty Commission — the state's segregation watchdog formed in 1956 — and for members of the racist Citizens' Council, who were among the most respected professionals in the state.

I always asked the same questions — Have you heard anything about Beckwith? Has he talked? Where is he? What is he doing? — and I almost always got the same response to my incessant grilling: "Myrlie, if we hear anything, we'll let you know, but why don't you let it go?" How, they wondered, could I constantly reopen the scar of my awful wound? What people didn't realize was that the wound had never closed. When one has been so critically hurt as I had been by Medgar's senseless death, and then by Mississippi's failure to punish his assassin, the wound only festers. I focused on my mission and, through prayer and self-talk, found the determination to carry out the charge. It wasn't so much that I believed Beckwith's incarceration would make the wound disappear, but I knew that justice at least would allow my children and me to start healing. My tenacity both amazed and angered people around me. Some even branded me a nuisance. But no matter who scoffed at my efforts, no matter what sensible arguments they advanced, I kept reaching down inside myself for strength, and I continued to weave into my life's tapestry a single thread marked "Byron De La Beckwith."

In the years that followed his inconclusive trials, Beckwith was very obliging, leaving traces of his malevolent activities throughout the South. Because he was active in the Citizens' Council, he kept cropping up in the news and in personal accounts, always attached to some evildoing. After his second trial, for example, his name appeared in a newspaper article about White picketers protesting the integration of the Leflore Theater in Greenwood. Delay loved the limelight and openly expounded his views to members of the press, refusing only when an interviewer was Black or Catholic or Jewish. One video news clip in my files shows him chasing a young Black reporter off his property. Over the years, Beckwith boasted that he found meaning in Christian Identity, a racist movement that he called "a religion." Its core belief was that all the non-White races are like animals and therefore soulless; and to Beckwith, an ordained Christian Identity minister, murdering Medgar was no more serious a crime than killing an animal. "God put us here to rule over the dusky races," he once told a TV reporter.

In 1974 the law finally caught up with him. He was apprehended by FBI agents in Louisiana, on his way to bomb the home of a prominent Jewish leader in New Orleans. Acquitted in federal court, he went to trial on state charges in 1975, and the jury, which included five Black women, found him guilty. He was given a five-year sentence for carrying explosives; in 1977, having exhausted his appeals, he went to jail. That same year, in a letter to the editor of *Attack!*, a White supremacist magazine, Beckwith referred to Medgar as "Mississippi's mightiest nigger." And he added smugly, "We have had no trouble with that nigger since they buried him — none!" He served three years and, on his release from jail, returned to his dilapidated cottage in a rural area south of Greenwood. Soon thereafter he remarried and moved in with his new wife in Signal Mountain, Tennessee. But I always knew where he was. ~

While I was following Beckwith's trail, he was keeping his eye on me. In 1987, during my bid to represent the Tenth Council District in Los Angeles, I, along with the twelve other candidates in the primary race, participated in a series of candidates' forums at which we were given a few minutes to discuss our platform and then answer questions from the audience. One evening, after finishing my speech, I excused myself early because of another engagement, left the stage, and made my way up the aisle toward the exit. Suddenly a man emerged from one of the rows of seats. He was in his late thirties or early forties, with stringy, dirty-blond hair, and was wearing an army-green Eisenhower jacket and an odd little hat. Thinking he was a well-wisher, I extended my hand, but he refused to take it.

"You've got to stop this," he said menacingly.

"I'm sorry," I stammered in as cheerful a voice as I could muster. Although he obviously wasn't referring to campaign issues, I turned to them as a defensive tactic. "I don't understand, but I'm sure that whatever the problem, we can clear it up. I'm late for my next meeting, though, so why don't you call my campaign headquarters and perhaps make an appointment?"

"No!" he shouted. "You've got to stop!"

At that point, heads in the audience began to turn toward us. I continued walking, but he kept following me. Just as I was about to open the door, I wheeled around and said indignantly, "Who *are* you? What is your name?"

He never answered, but just squinted at me with sinister, lashless eyes. I went out the door, but still he was at my side. As I made my way to the street, trying to ignore him, he said menacingly, "You've got to stop this now. You keep doing it to my family."

"Who are you?" I demanded once again.

"The Beckwiths are my family."

As I heard him say "Beckwith," I realized that he had his hand in his right pocket. I thought, *God, is this it? What should I do? Do I run? Do I fall to the ground? Push him off balance?*

Luckily, as I was fearfully weighing these options, someone called out, and he turned his head. In that split second, I ran across the street against the traffic and got into my car. I was so shaken, I skipped my next engagement and raced to my campaign headquarters.

The detectives who later came to question me acted as though I had invited the attack. "Why did you upset this man? What did you do to provoke him?" They grilled me relentlessly, and if I was foggy on a detail, they assumed I was lying. By that point in my life, I should have been accustomed to such treatment at the hands of the police, but one never does get used to it — nor should one.

Later several of the other candidates, almost all of whom were Black, had the temerity to suggest that I had invented the entire incident for publicity; the *Los Angeles Times* printed an article implying the same thing. Reading that piece, and hearing the gossip, I felt the anger of years past surface, and my body literally trembled with waves of fury. How could my own people question my integrity? *Get real, Myrlie,* I reminded myself. *This is politics, and anything goes.*

A week later, the police found my stalker not far from where he had accosted me. He was in a dingy one-room apartment, one of its walls covered from ceiling to floor with clippings and photos of Beckwith and Medgar and sketches of the Beckwith family tree. Although I was finally believed, because this man had done nothing illegal, he could only be held for questioning. I still have his mug shot, a reminder that I must always look over my shoulder.

I have no idea how many enemies may have been tracking me over the years. But after the stringy-haired man, I became increasingly hesitant about plunging headlong into crowds. I told a reporter in 1987, "I'm going ahead with my life and my campaign, but I'm a lot more alert these days — I don't relax." I kept Mace in my bag and was ready to use it if necessary. Walter, who constantly worried for my safety — as did my children — suggested I carry a hatpin, too, if not a gun. But what good is a gun? Medgar had one with him the night he was killed. Besides, I was single-minded; neither threats nor fear could deter me.

I have lived with both for my entire life. In Mississippi, the threats were bolder and darker, and the fear was the kind that made the hair on the back of my neck stand on end. Leaving the South relaxed my guard a bit, but when fear becomes a way of life, you never completely overcome the sense of foreboding. Even in California, my children and I were frequently under surveillance — our phones were tapped, strange cars often passed by slowly, and helicopters hovered overhead. We always knew there were people out there who would harm us because of what we represented *and* because of what we said. But in our family, silence is unacceptable. How then have we coped? By remembering that fear is a survival mechanism, and that if we manage it, rather than allowing it to manage us, we can turn fear into an asset, an acute awareness that protects us and even gives us an edge over our adversaries. ❦

My persistence in following Beckwith's trail finally paid off on a Monday morning in 1989, when Jerry Mitchell, a Jackson reporter who worked for the *Clarion-Ledger*, called to say he wanted to fax a story of his that had appeared the previous day on the front page of the newspaper. It was headlined, "State Checked Possible Jurors in Evers Slaying." Mitchell, with the cooperation of a variety of sources, including several Klan informants, had uncovered evidence proving that in the 1960s, at the same time that Mississippi was prosecuting Beckwith, the state agency created to thwart integration, the Sovereignty Commission, was secretly aiding the defense. Records showed, for example, that one of the proposed jurors was not recommended because the commission "knew his thinking," and another was questionable because he was "believed to be Jewish." In other words, while one sector of the Mississippi government was allegedly trying to jail Beckwith, another was simultaneously working toward assuring his freedom.

When Jerry asked if I thought his findings warranted reopening the case, I let out a resounding "Yes!" Two days after printing my written response to his article, the *Clarion-Ledger* supported my position, running a pointed editorial that led with an unequivocal banner: "Peters Should Reopen Murder Case." Ed Peters had been the district attorney in Hinds County, which included the city of Jackson, since 1972. The editorial argued that by returning to court to retry Beckwith, "the state could proclaim to the nation that indeed Mississippi has made a new beginning and is a place of hope and justice for all law-abiding citizens without regard to race or philosophy."

Not surprisingly, that editorial created a furor on both sides of the debate. The question of a retrial signified everything dark in Mississippi's past and the possibility of redemption in the future. I was pleased with the editorial and at the same time disdainful, knowing that this same newspaper had once been labeled the "Klan-Ledger." I couldn't help remembering that in the days before Medgar was killed, a boxed quote blazoned across the front page of the *Clarion-Ledger* predicted: "Blood will flow in the streets." The accompanying article had suggested that violence was the best means of preventing integration. Now, decades later, the sons and daughters of those editors were calling for justice.

Ed Peters was initially of the opinion that a new trial would violate Beckwith's right to a speedy trial under the Sixth Amendment. A twenty-five-year delay, in his opinion, didn't fall within any interpretation of what was meant by "speedy." But Jerry Mitchell kept applying pressure, by writing additional articles about the role of the now-defunct Sovereignty Commission (it was abolished in 1977) in Beckwith's trial. By late October, the Jackson City Council asked for the case to be reopened; a few weeks later, the Mississippi NAACP made a similar request.

Shortly thereafter, I called Peters to make an appointment to discuss the matter at his office in Jackson. I received a letter and a follow-up call from Bobby DeLaughter, an assistant DA, apprising me of the progress of the investigation thus far. Peters had assigned DeLaughter the thankless task of fielding telephone calls related to the case and authorized him to follow up any leads that seemed legitimate. Some callers said they had heard Beckwith brag about his views; others turned out to be potential witnesses who, years before, had been afraid to come forward or who had lied out of fear for their lives. At that point, though, Peters continued to reserve a decision about putting the case before a grand jury.

I wasn't hopeful, for I had heard a good deal about Ed Peters over the years. Tall, suave, gray-haired, and aptly nicknamed the Silver Fox, he was reputedly tough on crime. A self-proclaimed conservative, he had some supporters in the African-American community, but some of the more vocal Black leaders had warned me, "Don't trust him. He's all about show. Underneath, he's a racist too." Whether their assessment was accurate or not, I'd spent enough years dealing with the state of Mississippi and had seen enough to know not to face *any* DA alone, so I began to carefully plan my strategy. ℛ

Perhaps it was the result of my determination, perhaps it was fate, or perhaps a combination of the two. But as I got closer and closer to what I hoped was my final confrontation with Beckwith, I stepped back and realized how confident I had become. One of the hallmarks of maturity, I believe, is the ability to assess your accomplishments objectively and to appreciate the obstacles you've already overcome, the victories you've achieved. It's a useful exercise to remember how hard certain tasks once seemed and to revel in the knowledge that facing down such challenges has become second nature.

Thanks to my own growth and the perspective of time, Beckwith didn't loom as large in my life as he had twenty-five years before, when I was a young widow. Nor did the possibility of justice seem quite so remote. I had raised three children alone, and conquered the wilds of politics and corporate America. As the newly appointed Los Angeles commissioner of public works, I now had a hand in running a huge, sprawling city that seemed to have as many problems as it did people. How hard could it be for me to take on the entire state of Mississippi?

Equally important, the issues themselves now encompassed more than Medgar's death. Even though revenge at first propelled me and continued to play a role in my quest — I'm only human, after all, and I wanted Beckwith to pay — as always, I turned to my faith for guidance and to lift me out of negativity. I also heard Medgar's voice saying, "Myrlie, you must not hate." I knew he would have encouraged me to seek justice, but not to blind myself with vengeful feelings. Hence, I came to realize the larger and truly more important nature of my mission: Beckwith's freedom had come to symbolize the sad reality that the American justice system doesn't work for all of its citizens.

As the excitement of possibility began to energize me, it began to weigh ever more heavily on my children. Darrell and Reena, then in their midthirties, had no reservations about my going forward. They vividly remembered the night of their father's death; like me, they wanted to see Beckwith have the trial he deserved. Van, nearing thirty himself, felt "mixed," to use his word. "Selfishly, I sometimes wanted you to leave it alone," he later admitted. As the prospect of a new trial became a reality, though, Van set aside his own misgivings. "Bottom line," he told me, speaking for his brother and sister as well, "is that all of us support you, no matter which way you go. You've always been there for us — we're always going to be there for you. Always."

In early December of 1989, I arrived at the district attorney's office for the meeting; Morris Dees was at my side. Two months earlier, I had called this legendary crusader against segregation, who cofounded the Southern Poverty Law Center, to inform him of my conversations with the DA's office and to ask him to join me. I expected that I would be filled in on whatever evidence had been uncovered to date and would discuss the possibility of reopening the case. Dees had considerable experience in this legal domain, having tried a number of cases involving civil rights violations and racist injustices. I knew this was precisely the kind of case Dees relished and that he could bring to the meeting a level of expertise that I lacked.

I also suspected that Dees would not be welcomed in Mississippi. Still, I hoped that his knowledge of legal precedent in cases such as this would convince the district attorney to view Beckwith's situation in a new light. Instead, Dees's presence immediately put Peters on the defensive. To say we got off to a bad start is an understatement. I let Dees do most of the talking at first, and within minutes it was clear that he and Peters didn't see eye-to-eye with regard to this case. Dees informed Peters that he was ready to represent our family in a suit that would force the DA's office to act, and that he would bring in his own investigators to search for old documents in city and state files. Tempers flared, at which point I stepped in and calmly but firmly told Peters, "You have given me every reason possible that this case cannot be pursued. Now tell me what you *are* going to do to carry forth the pursuit of justice. If you don't, with my full support Mr. Dees will."

Bobby DeLaughter seemed more receptive at that first meeting; something about his quiet strength reminded me of Medgar. A solid son of the South, Bobby DeLaughter had been only eight years old when Medgar was killed. Initially, this case was just a routine assignment, but the more he investigated and the more we conferred, the more committed he became — and, of course, the closer I felt to him. It wasn't lost on the bright, fair-minded assistant DA that he was now almost the same age as Medgar when Medgar died, nor that he too had three children. Still, our relationship progressed gradually, with both of us keeping a cautious distance at first (I later discovered that he was somewhat shy). We agreed that we would speak at least every Friday to discuss our progress. He would keep me posted on his investigation; I would share whatever contacts I had made and pass along any information I'd heard.

Although Morris Dees and I kept in touch, there was no reason for him to get involved in the case itself. Over the course of the following year, DeLaughter assembled an impressive body of evidence. He located numerous old photos, records, and fingerprints; some items appeared on his desk seemingly out of nowhere. "It was as though the hand of God had placed them there," he told me. In addition, DeLaughter tracked down not only original witnesses but others who were now willing to come forth with testimony. And almost miraculously, he found the murder weapon. He remembered that his late father-in-law, Judge Russel Moore, had once told him about having a "souvenir," a rifle connected to an old civil rights trial. DeLaughter's heart all but stopped when his mother-in-law led him to a shelf in an upstairs bedroom closet in which her husband had stored the gun. Comparing the serial numbers with the court records, he realized he had a match.

As each piece of the puzzle fell into place, I became more and more optimistic, if cautiously so, for we still faced many obstacles before getting Beckwith into court. One day DeLaughter called sounding especially dejected: "Mrs. Evers, we have a problem. The original transcript is not to be found anywhere. You know," he reminded me, "we're looking at thirty-year-old records. Some are missing. I need the transcript in order to proceed."

"I have a copy," I said quietly into the phone.

He gasped; it seemed to take a few seconds for my statement to sink in. "You have one? Well, is it the legal document?"

Yes, I assured him, it was a three-volume carbon of the original — in those days Xerox machines were not yet in widespread use — but my copy bore the court seal. It had been stowed away for nearly three decades in one of several trunks filled with Medgar's writings, newspaper articles, and other items documenting his life and death.

"Please, Mrs. Evers, send it to me registered mail right away."

"I can't do that, Bobby," I told him. "I can't send it — not even by registered mail. Even if it means paying my own way, I'll deliver it to you personally."

Thanks to my years at ARCO, where I'd honed the art of corporate maneuvering and refined my own public relations skills, I was able to size up the situation and plan my strategy. This is an art one must learn and practice in order to survive in any arena. I had been patient and persistent for nearly thirty years. Now that I had reached a critical juncture in my crusade, I wanted to be certain both that the world was watching and that there would be no slipups. I did not want to risk even the slightest possibility that anyone might claim the document was lost in transit.

I also had learned how to make an impact and how to exploit every opportunity to make my cause visible. I knew that the right kind of dramatic and symbolic publicity would keep the case in the spotlight. So I promptly called Jerry Mitchell, informing him that I would personally deliver to the DA's office the 963-page transcript of the trial, which everyone had assumed was lost. He was more than willing to cooperate.

"I will arrive on a Delta flight," I announced, providing Jerry with the date and time. "Meet me at the airport with a photographer." Days later, a photograph did appear in the *Clarion-Ledger*, showing a jubilant Myrlie Evers, triumphantly holding up the bulky three-volume set.

In December of 1990, a month after Judge Hilburn had ruled that my copy of the transcript was genuine, a grand jury indicted Beckwith. Although no trial date was set at that point, we all knew that was the next step.

By then I had come to see Bobby DeLaughter as a true friend. We spoke many times a week, sometimes every day, depending on what was happening with the case. We laughed together on the phone, cried, even prayed together. Today, Bobby speaks of that burgeoning relationship as "two people coming from entirely different backgrounds being able to shove everything to the side and focus on simple justice."

I eventually came to understand and respect Ed Peters too — and vice versa — but our relationship developed much more slowly. Ed was more distant and a confirmed skeptic. But I tried to keep an open mind about him. For practical reasons, I wanted him in my corner, for he was known throughout the state as a rapier-sharp prosecutor. I also sensed that he wanted to clear the state's name; and winning the case would be a political coup for him.

However, I don't come to trust easily, and with good reason. Growing up Black in the South and experiencing as much violence as I have, I learned to proceed cautiously, ever mindful that facial expressions often say more about people than words. Many women have keen intuition, but sometimes we don't listen to it. By then, I had learned that I could trust both what I saw *and* what I felt in my gut and, deep inside me, I sensed that Peters was an honorable man.

Peters later admitted that he initially regarded me as "pushy," "antagonistic," and politically motivated. But as the investigation wore on, he began to realize I was neither a poor-me widow out for revenge nor a self-serving politician seeking the limelight. I was, in fact, simply doing what I claimed to be doing: seeking justice. At the same time, I came to see that he had not made decisions based on race, as some had warned he might; his office had come through for me and for my family. When the indictment was handed down, we sat in his office as colleagues.

We also knew that we were not quite there . . . yet. Peters and I acknowledged that the history of Southern justice is littered with evasive suspects, hung juries, and killers set free. Medgar's wasn't the only murder to have gone unpunished in the state. There were several, in fact, that Medgar himself had investigated. Beckwith could go to trial again. The question was, would any jury in Mississippi convict him? ⚘

One of the most painful ordeals during the long preparation for the trial was DeLaughter's request to have Medgar's body exhumed. Because the original autopsy report had not been found, Bobby explained, an examination of Medgar's remains was essential to the case. Not only did he need me to sign a release to legally unearth my husband's casket, but also my three children. Thus began a frantic series of family phone calls debating whether we should allow such an intrusion. I was devastated, constantly in tears, both angry and hurt. Because I was bone-tired at that point and weary of the whole process, the old wound ached even more. To disturb whatever was left of Medgar's physical body felt utterly invasive. I finally told Bobby, "No, just let Medgar be. Don't touch him. Let him rest in peace."

"Mrs. Evers," he patiently replied, "if you and your children don't sign the papers, I'll have to get a court order, because I *am* going to have the body exhumed." I knew that DeLaughter was doing what he had to do; and while I didn't like what he said, I respected him for taking a stand.

It was Walt, bless him, who guided me through this dilemma. He was the only one I would allow to see me fall apart, and usually all I needed to find my bearings was for him to hold me in his strong embrace, quietly reassuring me with his love. But when it came to pursuing Beckwith, he was as insistent and as urgent as a trainer spurring on a prizefighter, pushing me out into the ring for another round. He once again reminded me, "I'm here with you, and you must see it through. You promised Medgar." That was his constant refrain as well as mine: *You promised Medgar you'd go the last mile of the way.*

Once the family had signed the necessary forms, I assumed that it would be I who would go to Arlington National Cemetery with DeLaughter to see that Medgar's remains were safely returned to the casket and that the casket was properly resealed, but Van had his own plans. "Mom," said my youngest, who barely remembered his dad, "*I* am going to see Father. *I'm* going to see that he is okay."

Everyone tried to talk Van out of the idea, including DeLaughter, Charlie Crisco, who was the lead investigator, and even Michael Baden, the New York State chief pathologist, who had been called in by the Hinds County DA to perform the autopsy. (Among other illustrious cases, Baden had reviewed President Kennedy's and Martin Luther King, Jr.'s autopsy reports; more recently, he was called in to examine Nicole Brown Simpson's remains.) Thirty years had passed, these men all warned us. No one could predict the state of the body — it might be nothing more than a skeleton with fragments of skin. No matter; a stubborn streak runs in our family, and Van, who refused to be dissuaded, simply announced, "This is something I have to do, and nobody can keep me from doing it."

The casket itself was encased in an airtight sarcophagus, which would be unearthed in total secret at dawn, before the gates of the cemetery were open to the public. Once exhumed, it was to be trans-ported in a vehicle that accommodated a driver and a single passen-ger. Dr. Baden, Charlie, Bobby, and, we assumed, Van would travel from Virginia to Baden's lab in upstate New York in another car. But when the time came to depart, Van refused to leave Medgar's side. Instead, he crawled into the back compartment of the van and squeezed his sturdy six-foot-one frame into the narrow space next to the coffin. He lay there, beside his dead father, for a good six or seven hours with only a few rest stops along the way. His thoughts were muddled; what he recalls most about the trip is the smell, the noxious fumes of embalming fluid mixed with the odor of decay leaking from the coffin.

They arrived in Albany at night, and the following morning, Baden, accompanied by DeLaughter, Crisco, and several security men, opened the casket to inspect the body. Then Van was invited into the autopsy room. As Van recalls, "It was the slowest walk I ever took — fifty feet at most — but it felt like it took me half an hour to get there. When I was around two feet from Dad's body, I just stood there, looking at him. My father." With the exception of a little water damage to his fingertips, Medgar's body was perfectly preserved. It was nothing short of a miracle, Baden and the others agreed; it was as though Medgar had remained intact long enough for his youngest child to see and visit with him.

Van reached down and touched him and simply said, "Hi." The rest of their reunion was carried out in silence. Van caressed his father's head and felt Medgar's hair beneath his fingertips. Charles had arranged for Medgar's last haircut, instructing the barber to crop it in his brother's characteristic medium-short "low English" style. Medgar looked exactly as Van had seen him in photographs. Later, Van would say to me, "Now I know where I came from." He had finally met his father. Hearing him, I closed my eyes and reminded myself once again, *God is good all the time.*

As it turned out, DeLaughter was right. The autopsy X-rays — a technological advance that hadn't been available in 1963 — yielded some very important evidence: the trajectory of the bullet as well as the presence of bullet fragments that proved to match Beckwith's rifle. Oddly enough, the first autopsy reports were then found as well. I asked DeLaughter to send me the attached photographs. "No, Mrs. Evers, they're too graphic. I can't let you see them. It might upset you too much."

Visiting his office a few weeks later, I brought the subject up again, explaining that I *needed* to see Medgar. On the night he was shot, I told DeLaughter, my friends and neighbors held me back when they placed his body onto Reena's mattress and lifted him into Houston Wells's station wagon. Because they hadn't allowed me to accompany Medgar to the hospital, I'd never had an opportunity to say a proper good-bye.

After hearing me out, DeLaughter nodded and took me into a vacant office, where he handed me a large manila envelope. "Call if you need me," he said, closing the door behind him. After sitting in silence for a moment, I undid the clasp and, one by one, removed the photographs. All of them pictured Medgar from the waist up, on a cold metal gurney. His eyes were wide open. His shirt was torn — I deduced that the doctors had ripped it — exposing a gaping wound in his chest. In an instant, the old horror and guilt returned. If only I had done something — stuffed a rag or a towel into the wound — I might have been able to stop the bleeding to save Medgar's life. That thought had plagued me for years.

Looking at the wound now, in the hollow silence of the vacant office, I realized what everyone had told me was true: There was nothing I could have done. The bullet that killed my husband was the kind used in high-powered hunting rifles to kill deer and other large animals. The wound is small at the point of entry, but the bullet explodes lethally inside the body, tearing up the flesh as it exits. It looked as if Medgar's heart had been wrenched from his chest.

I didn't cry, and though I wanted to scream, I was afraid that if I did, I'd never stop. In a sense, though, I was able to accomplish then what I had not been able to do the night Medgar was killed. I placed my index and middle fingers on his eyes and pulled them down, as if I could magically shut the lids and put Medgar to rest. That, more than twenty-five years later, was my final good-bye. ℘

In all, it took another three years of continued investigation and legal maneuvers, including Beckwith's extradition from Tennessee, before the actual trial could begin. In the meantime, the threats against me escalated. The Pacific Northwest is home to many radical white supremacist groups. Less than half of one percent of the population is Black, and I was an easy target. Hate mail poured in from all over the country, and while this wasn't an unusual occurrence, it distressed me.

Needless to say, I was especially vigilant for my safety during this period. One morning I went to my mailbox, which stands at the end of the driveway, barely a hundred yards from my house. As was my custom, dating back to my years with Medgar, when the firebomb exploded in our carport, I always stood to the side when I opened a mailbox or any kind of package. This morning was no exception. Sure enough, inside the mailbox was a crudely made bomb with a wire attached to the door. Luckily, the malicious amateur who made it had not assembled the bomb properly, so it never exploded. Had it gone off, my habitual wariness — which those who have not lived in my skin have called paranoia — would have saved my life.

Because things were happening fairly quickly at that point, this was a difficult period for me emotionally. I coped by doing what I've always found effective in times of trouble: turning to the love and support of family and to God. My children called constantly and cheered me on. Walt encouraged me to play the piano, which always unburdened my soul. "I'll even sing," he offered, knowing that the promise of my hearing his clear baritone was added inducement. Sometimes we'd pray together and ask for guidance.

A trial date was finally set, with the voir dire — each side's questioning of prospective jurors — beginning on January 17, 1994. In order to select an impartial jury, the proceedings took place in Batesville, Mississippi, a city on the Delta in Panola County, with a population that is 51 percent White and 49 percent Black, approximately the same racial makeup as Hinds County, where Medgar was shot. Once the jury was impaneled, the trial itself was moved to a Jackson courtroom.

The lobby of the Hinds County Courthouse is adorned with an intricately detailed, hand-carved frieze depicting complacent slaves toiling happily in cotton fields, with satisfied plantation owners looking on. This was the history of the South as seen through White eyes. Each time I passed the sculptures, I couldn't help but remind myself that here, in this very building where so many injustices had been perpetrated against Blacks, it was almost inconceivable that the scales could finally be brought back into balance. Getting Beckwith into a courtroom again felt like the end of a long, hard night. To borrow a phrase from writer Terry McMillan, I had been waiting to exhale, and now I almost could.

I was the first witness called to the stand. I had recounted the story so many, many times over the years that, to protect myself, I'd become numb to the telling. In interviews and in lectures, I was invariably asked to describe "that night," and while the words came out, I barely heard them. This time, though, I knew that I had to let myself feel the pain of the experience. This time, I made myself believe that telling the truth *mattered*. This time, I took a deep breath and prayed. *Please give me the strength to go through this again. I've done all that I can. Help me accept whatever the outcome may be. God, your will, not mine, be done.*

After my testimony, DeLaughter and Peters paraded a series of witnesses who confirmed the technical facts in the case. Another set of witnesses, some who had testified years before, others who were new, attested to Beckwith's venomous character, including his having bragged about killing my husband. Hearing their accounts made me physically ill. "You would think after years and years I would be immune to it," I told Jerry Mitchell several days into the trial. "I'm not."

Though I realized that each of those witnesses bolstered the prosecution's case, it was a surprise witness who buoyed my spirits. Mark Reiley, a thirty-six-year-old former Louisiana prison guard, had called the DA's office from his home in Chicago only days before to say he had seen news of the proceedings on CNN. Was anyone interested in the fact that in 1979 he had heard Beckwith *admit* that he killed Medgar Evers? His story checked out. His appearance was, Peters later told me, every trial lawyer's dream.

On the stand, Reiley recalled being assigned to guard Beckwith when he had been confined in the Angola Prison wing of Earl K. Long Hospital in Louisiana. At one point, when a Black nurse's aide came into his room, Beckwith chased her out, saying, "If I can get rid of an uppity nigger like Medgar Evers, I would have no problem with a no-account nigger like you." Beckwith also tried to convert Reiley to Christian Identity, among other points explaining to him that God wasn't upset when a Black person was killed, "because they weren't human beings, they were beasts."

Like the others who testified, his words portrayed Beckwith as a self-congratulatory braggart, but one statement of Reiley's in particular had to have weighed heavily on the jurors' minds: "[Beckwith] told us if he didn't have the power and connections he had, he would be serving time in Mississippi for getting rid of the nigger Medgar Evers."

Naturally, the defense tried to discredit Reiley. "How much have they paid you to come here?" Beckwith's attorney asked.

"Well, sir, I got down here yesterday, and they put me in the Holiday Inn, but they didn't feed me dinner. This morning, I got up and got here and didn't get breakfast. I told them I was hungry, and they finally bought me a sandwich."

Testimony ended on a Thursday night, and by Friday, the twelve men and women were still sequestered in the Hinds County Courthouse. Though Peters and DeLaughter had presented an excellent case, which seemed to make the jurors care about Medgar and the overarching implications of Beckwith's crime, I was warned that, as a rule, long jury deliberations didn't bode well for the prosecution. Fortunately, though, conventional wisdom didn't bear out in this case, and the following morning we were called back to the courtroom to hear the guilty verdict announced.

The moment not only marked a victory for the Evers family but came to symbolize absolution for Mississippi's past sins. Still, my own victory was bittersweet. The trial itself, and the long work of preparation leading up to it, had borne out my concern that, despite my efforts to memorialize him, Medgar had faded from public memory. Many potential jurors, for example, had had no idea who he was. Though Beckwith was finally and fairly convicted for this crime, I knew my task was only half-completed, for I still wanted Medgar recognized for his contributions to the civil rights movement. ⏾

Medgar's work and what he stood for are both a lesson in history and a memorial to the sacrifices great men have made in the name of freedom. All too often, the advancement of African-Americans is taken for granted by younger people; and not understanding and appreciating the struggles of the past can only lead to errors in the future. Moreover, Medgar was more than just a civil rights leader; he was a good father and husband, a kind and generous soul, and a determined man who had a strong sense of justice. Such people in all communities need to be held up to new generations, but today, it seems, there is a dearth of these role models for our young.

The root of this problem is, in part, the nature of celebrity today; fame is often more about media coverage and money than about giving back to humanity. The "stars" our children look toward are high-paid athletes and people in the entertainment world, many of whom show little interest in motivating our youth. There are, thankfully, a growing number of superior athletes and entertainers who use their money and position to educate and inspire. But we need more Magic Johnsons and Oprah Winfreys, not just in sports and entertainment but in every field — people who give of themselves and give back to their communities.

Hence, whenever I address successful young men and women, I exhort them to recognize the greater purpose they can serve and to have a sense of responsibility toward younger generations. Go to schools and community centers, I urge, and help youngsters understand the work and commitment that success in any career involves. Help them understand that in the long run the intrinsic rewards of a job well done are as important as the pay. And tell them that even though they might spend hours on the playing fields or basketball courts, they need to pursue an education.

Among other inspiring programs, I applaud the effort of author and journalist Vernon Jarrett, who founded the NAACP's ACT-SO program — the Afro-Academic, Cultural, Technological, and Scientific Olympics, which Jarrett envisioned as an "Olympics of the mind." The program incorporates mentoring, coaching, and teaching and is designed to improve and encourage academic and cultural achievement among African-American youth. Throughout the year, students in grades nine through twelve compete for honors at the local level in twenty-four categories, which include the sciences, humanities, and performing and visual arts, and the winners then go on to a national competition. It is truly a thrilling moment, at the ACT-SO finals, when hundreds of these young people march into the auditorium to the music of *Chariots of Fire*. Even those who don't win one of the first-, second-, or third-place medals are victors for having put in the time, effort, and dedication.

Of course, our children must first be taught at home to respect achievement and to look for and emulate suitable role models. When I was growing up, we didn't have to look far; exemplary individuals were all around us, and we were taught at a very young age to respect our elders — first and foremost our grandparents, but also our teachers. When my piano teacher, Mrs. Ruth Rowan Sanders, brought me pictures of the young concert pianist Phillipa Schuyler on tour, she was purposefully holding up an example she hoped I'd follow — and it worked. I practiced longer and more diligently, thinking about the success of that young woman. I knew that she had worked hard for her attainments, and the fact that she came from a wealthy family and was the child of an interracial marriage had nothing to do with her enormous talent.

"Success" also had a broader meaning in my day. The people Mama held up as role models were not necessarily wealthy or famous — indeed, few were. Rather, they were smart, talented, good-hearted, generous, entrepreneurial, creative, hardworking, and honest. We need to help our children and grandchildren equate greatness with character, not cash. Also, we must not allow young people to limit their horizons. Athletics can be a noble endeavor, but children must be inspired to use more than physical prowess. Be sure that in your conversations at home you applaud the achievements of people in all fields — medicine, teaching, science, business, the creative arts. When you take your child to the pediatrician, remark about the doctor's intelligence, patience, kindness, and the hard work it took to achieve her position. When your child tells you about a particularly creative or insightful homework assignment, comment on the teacher's wisdom and ingenuity. Many such opportunities present themselves in the course of a day.

Finally, we must instill in our youngsters a sense of responsibility. Whenever I'm asked to speak at a college commencement, I beseech the graduates, "Use your hard-won degrees as a means to civic health, not just private wealth." When you achieve success, you must look back, you must tell your younger brothers and sisters the truth about what it's like at the top — the hard work, the dedication — and you must extend a helping hand. I remind them, too, that no man (or woman) is an island: Whatever doors are open to us, whatever we've achieved, we have accomplished because of what someone who came before us has done. That we have a Martin Luther King, Jr., Day is gratifying, but honoring the contributions of great citizens should not be a once-a-year event, because then we forget. We forget about the real people behind the holidays and about the very real ways their contributions continue to enhance our lives. We must see the entire picture — where we were, where we are now, and where we are going. 🎔

A few months after the verdict was handed down, I returned to Jackson for the dedication of the Medgar Wiley Evers Post Office. I was gratified that at last a federal building in Mississippi would memorialize my late husband, but with the trial publicity dying down, I wished there were more I could do to heighten awareness of Medgar on a national scale. It was in this frame of mind that I received a call from movie producer Frederick Zollo.

"Mrs. Evers, I'm sure you've already heard that I'm doing a movie about the trial," he told me. "I'd like to meet with you to discuss it."

My only knowledge of Zollo was that he had produced *Mississippi Burning*, a 1988 film that dramatized the story of Goodman, Schwerner, and Chaney, the three civil rights workers whose senseless deaths had marked a defining event during Freedom Summer in 1964. Many in the African-American community had criticized the movie for its portrayal of Blacks as frightened and somewhat indifferent to their plight, leaving the good guys — a group of White FBI agents — to save the day. The truth was that, particularly in the wake of Medgar's murder, many young Blacks had heard the call to action and were anything but complacent. Most were also understandably suspicious of the FBI; director J. Edgar Hoover abhorred Negroes and made it very clear that he had no intention of helping our cause. In fact, he was later shown to have spent years persecuting Martin Luther King, Jr.

Because of the inaccuracies in *Mississippi Burning*, as well as my own experience with Hollywood, I was somewhat skeptical about Zollo's plans for what was then called *Free At Last*. Still, after several calls I agreed to meet him in person. A lean, charming, well-spoken man, Zollo listened intently as I expressed my reservations. Based on his track record, I wasn't sure that he could be sensitive or courageous enough to make an accurate movie about the system that killed Medgar.

"That's why I want to do another movie about Mississippi," Zollo reassured me, adding, "and through this movie, we can tell your husband's story."

In fact, I had been trying for years to get a film made on Medgar's life. In 1983 Charles Fries, an independent Hollywood producer, had bought the rights to my first book and pieced together a two-hour docudrama based on it. The film, which aired on PBS stations, hadn't reached a wide audience. This new movie, which would be shown in theaters nationwide, seemed like a promising second chance. Zollo already had several top-caliber people associated with the production — among others, Rob Reiner had been tapped to direct the movie and Whoopi Goldberg, a good friend of Zollo's, to play me.

A larger strategic issue was at work as well, one that went beyond the question of lending support to a film production, which, admittedly, is a situation few ever have to deal with. It was a matter of knowing what cards I held in the game, knowing when to play, when to fold. Practically speaking, Zollo was already in preproduction and had engaged much of the cast and crew. I knew he could finish the movie with or without my cooperation, for the story of Medgar's life was in the public domain. Instead of trying to fight the process, I reasoned, I would get more done by becoming part of the production and speaking with the principal players.

I met Rob Reiner at his home in Los Angeles a few months later. I was familiar with Rob primarily from his role in TV's *All in the Family*, and I certainly knew about his father, Carl Reiner, a superb actor-comedian and a vigorous supporter of civil rights causes. I had read the first draft of the script by Lewis Colick, I told Rob, and I was disappointed: The film they were making wasn't really about Medgar, but rather about Bobby DeLaughter. Certainly, I had no desire to minimize DeLaughter's contribution; he was a good friend and an important ally, and without him I would never have seen justice done. But there would have been no trial in the first place if Medgar hadn't worked toward change in Mississippi. To the generations of young people who didn't understand the struggle in Mississippi and Medgar's role as the voice of change, Beckwith's desire to gun him down in cold blood just didn't add up.

"I'm White, Myrlie, and I can't make a movie about Medgar," Rob answered. "But maybe someone like Spike Lee will." I know that Rob was sincere. I suspect, too, that Fred Zollo and the executives at Castle Rock Entertainment also subscribed to the Hollywood presumption that to make a *big* movie, a White man, in this case Bobby DeLaughter, had to be the central hero.

Whoopi Goldberg and I met for the first time at the Polo Lounge in the Beverly Hills Hotel, having spoken on the phone several times before. Production hadn't yet started, and I wanted her to hear my opinions about the script, just as she was eager to study me. After a few minutes of small talk, I shared with Whoopi my concerns about the movie. Having seen some of her movies — though not *The Color Purple* — I also remarked that although I considered her a marvelous actor, I was a bit surprised that she had been cast as Myrlie. A fleeting look of disappointment registered on her face, and she acknowledged that she was anxious about playing me. Van, who accompanied me, probably didn't ease her mind. "This is my mom, and I love her," he told the actress, his voice thick with emotion. "And she has worked too hard to have her life misinterpreted."

That first meeting was, understandably, rather formal and stiff, but a few days later, Whoopi and I saw each other again at Van's photography studio. We were comfortable and casual, both of us in jeans and sneakers, and in such a relaxed setting, it was easier to talk more openly about ourselves. We discovered that our lives had been shaped by common struggles and misconceptions, and I expressed the hope that understanding our similarities would help her climb into my character. Like me, Whoopi puts on a facade in public and shares her personal face only with family and good friends. I explained to her that just as she has been typecast as the perennial cutup, associated primarily with comedy, I am often narrowly perceived as a prim, proper church-lady type. "But there's fire that burns in this Mississippi woman!" I assured her. "So, when you portray me, show some anger, some spunk, some life. Put some Whoopi into your Myrlie!" I knew she wanted to do right by me, and I was very appreciative of her efforts.

In contrast, my meeting with James Woods was rather sobering, though through no fault of his, I might add. One day on the set, when the crew was shooting several of the trial scenes, I was standing outside Rob Reiner's trailer, and as various people came up to introduce themselves, I became aware that someone had walked up behind me. "Myrlie, I want you to meet James Woods," said Rob, at which point I turned around. I knew Woods had the role of Beckwith, but seeing him in full makeup took my breath away.

Still in character, he extended his hand and said, "Pleased to meet y'all, Miz Evers." He looked and sounded more like Beckwith than Beckwith himself! Woods must have registered the instant hatred in my face, because he quickly dropped the southern drawl and said, "It's okay, I'm James Woods. I may look and act like him, but I don't think like he does."

Watching the shoot that day, I was amazed, for I felt as if I had been caught in a time warp. Alec Baldwin, playing Bobby DeLaughter, was questioning witnesses. The set designer had faithfully replicated the fleur-de-lis pattern in the dark wood paneling behind Judge Hilburn's bench, the blue upholstered chairs in the jury box, the eagles over the windows. The only difference between the movie courtroom and the one in Jackson was the presence of Rob Reiner's director's chair.

Ironically, although such pains were taken to accurately re-create locations down to the most minute detail, the script itself veered from the truth. Jerry Mitchell, the reporter who broke the story, was portrayed as a nuisance when in fact he was one of the central figures responsible for reopening the case. The film also implied that I had a strained relationship with Bobby DeLaughter, who for a long time was the only one I actually trusted. And Ed Peters, who conducted virtually all of the cross-examination as well as a summation, was depicted as a background figure. What concerned me most was that I knew the movie's version of history would eventually supplant the real-life events. In our media-dominated culture, people often take as gospel what they see on the screen.

I understood the concept of granting creative license for dramatic effect, and appreciated the fact that the film was supposed to be "entertainment," not a history lesson. But I also believed that the nature of the events that did take place would have been even more effective at keeping people on the edge of their seats. For example, could any screenwriter have invented a more powerful scene than when Mark Reiley, who became our star witness, just happened to take a sick day, tuned in to CNN in Chicago, saw news of the trial, and called the DA's office willing to testify?

A PR blitz had preceded the movie, with articles appearing in major newspapers throughout the country months in advance of its release. In an article entitled "To Bind Up a Nation's Wound with Celluloid," Rick Bragg of the *New York Times* wrote that the first third of the film would be "about Mr. Evers' life and death." But by the time *Ghosts of Mississippi* was screened for reviewers, that "first third" had been cut down to just a few minutes of newsreel footage and a scene or two devoted to Medgar. As a consultant, I was listed among the credits, as were members of my family to whom Rob had given small roles.

The end product, when it was released in December 1996, came as no surprise to me. I had seen most of the script changes and had made notations in the margins — and a few of my suggestions were actually used. Also, Rob Reiner had repeatedly stressed, "I can't make this movie the way you want me to make it, Myrlie." Still, I found myself in an awkward position when Castle Rock Entertainment asked me to help promote the film, for I was regarded as the keeper of Medgar's memory. I knew I would be asked at every juncture, particularly by African-Americans, "What did you think of the movie, Mrs. Evers?" If I praised the film excessively, I would have been somewhat deceptive. In the end, I made my peace by praising the direction, the acting, and the *effort* — and by expressing my hope that the film would herald a new beginning of public awareness.

That, in fact, was an accurate and honest assessment. The movie had at least put Medgar's name before the public and fostered people's interest in his life. Imagine my delight when this was confirmed in letters from strangers. I was particularly moved by one from a fifteen-year-old boy, in which he said, in part,

> *A lot of people, myself included, finally rightfully know the name Medgar Evers. And they know that Medgar Evers was a peaceful man who only wanted equality for all people. . . . I have never been a racist, but you and your husband have still managed to teach me so much. I don't believe that there are Black Americans and White*

Americans — only Americans. Maybe someday we will all get along and except [sic] each other for who we are. Your husband would have wanted it that way. He died a hero. He lives on in my memory, as you do, a hero. . . .

I also was genuinely touched by Rob Reiner's sincerity; I knew his heart was in the movie. Among other shows of good faith, Rob donated the proceeds of the Los Angeles premiere to the organization of my choice. The timing couldn't have been better. For years, I had hoped to establish the Medgar Evers Institute, a multipurpose think tank and youth leadership center that would embrace the principles Medgar lived and died for. Thanks to Rob's generosity, the institute became a reality.

When I appeared on *Oprah* with Rob and Alec Baldwin a few weeks before *Ghosts of Mississippi* opened, I expressed my hope that the film would "make people more curious" about that time in history. As I said that day to the millions of viewers who had tuned in, "You try to find positive things in the negative." That, in fact, has been a guiding credo of my life. Though tragedy has shattered my world more than once, I have kept on keeping on. My faith in God and the strength of my forebears are like pillars holding up my soul, giving me an inner reserve of courage and hope to draw from.

In the course of that *Oprah* broadcast, we all chatted amiably about the movie, from which several clips were shown. Later in the show, I turned to Rob and said, "I have a little surprise for you." From a small purse on my lap, I pulled out a wallet that had been in Medgar's pocket the night he died and was among the bloodstained personal effects returned to me by the police department. I could hear the audience gasp.

"Darrell, Reena, Van, and I have talked," I continued, "and we wondered, 'What can we do to thank Rob?' As you know, the Evers family does not give away things of Medgar's very easily." Rob, who was very emotional throughout the filming of the movie, started to tear up; so did Oprah. I first removed a five-dollar bill, remarking that it was ironic to see the face of Abraham Lincoln obscured by Medgar's blood. Finally, I took from the wallet a piece of white paper, which I slowly unfolded to reveal one of Medgar's poll tax receipts, also smeared with his blood.

Poll taxes in Mississippi dated back to 1890, when, in the interest of maintaining White supremacy in a state that was predominantly Black — or, as James K. Vardaman, one of Mississippi's most virulently racist governors, put it, "to eliminate the nigger from politics" — an amendment was passed. Any Negro who wanted to vote first had to pay a poll tax of two dollars, tendered well in advance and two years in succession. This was a tremendous financial burden on the Black populace, which had a median annual income of $601 in 1950 — less than twelve dollars a week — with many earning considerably less. Negroes also had to pass a test proving that they could give a reasonable interpretation of a section of the state constitution. If that wasn't hindrance enough, local officials in some counties added other "questions," such as, "How many bubbles in a bar of soap?" Before such practices were outlawed as unconstitutional in 1964 with the passage of the Twenty-Fourth Amendment — six months after Medgar's assassination — few Negroes held poll tax cards. For a Black man to have one, then, was nothing short of a miracle.

"Having this card meant one was entitled to the full rights of citizenship in Mississippi," I explained to Rob, handing him the receipt. Speechless, he gave me a bear hug. My gift was a statement and a reminder, not only to Rob but to the public, of why Ghosts of Mississippi was made in the first place. I may not have won my battle, but I certainly took another small step toward winning the war. I wouldn't allow anyone to forget that because Medgar fought for his right to be a first-class citizen, because he spilled his blood, justice was pursued and justice prevailed.

8

BEGINNING TO UNFOLD

Politics and the search for identity

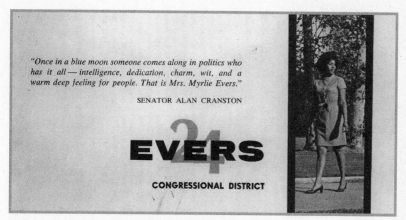

> "Once in a blue moon someone comes along in politics who has it all — intelligence, dedication, charm, wit, and a warm deep feeling for people. That is Mrs. Myrlie Evers."
>
> SENATOR ALAN CRANSTON

EVERS

CONGRESSIONAL DISTRICT

The cover of my congressional campaign brochure, 1970.

Surrounded by supporters, I announce my candidacy for the Tenth District city council seat in Los Angeles, 1987.

The starting point for a better world is the
belief that it is possible.

℘ *Norman Cousins*

Activism has been one of the defining forces of my life, and my experience with *Ghosts of Mississippi* reinforced a familiar lesson: You can often accomplish more by working from the inside. Even though the movie I wanted was not made, my presence exerted some influence over the production. More important, my involvement led to what I had sought for so long, an increased public awareness of Medgar's contributions. In my mind, that's what activism — according to the dictionary, "a doctrine or practice of vigorous action or involvement" — really means. It doesn't necessarily imply winning; my satisfaction always has come from putting myself out there, laying my values on the line, committing myself to a cause.

Like many southern African-Americans, I was born into a community of service and goodwill. The church was the hub of our lives, the spirit and backbone of our culture. When we had nothing but our hopes to survive on, we Negroes had our churches. Back in the plantation days, slaves had "meeting Sundays," where they sought solace in God. These prayer meetings sustained heart and soul, providing comfort and shelter from the harsh reality of life, not to mention serving as a hot line of information. Religious meetings also sowed the seeds of rebellion. Because slaves were forbidden to pray on most plantations, these services were hidden, often taking place in the woods. The words of hymns, which praised "freedom" or admonished one to "steal away to Jesus," took on a double meaning, particularly as the antislavery movement grew.

Later, during the civil rights movement, our spiritual centers played an important role. As the poet Margaret Walker Alexander recalls, "The people prayed and sang their songs, and they were so moved emotionally that they could go out in the streets and face the devil." African-Americans recognized that their churches were sanctuaries in which they not only praised God, but held secret planning sessions, dispensed medical assistance after demonstrations, and, when necessary, found a safe haven. Many church buildings were destroyed by opponents of the movement for precisely that reason. Church was the only meeting place we had in those days, barred as we were from restaurants, clubs, convention centers, and banquet halls. Particularly for women activists, the church was a training ground for cooperation and organization. Even today, churches not only continue to provide for our communities in many of the same ways, they continue to be the target of hate groups. Consider the recent rash of church burnings, particularly during the summer of 1996, when there were more than a hundred such incidents nationwide.

When I was growing up, church was less about political activism for my family and more about being part of a community of believers. Still, I learned the importance of doing my part. Mama always reminded me, "You weren't put on this earth to do nothing," and I followed her example. Whether it was organizing efforts to provide food, shelter, or medical aid for the needy, or working with neighbors who needed help around the house, we took care of our own.

Being raised by two women who were understandably frightened to challenge the status quo, when I met Medgar, I did not define activism the way he did. I remember the evening in Mound Bayou when he came home and said to his new bride, "Myrlie, I have a present for you." He extended his hand, holding what looked like a small piece of cardboard. "You're now a member of the National Association for the Advancement of Colored People," he proudly announced.

I was speechless. A *present?* A present was a necklace or a new dress, not some membership card. I had heard of the NAACP when we were in college, of course; but I believed that the organization had nothing to do with my personal life — except for Medgar's increasing involvement with it. Needless to say, in spite of my initial surprise, that little card came to be a badge of honor, a passport to full citizenship. And in time I became as bold as my late husband in the cry for equality.

Today, in fact, I believe that true fulfillment in any individual's life comes as a result of doing service, giving of self, embracing an idea or a principle and being willing to fight for it. Whether you act under the auspices of a house of worship, a volunteer organization, or an elected office, the joy is in the process itself and in the commitment. Sometimes the goal is met; sometimes not. In almost every instance, though, the experience is a positive one, for not only is the cause helped but the activist benefits as well.

My involvement over the years has taken me places I'd never even envisioned. In 1969, for example, John Mack Carter, editor-in-chief of *Ladies' Home Journal*, selected me to be part of a delegation the magazine was sending to Paris, where representatives of the United States and North Vietnam were trying to negotiate an end to the Vietnam War. Our mandate was to deliver to North Vietnamese officials a summary of readers' sentiments, drawn from some sixty-five thousand survey questionnaires about the war and the POW issue. Four delegates accompanied Carter to Paris, including Lenore Hershey, then editor of the magazine. I was the only Black woman. With us was Virginia Allen, a representative from the U.S. State Department, who tried to facilitate our meeting. We were stymied by red tape at every turn. Frustrated, the others returned to the States, leaving me with the responsibility of making contact.

After several more days, I was finally granted an audience at the North Vietnamese embassy with the top aide to Madame Nguyen Thi Binh, then chief negotiator for the Vietcong. There, in a somber gray meeting room, I began by presenting her with a small gift the *Journal* traditionally reserved for special occasions, a heart-shaped pendant inscribed with the magazine's motto: Never Underestimate the Power of a Woman. Through an interpreter I told her that I hoped the gift would be a reminder of our readers' desire for peace. As an American Black woman, a mother of three (my older son near draft age at the time), and a citizen of the world, I said, I was proud to bring her this message.

As she listened intently, a polite smile appeared on her distinguished face. When the interpreter finished, Madame Binh's aide turned to me and in perfect English said, "Yes, yes. We women *are* the strong ones." With that the ice was broken. She took my hand and led me into an anteroom, where display cases bore souvenirs of war, including artifacts and photos of American soldiers in captivity or killed. My heart sank as my eyes lit on a small replica of our flag. Regardless of the injustices against Blacks, America was still my country, and at that moment I felt that I was its ambassador.

"This figure represents *all* women," the aide said, directing my attention to a life-size statue of a woman holding a child in her left arm and a sword in her right hand. "We nurture our children, and we will fight to the death to protect them." *Indeed we will,* I thought. I left her with the book of signatures, as well as a clearly articulated statement representing our readers' position toward the war: It must end. In retrospect I suspect that our mission had little impact, if any, but that meeting, so far removed from all my previous experiences, made me understand with greater clarity that women worldwide have much in common. We struggle, we give birth to our children, and we support our nations; we are strong, we survive, and, yes, sometimes we even thrive. As I said my good-byes to the North Vietnamese diplomat, I couldn't help thinking, *How far you've come, Myrlie. The shy woman from Mississippi playing a part in the struggle for justice in her own country, and in the quest for peace in the world.*

My experience in Paris was, to me, a particularly dramatic and moving example of how activism can take many forms; but it is always a process, involving dedication, participation, and movement toward a goal. Good works nurture one's soul and build a sense of self-confidence. I have been accompanied on my own journey by fellow activists, particularly other women of my generation, who found themselves at similar turning points later in life. Through activism, we saw that we could make a difference and that we could be more than we had imagined. Even when others continued to see me in a widow's veil, I knew a more evolved Myrlie had emerged from that narrow portrait. ⵒ

Soon after Medgar was killed, a troublesome thought began to skirt the edges of my consciousness: If I didn't start to shape my own identity, I would be known forever as someone else's *something* — Mrs. Beasley's granddaughter, Mrs. Polk's niece, Medgar Evers's wife, Darrell, Reena, and Van's mother. Who, I wondered, was I?

Although my efforts for the NAACP and my position at the Claremont Colleges, as well as the trip to Paris, helped me make a name for myself, I truly stepped out on my own when I entered the world of politics. In 1969 several representatives of the local Democratic Party asked me to consider running in a special election being held to fill the seat of a U.S. congressman who had died in office. He had represented California's Twenty-Fourth District, a suburban sprawl that was predominantly White, conservative, and Republican.

I didn't have time to consider the proposal as seriously as I'd have liked; there was only a week before the filing deadline. My children — the older two of whom were in their teens and Van nearly ten — supported my decision to run. One reason I agreed was my sense that the community would benefit from hearing a liberal voice. The other reason was my desire to be someone on my own. *Here's an opportunity to really venture forth and test myself,* I thought. I suspected that my being "the widow of" was the main qualification the local Democratic Party initially valued in me — that, and the fact that no one else was willing to run. But I didn't care. I was flattered to have been asked at all.

Although I had worked at Medgar's side and organized voter turnouts in Mississippi, I brought only minimal political experience to my candidacy. Clearly, the race would be a challenge, especially since my Republican opponent, John Rousselot, was a seasoned politician who had already spent a term in Congress. He was also the former national public relations director of the ultraconservative John Birch Society — a group that, to my mind, was nearly as pernicious as the Klan.

Everyone knew that my campaign was a losing battle; the coffers were empty and, with the exception of Claremont and Pomona, I couldn't count on much support from the towns in Los Angeles

County that made up the Twenty-Fourth District. The party bosses who drafted me had no intention of helping me wage a *real* campaign, preferring that I attend teas and coffee klatches — the demure widow of a slain civil rights leader putting on her brave face.

One evening, as the race was heating up, I found myself sitting at campaign headquarters in downtown Claremont, pondering my situation. I was living out a plan designed by others. How did I get here? Granted, in accepting the nomination, I had tacitly agreed that the Democrats would showcase a "name," and that I in turn would have the opportunity to break into politics. But something didn't feel right.

It was nearly eleven o'clock. The office became quiet as the last of my volunteers walked out the door. I reflected on the unlikely assemblage of people who had come forward to do the grunt work of campaigning — energetic senior citizens working side by side with idealistic college students, nine-year-olds on street corners passing out my campaign literature. I looked around the stark space, strewn with posters and brochures and boxes of buttons. A lamppost outside the corner window illuminated a three-foot-high stack of brown shopping bags, the hallmark of my campaign. Designed by Leslie Stevens, producer of the 1960s TV series *The Outer Limits*, each was imprinted with a list of community concerns addressed in my platform: unemployment, violence, consumer and environmental protections, lower interest rates, community facilities for teens.

Suddenly I realized what had been bothering me: Every bit of material in that room had my picture on it, but the banners and buttons and posters all said, *Vote for Mrs. Medgar Evers.* "That isn't how I want to be known!" I exclaimed, needing to say the words out loud. "It should be *Myrlie* Evers — the woman, not *the widow of.*" At that moment, I realized I had my own ideas about running this campaign, and by God, I was going to express them.

Even then, though, a part of me drew back at the idea of being known simply as "Myrlie Evers." In truth, *Mrs. Medgar Evers* had been my security blanket. The name gave me stature; it was a passport of sorts, affording instant recognition and immediate respect. It was also an enduring connection to Medgar, enabling me to keep his name in the public eye. Did I really want to give all that up? Besides, as an African-American woman, having "Mrs." attached to my name was a mark of respect; it meant I was an adult, not some "girl" called by her first name. That's why I had insisted on being called "Mrs. Evers" in 1964 when I testified in the earlier Beckwith trials. And, I had never liked the feminist "Ms.", which was far too close to the demeaning "Miz" of the South.

Ultimately, my desire to establish my own identity won out, and my compromise was to campaign as "Mrs. Myrlie Evers." This was the beginning of an important transformation: Myrlie the activist bolstered Myrlie the individual. Something in me awakened, and I became more comfortable starting sentences with "I." I stopped saying, "I think," and instead said, "I know." I stopped trying to please everyone, and instead thought, *The heck with it. If I'm going to lose, I'm going to lose as me.* In short, I began to do what every woman needs to do: *I recognized and embraced myself.* I looked into the mirror and asked, "Do you really know who you are?" The answer was: "Now I'm going to find out!"

As the campaign progressed, I garnered support from surprising corners. People throughout the district formed a Republicans for Evers committee. Averell Harriman held a fund-raiser in my honor in his Washington, D.C., home. A well-known Pasadena attorney took an interest in my campaign, donating money and advice as well as hosting a fund-raiser. And in the final weeks before the election, just as I was running out of money, Bill Cosby performed back-to-back benefit concerts in Pasadena and Claremont. But by far my greatest support came from U.S. Senator Alan Cranston, without whom I would not have had a campaign. "Once in a blue moon someone comes along in politics who has it all — intelligence, dedication, charm, wit, and a warm deep feeling for people," he proclaimed to the press. "That is Mrs. Myrlie Evers."

In addition to his vocal support, Cranston loaned me one of his best campaign managers, a press agent, and a dynamic fund-raiser who presented me with lists of potential contributors — people with political clout, Hollywood stars, wealthy socialites, entrepreneurs in

Beverly Hills. I would go to the fund-raiser's office and get on the phone to make "cold calls," to introduce myself and explain my platform. Trying to convince strangers to contribute money and other resources was one of the most difficult things I've ever had to do. Ultimately, though, I raised more money for my campaign than anyone expected.

Naturally, in a district where Republicans outnumbered Democrats three to one and at a time when most women were uninvolved in politics, I also met with a fair share of disapproval, not the least of which came from women themselves. There were only eleven females in Congress in 1970; and, as *Time* reported in August of that year, "all too often, the electorate still views women politicians as sideshow curiosities." At one of the candidates' forums, a woman said to me outright, "You shouldn't be running. Politics is no place for a woman. You should be at home caring for your children." I reminded her that as a single mother I was the head and heart of my home. Another woman glared at me and said, "I can't vote for you — I don't like you." I don't know whether she was reacting to my gender, my politics, or my race, but in any event, her look of sheer hatred unnerved me.

I also encountered sobering criticism from my own people, particularly from African-American politicians. Many of those who had worked their way up through the ranks were mystified — and irked — by my sudden appearance on the political scene. Few detractors could deny that my visibility was helpful to the Democratic Party, but at the same time, they argued, my campaign would take money away from candidates who had the potential to actually win their races. Only Mervyn Dymally, a Black legislator who for many years had dominated the Democratic machine in Los Angeles, openly supported my candidacy.

Some also wondered about my long-term political commitment. Typically, Democratic and Republican Party bosses strategize years ahead, determining which local candidates have the potential for victory in state and federal races. It was almost unheard of for someone to jump in at the congressional level without ever having held any public office. Therefore, when Yvonne Brathwaite Burke, the only Black woman holding an assembly seat in the state legislature, heard the news of my candidacy, she was understandably surprised; I hadn't come up through the ranks. "I had no idea you were going to run," she said. "You know, *I* was next in line." (As it turned out, she made history: Besides being the chair of the Democratic National Convention in 1972, a few years later she became the first African-American to represent California in Congress.)

At one of the candidates' forums, during the question-and-answer period, an African-American man raised his hand. "I want to know why you're doing this," he demanded pointedly. Before I had a chance to answer, he added, "You know you're hurting Black men, don't you?"

"No!" I replied sharply, taken aback by his insinuation. "I was asked at the last minute to run because no one — no male, no female, Black or White — was willing to do so. I accepted the challenge. You live here; but you chose not to run, nor did any other Black man." He had no answer, but I knew that wouldn't stop him from viewing me, a Black sister, as someone who was taking power away from him.

Had she heard these voices, my grandmother would have been afraid for me. She believed in extending a helping hand, but she never liked confrontation, and in politics, you can't avoid it. The personal attacks upset my children too, and despite their initial encouragement, they had mixed feelings as the campaign progressed. "To me, it was just another thing that would cause you more aggravation," Darrell recalls. "You were honest and up front about issues, but that's a hard position to maintain in politics. I didn't want you polluted by manipulation and conniving. And I saw how it affected you."

I did, indeed, spend many sleepless nights reviewing my plans, weighing the criticism. Even if I were a "sacrifice candidate," as so many reporters called me, the race gave me opportunities to speak for myself and to put important social issues on the table. At least, this was *my* battle. Rousselot and I couldn't have been more opposite. He believed in "winning" Vietnam, and I wanted our boys out of there. I talked about quality-of-life concerns, all of which were nonissues in Rousselot's camp.

At one point a *Newsweek* reporter asked whether it was "practical" for a Black liberal to run in the lily-white Republican stronghold that was the Twenty-Fourth District.

"Well, it's something that needs to be done," I answered. "I say it is possible to win," I added, knowing that it would be a miracle. When he asked my qualifications, I didn't hesitate: "A heritage of service, an abundance of concern, and a good ear." I paused for a moment and smiled at him, recognizing that those traits didn't exactly define a veteran politician. "And I have lots and lots of sincerity."

In truth, one doesn't need special training to give to one's community. Activism often begins at the grass-roots level. I hear heartening stories every day of parents organizing neighborhood watch groups, of young men and women volunteering their time to be Big Brothers and Big Sisters, of concerned citizens working in local campaigns, just to get involved and to gain firsthand experience. Of course, there are books available that can help you learn how to be a leader, biographies you can read about those who have dared and won, courses you can take to help you write a more convincing essay or address a crowd. All of those are good means of preparing for political office or other forms of activism. But sometimes the best education is acquired on the front lines, by taking risks, by giving your time and energy, and by actually being there, witnessing, and maybe even directing the wheels of change. ⅌

I didn't defeat Rousselot, but I won 38 percent of the vote — a surprisingly good showing. My campaign gave me increased respect and visibility in the Democratic Party. Although I recognized that politics could be brutal, I knew it was an important arena for effecting change. And my first foray into the world of politics was an important personal milestone for an evolving woman: I had gained public recognition *as myself*. What is more, if I decided to run again for office (at that point I had not ruled it out), I now had access to powerful people.

I resigned from my position at the college in March of 1970, and began to devote myself to lecturing, my political campaign, and other forms of activism. Later that year, the founders of the National

Women's Political Caucus (NWPC) — the late Bella Abzug, Betty Friedan, and Gloria Steinem — invited me to be one of the convening members. At the 1968 Democratic National Convention, only 13 percent of the delegates had been women. Hence, the goal of the NWPC was to increase women's participation on the political front. A related objective was to make legislators more aware of "women's" issues, such as health, child care, credit laws, and education. We would raise funds for female candidates, offer training to their campaign staffs, and, ultimately, place and keep women in elected and appointed offices. Even women who didn't win the races they entered nevertheless provided role models for younger women considering a career in public service or government, because they exhibited a "can do" mentality and challenged long-held traditions in politics.

The seventies were a heady time for women in politics. "Women want more of the action," I told a reporter, summing up the tenor of the times. Yet only a relatively small group of women of color took part. For example, at the NWPC, I was joined by Congresswoman Shirley Chisholm, who would wage a lonely bid for the presidency in 1972; civil rights activist Fannie Lou Hamer; Dorothy Height, president of the National Council of Negro Women; Beulah Sanders, vice president of the National Welfare Rights Organization; and Native American activist La Donna Harris.

For African-American women, feminism was seen with a great deal of inner conflict. In the wake of the Black Power movement, which began in the late sixties and segued into the seventies, many of my sisters were ambivalent about joining feminist organizations. To whom did we owe our allegiance? Was our primary battle against racism or sexism? When Stokely Carmichael, who coined the expression Black Power, was asked by a reporter what the "women's position" was in the civil rights movement, he answered dismissively, "On their backs." Understandably, many of us found his comment unacceptable. We weren't just making coffee in the back room; we were right there on the front lines with our Black brothers. Now we found ourselves derided and perceived as sex objects, in that respect suffering the same indignities as all women.

Yet in many people's minds, liberation was fundamentally a White woman's crusade. For example, in July of 1971, at the first meeting of the NWPC, at the Statler Hilton Hotel in Washington, D.C., most of the three hundred participants were middle and upper middle class. Racial issues were different and more substantial, it was argued, and some minority women boycotted that conference, believing that Whites, no matter how liberal or well intentioned, simply couldn't understand their struggle. Even among the African-American women who attended, there was a degree of skepticism. If the White women in the room thought that they had problems, Fannie Lou Hamer said, "then they should be Black and in Mississippi for a spell."

To African-American women, "liberation" also didn't mean winning the right to work. We had no choice; we *had* to work — sometimes, *for* White women as their maids or as caregivers to their children. Moreover, my sisters were interested in building up their own confidence, but not at the expense of their men. As a result, the question of candidate support became a volatile issue. Should the NWPC assist female candidates only, or should we also support male candidates who embraced women's issues? The debate raged for an hour or more. I and several other Black women lined up behind the microphones, many of us uttering similar sentiments: "Don't force us to make a choice. We fully support the purpose of the NWPC, but we will not pledge to withhold our support from worthy male candidates, especially Black men."

Not everyone agreed. In the excitement of the moment, Fannie Lou Hamer maintained that the NWPC should designate its resources to women only. "We women have done all of the work anyway," she reasoned. "The men have done little or nothing for us in their battles." Hearing her argument, I could barely control my emotions. Stepping again before the microphone, I specifically addressed Sister Hamer's remarks and reminded her that, if it had not been for Medgar Evers's giving his life for the cause, making possible equal opportunity for *all* of us, she would never have had the chance in Mississippi to run, as she had just announced, for the U.S. Senate in the next national election. That moment drove a wedge between us that lasted for a few years. Fortunately, we reconciled before her death.

Believe me, I have never made excuses for patriarchal attitudes that designate a woman's place as the kitchen rather than the world. I worked hard to get through college and to establish myself in a career, and I truly resent any man, regardless of color, who begrudges me what I have rightfully earned. But I do understand the reasons for their attitude: African-American men have so often found themselves at the bottom of the social pecking order in our culture; keeping women subordinate at least provides them some illusion of dominance.

My priority was the civil rights movement, but I also wanted to participate in the women's movement. To make this a better world for my children and grandchildren, racism *and* sexism had to be addressed, and I was determined to work toward change on both fronts. In the struggle for civil rights, I had raised funds and motivated people to become involved at the local, state, and national level and had helped develop outreach programs in minority communities. My work at the Claremont Colleges was an extension of those efforts. Where women's issues were concerned, as a member of the advisory committee of the NWPC, I assisted in developing position papers and supported various female candidates throughout the country. Wherever my work took me, wherever I traveled and was asked to speak, I looked for ways to advance both causes.

One such opportunity came along late in 1971, when Senator Edmund S. Muskie of Maine, then one of the leading contenders for the Democratic nomination in the 1972 presidential election, asked me to become cochairman of his National Citizens' Committee. This position involved my making speeches and public appearances on his behalf and assisting in fund-raising efforts, as well as offering my input about national issues and the campaign. There were those who believed that my appointment was a defensive strategy on Muskie's part, to counter criticism from Black leaders responding to his remark that a Black vice-presidential candidate was not feasible in 1972. However, I thought Muskie would be a good president and agreed with most of his politics — among his other achievements, he had helped draft and push through major civil rights legislation. As cochairman of the NCC, I was active on the Women's National Advisory Council and also traveled throughout the country on Muskie's behalf, often criticizing Richard Nixon, the incumbent, for not addressing civil rights issues. Among other serious miscalculations, the president's moratorium on busing, I told the press, "set the country back years."

Looking back, being named one of the movers of the Muskie campaign was a monumental coup for me, and I was disappointed when he failed to win the nomination. On a personal level, though, I had gone beyond what I thought I ever could. I wasn't playing the piano in Carnegie Hall, as I had once dreamed I might, but I was doing something even more important for our people.

On a professional level, the work confirmed that more could be accomplished from working within than by protesting from without, which is often seen as antagonistic. Working from the inside is typically viewed as a more acceptable method of effecting reform, but it can be a more intricate endeavor too. It's not a matter of simply advancing your own agenda; you must first study the players and understand their objectives and then assess where and how change can be best implemented. Another difficulty presents itself in the form of criticism from peers who are outside looking in. Especially when a Black woman gives her support to a White male candidate, she risks being viewed as an Aunt Thomasina — a "sellout." I didn't need to answer such charges; I only had to know my own goals and motivation. No matter how harshly some viewed me, I knew that my involvement opened the doors for others. ⁊

Activism remained a priority even after I joined ARCO in 1976 and became more occupied with corporate duties. I continued my long-time association with the NAACP and other organizations, such as the Urban League, because I knew that one can accomplish a great deal through such work. The roots of Black civic organizations can be traced to Negro fraternal organizations and women's clubs, many of which were founded when the landmark *Plessy vs. Ferguson* ruling of 1896, with its separate-but-equal doctrine, essentially legalized racism in this country. At the turn of the century, reformers like antilynching activist Ida Wells-Barnett, president of the Afro-American Council, and Mary Church Terrell, president of the National Association of

Colored Women, recognized that White America wasn't going to aid the advancement of our race; any education and social reform must come from within the Negro community itself. Their activism and philanthropy led to the establishment of schools, orphanages, hospitals, old age homes, and other social service centers. The motto of the NACW said it all: Lifting As We Climb.

Those early women's clubs set the tone and laid the groundwork for other civic groups, among them Negro sororities, which not only supported young women in college but inspired them to give back throughout their lives. I myself was an involved member of Delta Sigma Theta sorority. In the undergraduate years, the all-Black sororities were very much like their White counterparts, and served for the most part as social clubs. However, they took on a far more important function for alumnae, providing links of sisterhood and service. To qualify as a bona fide member of Delta Sigma Theta today, one must participate in the community work of local chapters, which provide education and outreach programs designed to support young women's endeavors. One, for example, identifies and secures start-up funds for new businesses; another helps promote the careers of exceptionally talented young artists.

In the 1970s I also found unexpected sisterhood in a mixed-race group of women in Bunker Towers, the enclave of apartment buildings in Los Angeles where I and many other professionals lived. Several of us traveled in the same social and political circles as well. Realizing that we had interests, goals, and schedules in common, we decided to meet regularly to share information, encouragement, and laughs. We called our informal support group the Brown Baggers, because we met over sandwiches in the community room of the complex. We were all accomplished to some degree, but society still didn't welcome us as full-fledged members in the halls of power. Whenever any of us did manage to wedge a foot in the door, we sought ways to exploit every opportunity and bolster one another, by sharing contacts and discussing strategies.

The Brown Baggers was a group that accomplished its mission. We became active members of the newly formed Women's Education

Fund, a national organization that grew out of the National Women's Political Caucus. And we made considerable strides in our professional lives as well. Maureen Kindel, who accompanied me on my ARCO trip to Alaska, was persuaded to join Tom Bradley's reelection campaign, and in six weeks managed to raise over a million dollars for him. She moved into the mayor's inner circle and eventually landed a top position as president of the Board of Public Works of Los Angeles.

Other Brown Baggers enjoyed similar degrees of success in politics and commerce. Maxine Waters at the time was chief deputy to City Councilman David Cunningham and even then one of the highest-ranking Black women in City Hall. She went on to win a seat in the California Assembly, where she became the powerful majority whip, and later was elected to the U.S. Congress and served as chair of the Congressional Black Caucus. Kathleen Brown, daughter of Edmund and sister of Jerry — both were governors of California — became the treasurer of the state, ran for governor, and is now a top executive at a major bank. Willie Campbell, an international activist who focuses on the plight of women in third-world countries, eventually became a presidential appointee under Jimmy Carter. Diane Watson became a member of the Los Angeles Board of Education, and a few years later, was elected a California state senator.

The most interesting thing about the Brown Baggers was that our collective vision was bigger than any of the dreams we had for our individual selves. Most of us started out having no idea of how far we could go — that was the mark of many of the women activists of our generation. As Maureen reminded me, "You always used the word 'green' to describe yourself. I'm sure when you were ironing Medgar's shirts, you never in your life imagined that someday you would be chairman of the board of the NAACP.

"That's how it was for many of us," she remembered. "We got married and couldn't conceive of anything else — it just wasn't in our lexicon. And then all of a sudden, in the sixties, everything changed. By the time we all met, there was a feeling among the women in that room that there were important things to do in this world, and we wanted to be part of getting them done. We wanted a voice." ❧

After I lost the 1970 election, I vowed I'd never run for office again, unless I could wage a decent campaign and had a good chance of winning. One thing I've learned since then: *Never say never.* In 1987 I was approached by a group of people involved in Los Angeles politics, who told me, "Myrlie, we need someone with character to run for the Los Angeles City Council." I knew that the Tenth District seat had become vacant when Councilman David Cunningham had resigned, but *twelve* other candidates were vying for the position.

"No way," I answered quickly, explaining that running against a pack of candidates wasn't my idea of a winnable election.

"But we need your help," they pleaded. "We need a strong voice."

I've never been good at refusing such requests. I was certain I couldn't win the race, but I had to give it a try — both because the campaign would enable me once again to address community issues and, frankly, because the opportunity would serve my own purpose. Taking a leave from ARCO just then would buy me time to think about what I might do next with my career.

Los Angeles, a city in the middle of conservative Southern California, is an interracial oasis, divided into fifteen council districts. The Tenth District was home to some 200,000 people — 44 percent African-American, 22 percent White, 22 percent Latino, and nearly 12 percent Asian. It had been a fertile ground for biracial coalitions since the early sixties, when Blacks were just beginning to demand participation in a city where they comprised over 13 percent of the population. Bounded on the west by the mainly White areas of Culver City and West LA (the Fifth District), on the south and southeast by the predominantly African-American Eighth and Ninth Districts, on the east by the mainly Hispanic First District, and on the north by the heavily Asian Fourth, the Tenth District tended to attract a higher-income population than other predominantly African-American areas.

By 1987 the Black community was divided into two opposing forces, and the behind-the-scenes game-playing was intense. On one side were the "Dymally regulars," old-time politicians led by Mervyn Dymally, who dominated the Eighth and Ninth Districts; they represented a fairly staid, working-class orientation, typical of the traditional

242 ¾ WATCH ME FLY

Democratic approach. On the other side were the so-called Bradley reformers — a biracial coalition of upwardly mobile Blacks, some Asians and Hispanics, and liberal Whites, mostly Jewish. The White liberals first flexed their political muscle to support Tom Bradley in a successful bid for the Tenth District seat in 1963; thereafter, the area became a laboratory for their ideology, even more so by the time Bradley became mayor in 1973.

Some political observers would later mark the Bradley years as the heyday of multiracial politics in Los Angeles. Under his leadership, the city hired many minorities and women, aggressively pursued federal funding for social programs, called for police accountability, and supported downtown development — all directives that appealed equally to progressive Whites and non-Whites.

I had friends in both camps but because of my late entry in the race was endorsed by neither Dymally nor Bradley. Maureen Kindel called to tell me that she regretted she couldn't support me, because she already was working for Homer Broome, a candidate handpicked by Bradley. I understood; friendship was one thing, politics another. It was extremely rare for a city council seat to become available; most councilpersons remained unchallenged for years. When such a political office is challenged or vacated, candidates immediately line up their support — ideally, from people who have power and the visibility and money to finance the campaign. In this race, twelve others had tossed their hats into the ring. At least I had the support of a new coalition of powerful women, and several celebrities, such as actress Alfre Woodard, but I knew that with so many candidates vying for the seat, the best I could do was qualify for a runoff.

I was determined to at least make a good showing, raising my voice for people who wanted more jobs and less crime in their lives. But with only two months to plan a campaign, secure financing, and find a staff, I needed help desperately. Several of my other Brown Bagger friends — Assemblywoman Maxine Waters, State Senator Diane Watson — came to my aid, as did Assemblywoman Gwen Moore, attorney Geraldine Greene, with whom I'd worked at ARCO, and a few of the other top women in LA politics. I appeared on the front steps of City Hall to announce my candidacy. Numerous reporters turned out, still curious about the "widow of," although by then many in the press knew me from my own work.

The furor began once my campaign became public. "Why is she doing this?" people asked. "She doesn't even live in the Tenth." In fact, I literally lived across the street from the district's western dividing line. To ward off the criticism, I moved into an apartment complex owned by Maxine's husband. But that didn't stop other candidates from labeling me a carpetbagger. Walter alternated between our house and the little apartment, but I dared not do the same. Cameras and reporters were everywhere.

As the campaign heated up, the backbiting only got worse, and my opponents' tactics became even more aggressive. At night, I'd attend the various candidates' forums and try to make my voice stand out among those of the other twelve. During the day, my staff and I would go from neighborhood to neighborhood, passing out campaign literature and putting up posters; the next morning we'd find the posters on the ground. I met thousands of people personally, going to churches, nursing homes, supermarkets, and strip malls to shake hands and encourage citizens to use their power to vote. Walter was by my side the entire time; our children helped too. But it was a disheartening experience for all of us. At one point, Walter had enough. "If you ever decide to run for public office again," he said to me, "count me out. I can't bear to watch what they're doing to you."

Unlike the 1970 contest, in which I was the only candidate of color on the podium, now all but one of the contenders were African-Americans. One of my opponents was Jessie Mae Beavers, the society editor for the local Black newspaper, the *Los Angeles Sentinel*. She knew almost everyone in the Black community, was quite influential, and naturally had received the paper's endorsement. It wasn't long before she began to cross over from her society beat to the political arena, criticizing the other candidates, especially me. At one of the candidates' forums, I noticed her publisher seated in the first row, and I immediately sensed trouble. During the question-and-answer session, he raised his hand and fired a series of questions at me:

"Why is it that you're not honest? Why don't you use your real name, Williams?" he asked. "Why are you misleading the public? Why are you using the name Evers?"

I took a breath and responded, "How dare you question me and the name that I choose to use? I *am* Myrlie Evers. I always will be." I offered a summary of Medgar's accomplishments, noting that he had helped pave the way for precisely such Black enterprises as his newspaper. I added that I had worked side by side with Medgar and saw this campaign as carrying on his work. Finally, I pointed out to the publisher that he had a double standard; his society editor was using her maiden name as well. What was the difference between her situation and mine?

"Well, we have to protect the name of Medgar Evers — you are abusing it," he countered.

I was incensed, but instead of allowing my anger to control me, I simply said, "I would like to invite you to lunch. Perhaps I can help you understand the history here. You are extremely insensitive to it. Medgar didn't belong to you; he was my husband, my children's father. And I think it would be best if we discussed this privately." Weeks later, I did take the publisher to lunch, but I never got another line of coverage from his paper.

The election was narrowly won by State Senator Nate Holden, who beat the Bradley-endorsed candidate, Homer Broome. I didn't take the defeat personally. At least I had made myself heard. I had used the same skills that made me an effective speaker, being a quick study, knowing my audiences, observing body language, and really listening before responding. People thrive on direct contact; they want to feel that a candidate is paying attention to them and to their concerns, not simply spouting his or her own ideas.

Of course, anyone who considers becoming involved in politics needs not only a thick skin but an especially strong set of ethics. No matter how much mud was slung in my direction, I resisted resorting to similar tactics. I refused to spread lies or gossip. At the same time, to be successful in politics — whether it's in a corporation or a campaign — a contender can never appear weak; no one wants to support a losing cause. But the opposite is equally true: no one wants to be bossed around; people desire strong, but fair, leadership.

In retrospect, the maturity and self-confidence I gained in the political process was different from the growth I experienced working for the Claremont Colleges or even afterward, as I achieved success in the corporate world. One reason, I suspect, is that when you undertake a political campaign or are part of an activist movement, no pay is involved. The decisions you are forced to make grow from interests close to the heart, and the work directly affects people's lives. And you often have to act alone, without the benefit of a structure to protect you.

Without winning either election, I gained self-esteem by standing up to the challenges of my 1970 and 1987 campaigns. The mere act of being a candidate and holding my own in such a brutal arena gave me the courage to take further risks. (Little did I realize that the greatest test of my mettle and my leadership was still to come, when I ran for chairman of the NAACP.)

The truth is, I never put my activism on a shelf. It doesn't matter where I am — on a podium or a plane, addressing a room full of strangers or talking to my grandchildren, slogging through a heated session at the NAACP or shopping for a pair of nylons. My work takes me on surprising journeys. Through it all, I've tried to be as tough as the problems I've set out to conquer. I've had to pull back and *think*, to plot and plan. When a need arises, or when a debate is aired, I can't be silent — I'm there.

Recently, for instance, I was in a department store in Bend, and a woman came up to me on the checkout line. "You were recently widowed, weren't you?" she asked.

I looked at her a bit suspiciously and waited a beat before answering. As it turned out, she had seen me on a public-service commercial about the Bend Hospice, for which I acted as spokesperson. "I just lost my husband," she explained, her face strained with grief. "Do you have a moment to talk to me?"

I was late and, as usual, very busy, but I listened. You see, taking time for someone else is the essence of activism — seeing another human being's pain, responding to it, lending support, rather than just walking away. Whether one-on-one or in a crowd of thousands, activism means being *involved*.

That's why I have sought the political offices, run the campaigns, made the backroom deals, lobbied for change, and put myself out there, risking criticism. That's why, even when I look back over the long years of struggle, although I sometimes get weary just thinking about the crusades I've fought, I know I'll keep on keeping on. Hopefully, my work will inspire others to join me — and, shoulder to shoulder, we'll fight the good fight.

9

MADAM CHAIR

Coming full circle

At a White House meeting representing the NAACP, July 1995.

Addressing the NAACP convention, Atlanta, Georgia, July 1998.

Lose not courage, lose not faith —
go forward!

ϟ *Marcus Garvey*

*M*yrlie Victorious!" trumpeted one of the headlines on February 19, 1995, the morning after I became only the third woman since 1909 to head the NAACP, and the first on a full-time basis. As had been the case with my campaigns for public office, I had not sought this nonsalaried position but agreed to run out of a sense of duty. "Medgar died for the NAACP," I told reporters after my victory. "I will live for the NAACP."

Although I still had ambivalent feelings about the organization because of how little had been done to protect Medgar, the NAACP had nurtured my children and me when our situation was precarious, for which I've always been grateful. But by the early 1990s, the NAACP was threatened with extinction. Some critics questioned the organization's very "relevance," often citing its name as one of the problems. To those who grew up hearing "Black is beautiful" and identifying themselves as African-Americans, the word "Colored" seemed at best sorely out of date, at worst, offensive. For several years, membership had been decreasing and the group's financial state deteriorating, and the infighting, coupled with many of the same internal problems that had plagued the organization in Medgar's day, exacerbated the situation. There also was poor communication among the managers of branch, regional, and national offices. Many board members, too, complained of being uninformed and therefore ineffectual. The politics of Executive Director Benjamin Chavis, which many felt bordered on militancy, were out of sync with the historically moderate organization. William Gibson, a dentist from South Carolina, who had been reelected chairman of the board of directors every year since 1985, had browbeaten the board into accepting Chavis over more moderate activists like Jesse Jackson. Those of us who perceived the gravity of this situation were desperate to find a remedy.

In 1994, when it was first suggested to me that I challenge Gibson in the next election, the NAACP was virtually collapsing under the weight of its $4.7 million debt and its internal discord. During a trip Walt and I made to Washington, D.C., that June, board member Joe Madison invited us to have lunch with him for the express purpose of trying to persuade me to run for the position of chairman the following February. He and the board members he represented wanted an answer by August. I was flattered and even a bit intrigued by the idea. Over the years, I had given time and energy to the association, raising funds and making speeches on its behalf, as well as serving on the board of directors for nearly a decade. But because Walter had been in declining health during the last several months as the result of prostate cancer, running for chairman was certainly not high on my list of priorities.

In August, though, the most serious assaults against the organization began. The influential syndicated African-American columnist Carl Rowan began publishing a controversial series of critical articles that detailed the NAACP's problems. Many board members were as angry at Rowan for exposing the news as they were disappointed in Executive Director Chavis for alleged wrongdoing. Rowan's series charged that Chavis had covered up a sexual harassment suit brought by a female employee and was now paying her off with association funds. The columnist also uncovered evidence about Gibson, maintaining that he had misused NAACP pension and tax-exempt grant funds and was guilty of "double-dipping" — charging the organization twice for expenses. Even worse, Rowan implied that the NAACP was so mired in its problems that it was "virtually paralyzed" and had neither the time, money, nor inclination to wage the important battles it was meant to fight. Rowan acknowledged that the NAACP had once been a legal powerhouse, spearheading important civil rights legislation and combating discrimination in many industries. But what was its purpose now?

In the wake of the bad publicity, several foundations immediately began to withdraw funding. Chavis was forced to resign, but Gibson let it be known that those who wanted him out would have a fight on their hands. The board members who implored me to run believed that I could unseat Gibson, but I wasn't sure I even wanted to try.

Walt, who was getting weaker by the day and needed me more than he ever had, was furious about what was happening in the association and remained wholly in favor of my running. "Why are you procrastinating?" he asked. "I don't have long, and this is my fight too. It will be good for you and good for the NAACP." He waited a minute and then added, "This is the last thing I'll ever ask you to do. Run and win!" (Walt lived long enough to see me do just that, but sadly he died only two days after my election.)

Despite his urging, I wondered to myself, *How can I choose civic duty over spending his last days with my beloved?* A painfully cruel irony was that I had really begun to enjoy a carefree life with Walter at that point. My years of being on the road had taken a toll on my health too, and I finally had begun to curtail my incessant traveling.

Over the next few weeks, I soul-searched and conversed with friends. I turned to Maureen Kindel, who also had heard from Walter; he knew that she would be one of the people I'd depend on for advice. "Walt told me he wanted me to talk to you," Maureen recalled recently, "because he knew I would say, 'You have to do this.' Even though it meant stepping into the job at the worst possible moment in your personal life, clearly the opportunity was a big *click!* that resonated down to your inner core. Myrlie — the public icon, the activist, the wife of a slain civil rights leader — *had* to do it."

That summer the phone rang constantly, with members inquiring about my intentions, reporters trying to get a jump on the story. Meanwhile, I agonized, watching Walt, now bedridden, become weaker, while Rowan's investigation continued unabated. A friend wisely suggested that prayer might help. I took comfort in the well-known Bible passage "Ask, and it shall be given you; seek, and ye shall find," and pleaded, *God, send me a sign.*

One day, after I hadn't been out of the house for three weeks, I asked the Bend Hospice to send someone to stay with Walt so that I could catch up on some errands. I hurried through town, and as I stepped out of the bank, suddenly in the sky overhead was a double rainbow. I had never seen such vivid colors before, and certainly never two rainbows at once. Filled with excitement, I drove home but decided to take a different route — almost literally, the road less traveled. As I rounded a curve, I saw a more amazing phenomenon: the end of the rainbow. Science tells us there is no such thing. Science is wrong, for I drove right through that wash of color, proclaiming loudly, "My prayer has been answered. *This* is my sign!"

I started crying and laughing at the same time, and when I got home, I didn't even stop to put the car into the garage but ran inside and shouted, "Walter! Walter! You're right: I *am* supposed to do this." I hugged him and told him what I had just witnessed, and he with a grateful smile said quietly, "I told you so."

I finally made my candidacy official in early February, explaining to the crowd of reporters, "There is no way I can disassociate myself from this organization, and no way I can stand by and watch it go under." I ran as Myrlie Evers-Williams, honoring Walt's role in my decision. Then, on the Sunday before the election, CBS's 60 *Minutes* aired a special investigative report during which Lesley Stahl featured interviews with Carl Rowan, who discussed the mass of evidence he had uncovered; Gibson, who claimed he could "explain" his spending; and me. I purposely did not campaign on camera but stressed that this was no time for America to be without the NAACP. The organization needed to heal and to strengthen itself from within so that we could fight the civil rights backlash threatening from outside. "I can imagine," I told Ms. Stahl, "those who wish to see the NAACP destroyed laughing as we destroy ourselves."

As with any political contest, backstabbing and innuendos quickly followed. Gibson's supporters offered a litany of reasons I would be unable to handle the position. Even though I had stepped out of a government job in which I had managed a $900 million budget and seven thousand employees, I lacked experience. Even though I had been involved in the NAACP for my entire adult life, I didn't understand the organizational structure or the issues. Even though I had traveled incessantly on the association's behalf, I didn't have the wherewithal to handle the chairmanship. My back would give out; I wouldn't have the stamina; I didn't have the knowledge; I wasn't tough enough. Of course, they also leveled the most stinging criticism of all: I was *only* Medgar's wife.

Unspoken, but at the heart of much of the condemnation, was the fact that I was a woman. I had experienced the same discrimination in corporate life. Somehow, though, in an organization committed to equal rights, the insult went even deeper. Women worked behind the scenes; men got the credit. Women did the legwork; men met with influential outsiders. Women's salaries and their titles were affected by sexism, and so were their chances of gaining real power within the organization. The board of directors was predominantly male — only fifteen of the sixty-four members were female — and the organization itself had a long-standing tradition, albeit unacknowledged, of limiting women's roles. Fewer than 20 percent of the local chapters had women presidents; in the organization's almost eighty-five-year history, there had been only three female secretaries at the national level, three female presidents, and, at that juncture, two female chairmen. "It's a dirty little secret among the Black brotherhood in most civil rights groups," wrote Barbara Reynolds in a *USA Today* article that came out shortly before the election, referring to the problem as "sexism within."

Two years earlier, in fact, Jewel Jackson McCabe, president of the National Coalition of 100 Black Women, was among the finalists under consideration as a replacement for Executive Director Benjamin Hooks, who had then announced his retirement. Ms. McCabe made her presentation before the full board and was allotted the same amount of time as the male candidates, but many, including the candidate herself, insisted that she didn't get a fair hearing. Allegedly, letters sent on her behalf — some of which promised sizable donations if McCabe was chosen — weren't even read by some board members. Ultimately, Chavis was selected for the position. McCabe had the courage to challenge the system, and her complaints helped women make some inroads, but she and other women were understandably not optimistic about my chances.

Those who championed my candidacy pulled out all the stops. The *60 Minutes* exposé played continuously on a television monitor strategically placed in the registration area of the annual meeting, which was held at the Hyatt Hotel in New York City. Although the votes for chairman would be cast only by members of the board, it was important to enlist the support of the rank and file, whose opinions would have an impact on directors' votes. The night before the election, my supporters canvassed every floor of the hotel, slipping campaign literature under delegates' doors. Caucuses were held long into the night, most in secret. Early in the morning, the telephone calls started, and deals were cut on both sides: "If you support my candidate, you can get this committee appointment."

During the annual meeting, which took place on the day of the election, prior to the board meeting, participants were uncharacteristically rowdy. Some members waved placards, trashing the old regime: "Gib$on Loves $$$$. We Love the NAACP!" Others supported it, among them a bloc of South Carolina faithful wearing bright yellow windbreakers to symbolize their solidarity with Gibson. Several delegates walked around with $10,000 checks in their pockets, which they refused to give to the organization until a new financial policy was in place. The word was out that an ever-increasing number of individual and corporate benefactors also had threatened to withhold funding until the NAACP demonstrated that its house was in order. And when it came to voting on the financial report presented to them by the treasurer — normally a rote process — the attendees refused to accept it. At that point, Enolia McMillan, a highly respected former president of the NAACP, took the microphone and called for a vote of nonconfidence against Gibson. The crowd went wild, and the motion passed.

The board meeting that followed was one of the best-attended and most heated in the NAACP's history. Gibson called the meeting to order standing at the head of a mammoth U-shaped conference table, large enough to seat the fifty-nine board members who attended that day. Gibson supporters sat on one side of the table, Evers-Williams partisans on the other. Behind the table stood a throng of delegates — observers who couldn't vote but who nevertheless voiced their opinions in loud, angry tones, making it impossible to conduct the business at hand. Pounding the gavel, Gibson warned that if the group didn't quiet down, he'd call hotel security, and if that didn't work, New York's finest. He finally asked the observers to leave. When no one budged, Gibson enlisted my aid.

"Please, please, hear me!" I bellowed above the throng. "Go into the hallway and wait for the vote. We can't settle the chairmanship until you leave the room."

One man, then another, one woman, then another, began to chant as they filed out of the room. "Only for you, Myrlie, only for you!" I accompanied them, and found myself facing a sea of reporters and camera crews in the hall. I was pushed, pulled, and yelled at by the incensed delegates — why had they been asked to leave? I stood on top of a table, shouting the answer: "So you can have a new chairman!" An ear-splitting cheer rose from the crowd, and I went back into the board meeting, thinking, *Walt, what have you gotten me into? If I win, this is going to be the challenge of my life.*

As the designated counters began to tally the votes, I sat there truly believing that victory once again would be Gibson's. As is the custom, each vote is read aloud. The first was cast for Gibson, as was the second, the third, the fourth, and the fifth — twenty-nine votes in a row, in fact. *It's just as I expected,* I told myself, gratified to have played the part and relieved that I would soon be free to return to Walt. Then one vote was announced for Evers-Williams, then another, and another, until I too had twenty-nine votes. To my utter astonishment, the last vote was cast for me. It was hardly a resounding victory, but it was a victory nonetheless. (I often relate this story to people who say to me, "My vote doesn't count." One vote *can* change history.)

Minutes later, President Clinton called and, via speakerphone, congratulated me and pledged his support in renewing the association. Then, as protocol required, Gibson handed me the gavel, addressing me as "Madam Chairman," and I began to officiate my first board meeting. The delegates who had been waiting outside now crowded into the room, most of them cheering me on. But the board itself was still divided, and many were obviously angry at the outcome. Lacking the parliamentary expertise to handle their rudeness, I called a recess, regrouped, and prayed for strength and wisdom. That

Saturday night, after what the *New York Times* described as "a raucous day of chants, shouts, and loud complaints," the results of the election were officially announced to the general membership. I faced the nattily attired crowd in the grand ballroom of the hotel and blew a single kiss to the audience. "Her work began with that symbolic kiss," the *Times* reported, "but it was a kiss from an old friend." ♭

When I took the helm of the NAACP, I had a particular vision of unity and renewal for the organization. In my platform I had promised to restore credibility, step up fund-raising activities, recruit a new executive director, increase membership, and enhance youth participation. But because I had inherited a sprawling, 500,000-member organization with a disorganized network of some 2,000 chapters, before anything could be accomplished, I had to assess our situation with the eye of a cold, calculating entrepreneur. I had often decried the fact that the association was essentially a business and yet we failed to operate as one. Now I had to identify the deeper problems we faced, in addition to analyzing the obvious ones that had surfaced.

There were four interrelated and overlapping areas that needed attention: revamping the internal structure, which included staff, management, and leadership; funding (we were taking in $5,000 a day at the national level, when we needed $12,000 a day to keep the association operating); coalition-building, both within the organization and with other organizations; and the development of policies and programs. The 104th Congress was in session, and Speaker of the House Newt Gingrich was threatening to turn back the clock with his party's Contract with America. (Regrettably, he has succeeded to some degree.)

I knew I had to bring to bear all the leadership qualities and skills I'd developed both as an activist and as an executive. And if ever I needed my people skills, my ability to size up a situation, to know when to wait and when to charge ahead, it was now. My strategy was to determine the most pressing problems, to assess the best way to attack them, and to develop a step-by-step game plan to address them.

Because every issue facing the NAACP was of grave importance and called out for an immediate solution, I formed a Crisis Management Committee, a team whose nine members — all of whom were on the board, and some of whom were Gibson supporters — met weekly via conference calls and monthly at the NAACP headquarters in Baltimore. The members brought to the table expertise, organizational knowledge, credibility, and links to each region. The historic strength of the NAACP has always been its ability to truly represent its constituents. No other civil rights group has more members, more branches, more laypeople actively engaged in doing the organization's work. Our grass-roots support was threatened now, unless we could demonstrate openness and accountability, and restore trust.

One of my tasks, then, was to crisscross the country, appealing directly to the branches, letting them know that I was open to advice and that I needed their help. At each stop, I made inquiries, gathered facts, took voluminous notes, and wrote countless to-do lists. From this input, I tried to determine what goals were feasible to accomplish within a particular time frame. These personal visits helped me gauge members' attitudes directly and better understand their concerns. In effect, I became their connection to the national office. Equally important, whenever I made these visits, we tried to schedule fund-raising events, which earned money for both the branches and the national office.

During the early months of my tenure, the Crisis Management Committee and I made a series of painful cost-cutting decisions, ordering three of our seven regional offices closed and laying off twenty-five longtime employees — nearly half the staff in our national headquarters. This was a particularly difficult decision, because many had worked without pay during the decline of the past administration and were personal friends of years gone by; but the measure saved the organization close to a million dollars that first year. To lift morale, I hosted a luncheon meeting for the remaining support staff, informing them of upcoming plans and acknowledging how valuable they were to the NAACP. I was shocked when one staffer told me, "No one since Mr. Hooks has ever bothered to thank us." It took very little effort, but that small show of my appreciation gave so much in return.

I visited the Ford Foundation during my earliest days in office as well, to insure its continued support; at that juncture, it was the only foundation willing to support us. However, Ford insisted that we engage the services of a financial management firm to update years of badly kept financial records and to develop a system of checks and balances. In years past, there were practically no internal controls over finances, and communication about monetary matters was often highly restricted. Under the management firm's direction, a chief financial officer was hired, which guaranteed that all income would be accounted for and spent only as designated. I also made a necessary but unpopular cost-cutting decision to discontinue the practice of paying board members' travel and lodging expenses and a per diem fee for each of the quarterly meetings they were asked to attend. When funds were reimbursed for miscellaneous job-related expenses, more stringent reporting and reviewing requirements were now in place. We knew that these steps, along with other formal accounting practices, would not only put our financial house in order but also encourage new sources of funding.

Although some of my corporate life had been spent soliciting donations, I was offered truly invaluable assistance in this area by my supporters. Carl Rowan himself and activist C. DeLores Tucker cochaired the first-ever Chairman's Inauguration, a star-studded fundraiser that drew luminaries from every field. The honorary chairs of my inaugural committee included Maya Angelou, Jesse Jackson, Rosa Parks, Colin Powell, and Leontyne Price, and the members of the committee made up a veritable Who's Who. At the swearing-in ceremony on May 14, 1995, which was held at the historic Metropolitan AME Church in Washington, D.C., before an audience of one thousand supporters, I took the oath of office from an unprecedented assemblage of seven African-American federal judges who had come from different parts of the country specifically for the occasion. During the program, which lasted for more than three hours, many wellwishers greeted me with checks in hand.

The following evening, at Rowan's urging, the Freedom Forum bestowed upon me its highest honor, the Free Spirit Award, and the $100,000 check that accompanied the award was given to the association in my name. In all, over $1.5 million was raised, the major portion allocated to retiring the organization's debt. The two events clearly marked a turning point; my ability to attract funding and support changed the perceptions of board members and corporate America about the new chairman of the NAACP.

Gratifying as that experience was, I knew I had to continue to demonstrate to skeptics and supporters alike that I was strong, determined, and decisive. The first serious test of my authority came within a month of my election. I had just had eye surgery and was required to live as an outpatient at a residential hotel near the hospital in Portland, Oregon. Returning from the hospital that first day, I was presented with a two-inch stack of curled faxes by the concierge. Each memorandum concerned T. H. Poole, who for years had controlled the NAACP's Image Awards, an annually televised program designed to highlight the progress of minorities in the entertainment industry. Poole, who had allegedly mismanaged funds in the past, had finally gone a step too far. In direct disregard of my instructions and the board's order, he illegally signed a $500,000 contract with a television production company to coordinate next year's broadcast. I was half-blind from the surgery but had no trouble seeing what I had to do. *You knew you would be tested, Myrlie,* I told myself. *Stop this trouble before it gains momentum.* I immediately dismissed Poole, and put our attorneys on alert.

Another debate flared up over William Gibson, who after losing the election continued to sit on the board. Although he had accomplished much good in his home base, South Carolina, and at the national level as well during his earlier years as chairman, his presence on the board of directors was divisive. I knew there could be no chance for unity with his remaining there, so I included the issue of his removal in the agenda for my second board meeting.

Remembering the chaos of my first meeting, I engaged the services of a full-time parliamentarian, who sat at my side, ready to assist me with the subtleties of *Robert's Rules of Order.* I wanted to be certain that no one could accuse me of any breach of protocol and that no discussion would get out of hand. Even so, the meeting lasted eleven hours. I didn't leave that session once, fearing that even a trip to the ladies' room could risk my losing control of the group. I was stern, fair, and in charge throughout the meeting. When it was time for Gibson to present his case, rather than cut him off I allowed him as much time as he needed. In the end, he was dismissed, and I had gained the respect of my fellow board members.

In an organization as large as the NAACP, politicking is almost inevitable, and an effective leader has to be prepared to meet such challenges head-on, and sometimes to do a bit of fancy footwork and maneuvering in order to get the job done. For example, when I conducted an exhaustive search for a new executive director, I knew there would be forces within and outside the NAACP working to undermine my efforts. To avert that possibility, I named a seven-member search team, composed of loyal supporters within the NAACP and, for the first time ever, outside professionals from the legal, academic, and business worlds; I convinced retired federal judge Leon Higginbotham, Jr., to chair the team. A search firm was also brought in as consultant.

During a fourteen-month period, more than two hundred people applied for the job, and what I had learned at ARCO about tough negotiation and savvy gamesmanship came in handy during the course of selection. When, late in the process, Congressman Kweisi Mfume emerged as a front-runner, I conducted my meetings with him in private, in out-of-the-way places. He had expressed concern that media attention would detract from his congressional duties and disturb his staff, and I suspected that Gibson's cadre on the board might try to sabotage anyone I and the search committee suggested.

I asked Mfume, among other questions, whether he might have problems reporting to a woman. Given both the NAACP's old-boy mentality and his own take-charge stance, it was a question that needed an answer. To my satisfaction, he indicated that he was indeed willing to be part of an association that had a woman in command. Mfume readily acknowledged that he had reported to no one in the past, however, and we both knew that this arrangement would be a challenging transition for him.

After a series of interviews, the search committee and I were satisfied that Mfume's vision for the organization was similar to ours and that he would be a team player. But to ratify that decision we needed the approval of our seventeen-person executive committee, which consists of members appointed by the chairman as well as others (such as the treasurer) who are designated by constitution to serve. The timing was perfect: a regular board meeting had been scheduled, and members of the executive committee were readily available. We met over a late-night dinner at Judge Higginbotham's office, a location chosen intentionally because it was far from the hotel, preventing word of the committee's first choice from reaching board members prematurely. The following day, Mfume's candidacy, which included his demand that the title be changed from executive director to president/CEO, was officially presented to the board, and various directors were then given the opportunity to fire questions at Mfume regarding his qualifications. When it came time for them to vote, sixteen board members actually voted against the executive committee's decision to hire Mfume. A motion was then passed to present a full-consensus vote of approval. The end, in this case, justified my means.

Once Mfume was hired, it eased my burden somewhat, because he now made most of the visits to the branch offices and was responsible for the coordination of all operations. Still, my life as chairman was a twenty-four-hour-a-day commitment, leaving me absolutely no time for myself. I traveled constantly and spent long stretches of time in Baltimore, typically putting in fourteen-hour days at the national office. My first year in office, in the wake of Walt's death, I spent a total of six weeks in Bend, the second year, ten weeks, on each visit returning home to baskets of mail and a house full of dust and spiderwebs. A once meticulous housekeeper, I was lucky if I managed to get my dirty clothes to the cleaner's. Friends in Bend worried about me and warned me to slow down. I often had dark circles under my eyes. Even when I slept, my mind mulled over NAACP problems. But I was determined to set the organization on a smooth course.

The greatest test of my leadership, at both the personal and professional level, came near the end of my third year as chairman. In October of 1997, during a series of meetings at which the Harvard Business School was presenting a report to the board, Mfume and our press liaison abruptly called me out of a session.

"Have you had any calls from the media?" they asked, looking distressed. "Have you seen the New York newspapers or any television coverage about Mrs. Dukes?"

"No," I replied, alarmed. "What's wrong? Is she all right?"

Hazel Dukes was a friend of long standing. She had served on the board of directors for years and had been president of the NAACP between 1990 and 1992. During her tenure as New York State Conference president, thousands of new members joined and thousands of dollars were raised. She also had been a staunch supporter of my candidacy; it was she who had organized and underwritten the conference calls with the other board members who had urged me to run for chairman. And now I learned that, according to the *New York Post*, Hazel was accused of misappropriating funds. I was shocked and felt tremendous pain. I simply could not believe the charges leveled at this sister who had given so much to so many.

That night someone slipped a copy of the three-page *Post* article under each board member's door. In no time, the accusations were circulating throughout the entire organization and in the media. We seldom received news coverage for our progress or for the programs we'd implemented, but reporters were more than eager to publish our problems. Making matters worse, the Dukes exposé came on the heels of recent allegations involving three other board members. The press, gleefully it seemed, linked the various accounts, typically under such headlines as "NAACP Rocked by Scandal Again."

Thus began a most painful period in my administration. Letters flooded the office, all expressing opinions, some once again threatening withdrawal of financial support. Until the matter was properly disposed of, no other board business could be conducted. I was deeply concerned on two levels: I feared that all the progress achieved over the past two years would be overshadowed by this crisis; and I found it personally trying because Hazel Dukes was a friend. We had many conversations during this difficult time, and she understood that my mandate was to act as a leader; but that didn't ease my discomfort.

I tackled this challenge as I had others, by being open, fair, and decisive, and by following the guidelines set forth in the NAACP constitution. That document clearly dictates the actions to be taken if a board member is "found guilty of conduct not in accord with the principles, aims and purposes of the NAACP . . . or is guilty of conduct inimical to the best interest of the association." The guidelines allow for such a member's removal, after a full hearing and an affirmative vote of two-thirds of the board.

After a highly contentious executive committee meeting via a telephone conference call, the members voted to ask all four individuals to resign. I was enraged the next morning when an article appeared in *USA Today* entitled "Chairman Made to Act," implying that I was no more than a political puppet who had been forced into action. Even more upsetting, the article appeared before I had had a chance to notify anyone of our vote. Obviously, someone on the committee had leaked the information. I sent a harsh rebuttal, which the newspaper promptly printed, but the damage had been done. The article not only hurt those under investigation, it added fuel to what had now become a bonfire. Other accounts that followed criticized my handling of the matter, some accusing me of betrayal — I had turned my back on a friend. One editorial even charged that I was an unknown until Sister Hazel put me "on the map." Other board members and public figures expressed surprise that I had not caved in under the pressure and gained greater respect for my strength.

In accordance with her rights under our constitution, Mrs. Dukes requested a hearing. For her hearing committee I sought neutral board members who could put personalities and politics aside, stressing that, before making a recommendation, they should consider only the evidence and the best interest of the organization. After the hearing, the board would convene at a special meeting in Chicago to consider the case in light of the committee's recommendation.

In the weeks prior to that board meeting, however, various members asked me regarding Mrs. Dukes, "What is it that *you* want us to do, Madam Chair?" Although I believe in exercising authority, I was adamant about not robbing my constituents of their voices. "You do what you believe is right," I told each and every one. "You know our rules and regulations. You stand up and vote the way *you* want."

I didn't waver in my resolve to remain impartial, and that was unnerving for many of my colleagues. Those who were used to unquestioning compliance with the wishes of the chairman, which had often been expected under Gibson, were unaccustomed to finding their own direction and felt at sea. Those who wanted to trap me were disappointed. I knew that in asking my opinion, their goal was to stand aside from the dispute and to claim later, "Well, I voted for [or against] Mrs. Dukes because the chairman told me to."

When we finally met in Chicago, after allowing Mrs. Dukes to again present her case, the board voted to accept the hearing committee's recommendation to dismiss her for a period no longer than four years. For me, the experience was indeed a painful one, but it proved once again that personal feelings cannot take precedence over intellect and reason when one is in a position of leadership. I believed in the NAACP and in its constitution, and I had to allow myself to be guided by my love for what the organization stands for, no matter how others tried to bait me or embarrass me. ❧

Divisiveness in an organization can never be allowed to go unattended, for partisanship inevitably works against progress. Even as I set in motion new procedures and bolstered the organization by bringing in expert consultants and more competent management, even as I dealt with the various crises, there were long-standing troubles at many levels of the NAACP which, as chairman, I needed to address. Some women in the organization felt disrespected and excluded; the small number of younger members were often at odds with old-timers; and the board itself was still divided between Evers and Gibson supporters. From the outset, I knew that the success of my regime and the magnitude of what we could accomplish would depend in large part on healing those rifts.

I certainly understood the women's grievances, for the sexism I had faced during my campaign continued to plague me as chairman. My first six months in office, I had no secretary or assistant assigned specifically to me. When two female managers from Sears came to my office for a meeting about potential funding, they asked incredulously, "You have no one?" Concurring that no man at the head of an organization would be expected to work under such conditions, they made a grant of $80,000, earmarked for a staff person and travel expenses. One wealthy African-American man in Atlanta whom I had approached in the past for funding came to me after Mfume was hired and actually said, "Now I will make a contribution — a man is at the helm." Sadly, he was not the only man who adopted a wait-and-see position. *How many times,* I often wondered, *must I prove myself? How many insults, how many slights, must I endure?*

Instead of railing against the discrimination or trying to discredit those who stood in my way, I remembered what I had learned in business: Concentrate on advancing your goals, not on quieting your detractors. Accordingly, I encouraged more women to participate in the association. During my term as chairman, the number of women on the board rose from fifteen to twenty-four. A plenary session at the 1997 convention, entitled "Mothers, Daughters, and Sisters — Paving the Way for the Future," paid homage to my dear friend Betty Shabazz, who had recently died, as well as to other women who led the charge and are now inspiring a new generation of young women. This sent a clear message to the five thousand people in the audience that the work of civil rights and politics has not been solely the province of male leaders. I would hope that at regional and national meetings in the future, additional sessions that speak to women's involvement will be added to the roster. I recognize that it takes time to change attitudes, but as more women move into powerful and visible leadership positions, the gap between males and females will be bridged by common goals and understanding.

Much of my hope is with the younger generation, which is why I encouraged the reinvigoration of our educational programs, urged our young adult members (aged eighteen to twenty-five) to take part in the everyday workings of the organization, and, for the first time ever, included a young adult member on the search committee that evaluated candidates for the position of executive director. It is the attitudes and commitment of our young people that will shape the future and, in the coming century, their efforts will ensure the completion of projects we are now developing and breathe life into the cause. In the past, the young people who attended board meetings would typically sit together, say very little, and later complain about not having a voice. Although their number has not increased over the last several years — it is set by our constitution — I invited these young men and women to state their concerns at the meetings and to offer their solutions to issues. As a result, they felt welcomed and became more involved.

We now have a full-time national youth director, who is very outspoken and charismatic and, most important, can motivate and communicate easily with young adults. We need to help future generations understand that apathy solves nothing. Get into the fray, make yourselves heard; we may debate with you, but we need your input. The NAACP has always served as a training ground for the leaders of tomorrow. Trailblazers like Julian Bond, the new chairman, and former board member Ernest Green, one of the first students to integrate the Little Rock, Arkansas, schools in 1957, have come up through the ranks and achieved status not only within the organization but in their communities and in the world at large. With our guidance, I believe that young people will carry on the work and achieve more than we ever dreamed, because they have new eyes with which to see new solutions.

However, a family in turmoil cannot adequately nurture its young, which is why, during my tenure, I dedicated myself so fervently to restoring unity to the board itself. Sixty-four members strong, it is, most admit, too large for its own good. Although I investigated the possibility of reducing its size, I knew that in my administration we would not see such a radical change, for it would require both a constitutional amendment and the willingness of members to relinquish the perceived power of being on the board. Still, I believed that steps could be taken to improve efficiency, trust, and communication among board members. We developed a code of ethics, which in spite of some initial reluctance was unanimously approved. The document needs to be strengthened, but it is at least a step in the right direction. I also instituted our first board retreats in a decade. During these meetings, in places removed from our daily responsibilities, we dealt with issues of governance, troubleshooting, planning, building consensus on issues, and developing clearly defined guidelines for the duties of board members.

Using funds raised at my inauguration event that were designated for special projects, I contracted with the Harvard Business School to carry out a three-part mandate, which culminated in the first of such retreats. Board members were initially interviewed by phone and in person and asked their perceptions of the many issues and problems we faced. Then the results of those inquiries were analyzed and the information disseminated to the board. Finally, we addressed those concerns as a group. Although there is still some discord, the board has come together in a stronger way, armed with information and concrete strategies. Such coalition building paves the way for the board to give full attention to our primary agenda: the advancement of social justice and human rights. ⋟

America today is at an important crossroads, its people polarized by such social issues as health care, education, affirmative action, the environment, abortion, and privacy — not to mention all the "isms." But recently, these concerns have tended to overshadow the fundamental questions of human rights involving minorities, women, immigrants, and migrant workers — the oppressed of our civilization. How can the powerless answer the call to action and attain power? How can we learn from the past, teach its lessons to our children, and not become bitter in the bargain? How do we achieve freedom and hold on to it? How do we climb up without stepping on our own? I've learned that we should never be afraid of not knowing the answers — only of refusing to consider the questions. And as we ponder them, we can, and should, turn to history for guidance in seeking solutions.

Discrimination — the societal disease that the NAACP set out to cure in 1909 — continues to infect our citizens and weaken America. Leaf through any newspaper, watch any television news program, and you'll see stories of police brutality, hate crimes, fringe groups who want to oppress (or harm) anyone who's not White or not Christian. Conservative forces are eroding our civil rights; the Byron De La Beckwiths of this world continue to thrive and advance their agenda. Single mothers are more alone than ever. Serious failings in our educational system threaten to have long-term effects on children of all races and ethnicities. Violence wreaks suffering in our families and in our communities. And the country is experiencing a racial divide different from, but just as serious as, that seen during the sixties. As President Clinton himself has said, "The evidence doesn't just speak — it shouts!" In other words, our work is far from done.

The NAACP and other organizations must rededicate themselves to the cause of integration; we must strive to achieve equal opportunity and equal access on all fronts. A "separate but equal" society did not work in Medgar's day; it does not work now. We need to promote educational excellence as well as economic development, both of which will help reduce dependence upon government agencies and enable people to take control of their own destinies. And because our problems have reached such mammoth proportions, civil rights activists must work hard to link hands with others who believe in and fight for policies of fairness and inclusion. As one NAACP member remarked, "We are all in the same boat, so let us row together to safety."

In our collective strength we will find our power. If politicians who don't represent our values are elected, we have only ourselves to blame. Americans of common purpose must stand together. In 1992, when African-Americans, along with other minority groups, voted in record numbers, we made record gains in Congress and in local elections; because we sat out the 1994 election, however, we lost ground. In response, the NAACP launched a voter empowerment initiative. Our goal in that campaign was to register one million voters in time for the 1996 presidential election, and we succeeded. However, the struggle to achieve solidarity shouldn't stop at our door; I suggest that the NAACP and other like-minded organizations develop a "justice bloc" — a group of citizens combining their voting power to support progressive candidates who refuse to accept intolerance.

We must remember, too, that the dollar, as much as the vote, dictates America's direction. Inequality is rooted in economic disparity. The hands you see in the citadels of power and privilege are not calloused, nor are they reaching out for training or education, family assistance, or community support. Nor are the faces you see anything like the faces of those who do America's most menial jobs.

The current right-wing agenda uses terms like "quotas" and "welfare queens" as racial code words to encourage middle-class Americans to blame their problems on those who are having an even harder time staying financially solvent. Such strategies, in my opinion, are aimed at both minorities *and* women, a backlash to the gains attained on both fronts. Case in point: Three years ago, California's Proposition 209 began a national movement to dismantle affirmative action programs. Leading the charge was Ward Connelly, an African-American professor on the California Board of Regents, who insisted that "we" no longer need that extra boost. Politicians in his camp argue that America has achieved a level playing field. If that is true, why do I and other women, as well as men of color, keep stumbling?

Because of affirmative action, many citizens have gained access to fields previously closed to them, have gone into business for themselves, and have expanded those businesses. With the demise of these programs, we must learn to be more resourceful. For example, the NAACP, under the guidance of CEO Mfume, recently developed an Economic Reciprocity Task Force as a response to policies that seek to undo the economic gains made by minority workers over the last decades. The task force objective is to unite industry representatives and business owners in an effort to design and implement entrepreneurial programs, thereby helping African-Americans and other minorities to recognize and profit from their talents. Seasoned business leaders, as well as young people who are just starting careers, also must help to create new opportunities for their brothers and sisters by actions that include developing mentor programs and offering on-the-job training to workers who then might advance through the ranks.

The responsibility for undertaking these initiatives belongs to all of us — women and men, young and old — who have felt the sting of discrimination, and to those who have empathy for the victims. We wage a common battle, which is why our work and even our name — the National Association for the Advancement of *Colored* People — is as relevant today as it ever was. We are fast becoming a nation of color. By the middle of the next century, the majority of Americans will be citizens with roots in Africa, Asia, South and Central America, or the

Caribbean. It is ironic that the future of our country depends on the very people who have been so often held back.

How, then, do we overcome the barriers of divisiveness, discrimination, and deprivation? Dialogue, an honest discussion of ideas and feelings, is a vital tool. We must encourage community leaders, politicians, educators, clergy, and parents to come together in a variety of forums — focus groups, retreats, and town meetings — that foster a thorough exploration of matters of mutual concern. When people get to know one another and acknowledge their common goals, racial and ethnic stereotypes shatter, and everyone becomes part of the solution.

I applaud efforts like the President's Initiative on Race; though it fell short of its potential, it was at least a beginning. Similarly, *Glamour* magazine sponsors an annual Women of the Year program, which in 1995 chose me to be among the honorees. Coming together from a variety of endeavors and industries, we brainstormed about race, family and financial issues, and other contemporary concerns. Follow-up recommendations were then printed and distributed to the editors for consideration regarding future articles.

I always keep my eyes open for such opportunities. Recently, when *Vanity Fair* included me in one of the group photographs that appeared in its November 1998 issue highlighting "America's Most Influential Women," I was pleased to make the acquaintance of the accomplished individuals featured in the spread, women such as Patricia Ireland, president of the National Organization for Women (NOW), and Dr. Mathilde Krim, chairman of the American Foundation for AIDS Research (AmFAR). We exchanged business cards and information, hoping to learn about one another's programs and investigate the possibility of working together on joint projects.

At the organizational level, we must build new alliances and reaffirm old ones. The NAACP, for example, has renewed its partnership with a number of African-American groups, including churches and national fraternities and sororities. We have made an effort to heal the rifts with Jewish civic organizations. In times like this we must remember that what happens *among* us will have deep consequences for what happens *to* us. In 1997 the NAACP held a National Religious Leaders Summit, bringing together leaders of various denominations

representing more than 15 million people in an effort to work cooper-
atively on a range of social, civil rights, and religious problems.

One doesn't have to be the head of a foundation or chairman of
an association to plan or engage in dialogues such as these. When
you converse with a neighbor, have a conference with your child's
teacher, or meet a colleague for a business luncheon, use these occasions to explore each other's ideas about solving racial problems.
When you meet an exceptional thinker or an inspiring person, invite
him or her to your local community center or church, or arrange an
assembly program at school.

Last, and certainly not least, all of us can benefit from looking
inside our own hearts and taking stock of our souls. If we learned anything from the O.J. Simpson trial, which forced everyone to examine
his or her feelings about race, as well as attitudes toward women, it is
that streaks of prejudice run through most people, sometimes sublim-
inally, sometimes surfacing in more obvious ways. Each of us has to
accept and take responsibility for the fact that too often we still classify
and judge one another in terms of race, ethnicity, faith, sexual orientation, class, even age. Take a hard look at your own attitudes toward
different groups, and be mindful of the overt *and* covert ways you
express them. Be especially aware of the lessons you are teaching your
children. Discuss television programs, magazines, books, and advertising, pointing out positive and negative portrayals of issues and
people. Explore or even plan multicultural events with your family.
Most important, listen. How do your children feel about themselves
and others? How do they experience and handle prejudice? Are they
themselves inclusive or intolerant? It is upsetting to see how many
parents do not make these issues a part of everyday family conversation.

I'm equally distressed when I hear some young people who
encounter discrimination express apathy ("What's the big deal?"),
skepticism ("The system is never going to change anyway"), and even
self-centeredness ("I got mine and I worked hard for it — so can other
people"). In part, their indifference comes from ignorance. They may
not be aware of it, but many of our hard-won gains are slipping away.
Those of us who grew up before the civil rights movement achieved
its victories have tried to shelter our children and grandchildren from

the trauma we've been through. In essence, we have said, "Go off, my darlings, and have a good time. Take advantage of the opportunities we've created for you." And they have. The trouble is, we have made it *too* easy, and I fear that too many of our young people lack an understanding of where they came from.

A few years ago, the *New York Times Magazine* featured an article by a young Black woman about the civil rights movement. The author suggested that "the queens" — Coretta King, Betty Shabazz, and I — along with sixties radical Angela Davis, ought to "move out of the way" and make room for the younger generation. I could have felt wounded, but I chose to catch the arrow and hurl it back, to enlighten rather than injure. I have since used the *Times* article in many talks, to illuminate how important it is for all of us, especially our youth, to have a sense of history. Our goal should not be to live in the past, but to *use* the past — the struggles, the strengths, even the mistakes. Just as Jewish people vow they must never forget the Holocaust, we too must remember our past. If we don't learn to cherish our history, we will not have earned our place in the future.

10

A LITTLE OLDER, A LOT WISER

Reviewing the past and celebrating the future

Walter and I on a walk in Bend.

Every exit is entry somewhere else.

⋟ Tom Stoppard

A good friend recently described us in our sixties as enjoying a "delicious time — a time to do everything we ever wanted to do." For me, it also has been a time of deep reflection and poignant recollection, enabling me not only to look back but to make certain decisions about my future. It is a time of coming to terms with myself, acknowledging the force of my influence while also accepting the limitations of my power. It is a time of choice, too, an opportunity to fully be who I am: a woman hell-bent on slowing down and equally determined to continue to make a difference in the world.

It is often said that when you are older, if you have lived a good, honorable life you are permitted to enjoy it a second time. You will have righteous acts and beautiful memories to look back on, and your life will be filled with the wonderful people your heart has touched. Though some of your recollections evoke sadness, through the grace of God and your own inner strength, when you have come through the hard times with dignity and insight you are filled with gratitude.

I myself have so much to be thankful for, so much to be proud of, so much to remember. When I began writing this book, however, I had no idea how arduous it would be to review my life in this way. In the service of careful recollection, I have had to rifle through files and boxes, read letters I had long forgotten, pore over old photo albums, and revisit my ghosts in Mississippi. The process has been at once discomfiting and thrilling, puzzling and illuminating, gut-wrenching and spirit-freeing. Each chapter has plunged me deeply into the different arenas in which I have lived my life. In many ways this chapter is one I am still living. ⋟

It is 1997 and I am in Claremont, visiting the house on Northwestern Drive that was our home when the children and I moved from Mississippi to California. Reena and her children live here now. This December morning, Reena is at work, the children are at school, and I am taking a walk, hoping to clear my head. The streets are as they were when I first visited with Althea Simmons, lined with poplar, maple, and birch trees and graced with lawns that evidence constant care. Only a few cars pass by, all of them honoring the twenty-five-mile-per-hour speed limit. It is quiet, quiet enough to hear the wind whisper through the leaves. All seems calm and peaceful, a world removed from the pressures of daily life.

Yet I am in turmoil. Peace evades my mind, my heart, my very being. My feet are on the pavement, but my mind is soaring. It is as if I am rocketing away from Earth, watching myself from a completely different perspective. I am struggling with the beast of uncertainty that forces me to face my future. It is time once again to change the course of my life.

Every five years, from the time I was widowed at thirty, I have experienced an impetus for growth, a spurt, if you will — ultimately with positive results but always accompanied by some degree of pain. At thirty-five, a proud college graduate, I met the test of independence and began to realize that I could have power over my own domain. At forty, I experienced a new sense of self-acceptance and confidence as I made my first tentative forays into politics and corporate work. At forty-five, settling in at ARCO, I was able to accept my weaknesses and build on my strengths, and I tackled anything that came my way. Even better, Walt had come into my life by then, and I rediscovered love and passion. A few weeks before my fiftieth birthday, in the midst of ARCO's restructuring, I sent out invitations that read, "Come join me in celebrating a half century of life," and I meant it. I knew that even if I decided to leave ARCO someday, I could take on just about anything I set my mind to do. At fifty-five, when I could have rested on my laurels, I took a risk again, becoming commissioner of public works. And by my sixtieth year, I had moved out of Los Angeles, promised Walter I'd slow down, and was ready to enjoy the good life in

Bend. Then, once again, I experienced what I had learned many times before: Just when you think you have reached a contented state of equilibrium, life has a way of undoing what's done, and everything changes again.

Walking along the streets of Claremont, reflecting on my cycles of transformation, I ponder my approaching sixty-fifth birthday. In many ways, I feel spiritually at my strongest and most centered — younger than ever. But what a ride this last five years has been.

Rejoice! a small voice inside me says, trying to assert itself with authority. And yet another voice, hastening to remind me of my mortality, also speaks. I can hear them both, competing, cajoling, arguing, but agreeing on one point: *Come on, girlfriend, it's DT time again. Like it or not, decision time is here.*

Deep in thought, I absently take a seat on a park bench in the quiet cluster of stores we affectionately call "downtown" Claremont. Why am I in such a state? I consider all that is looming before me in the coming months, all that I must do. Could it be that I am missing my beloved Walter, who died three years ago and for whom I have not yet found the time to mourn? Could it be that I know it is time for me to step down from my position as chairman of the NAACP? Could it be that the prospect of returning to Mississippi — to stir memories of my past for these pages — is so unsettling? Could it be that, while my general health is excellent, I am suffering a number of physical problems due, I suspect, solely to my inability to diminish the stress in my life? Or could it be that seeing how fast my grandchildren are growing up makes me realize how much I am missing? Like a scratched record, the questions play and replay in my mind.

Clearly, I have to confront many critical choices. I smile at the paradox of my counseling young women to develop a chart displaying their opportunities — personal and professional — and to include options they might fall back on should their original plans fail. Why can't I heed my own advice? I frequently advise women to be aware of a common trap we set for ourselves — doing for others while neglecting ourselves, taking on more than we should and rarely asking for help. Find quiet time to meditate, I urge them. Regroup and renew.

Broaden your horizons. Don't be afraid of change. Keep the spiritual level high. Be kind to yourself. All easy to say but difficult to do.

I laugh out loud, recalling a sign I recently saw in an airport gift shop:

I am woman
I am invincible
I am tired

I recognize how apt this is, for in at least six years of doing, going, doing, and going again, I have not taken a break. A fine role model you are, Myrlie Evers-Williams. My own words of wisdom — "People will demand of you only what you will allow" — come back to haunt me. Only *I* set the expectations for me — I have no one else to blame for my fatigue or my frustration. And only I can readjust the demands I make upon myself.

I look at my watch and see it's time to walk back to Reena's — everyone will be home soon. *If I'm gone too long my overprotective daughter will worry,* I say to myself, easing my tired body off the park bench. As I begin to head back along Harrison toward Northwestern Drive, my thoughts turn, as they so often do these days, to those I've lost and left behind. ℞

I've loved two great men, and I've lost two great men. Whereas Medgar was wrenched from my life in seconds, Walter's passing was devastatingly slow but equally painful.

"It's prostate cancer," announced Walt one day in 1992, hanging up the receiver after a telephone call from his doctor.

He reached for me, and I started to cry. Sobs shook my body as I balled up my fists and beat his chest as hard as I could. "I tried to get you to go to a doctor!" I screamed. "For three years, I've begged you to take a PSA test. Look what has happened!"

My husband didn't need to be made to feel guilty on top of the bad news. But I quickly realized that my anger at his stubbornness and fear in avoiding the test was a function of my own terror. I pulled myself together and placed my hands on his face: "We — not you —

are going to beat this." Walt just held me, and I knew he must have been thinking about his errant father, who reentered his life when Walt was in his forties. When his father was bedridden with prostate cancer, it was Walt who had nursed him; he knew too well how awful this disease could be.

Like many people who learn they are seriously ill, Walt first went into denial. Then, when additional tests revealed that the disease had spread and that he had at most three years to live, denial turned to anger, especially when his doctor added that, statistically, African-American men have higher rates of prostate cancer.

"Oh no, I'm not listening to any racist doctor," Walt announced as we left the office. To him, this prognosis only seemed the culmination of a lifetime of closed doors and angry assaults. He had been jumped, chased, and shot at by Whites as he challenged inequities in the produce industry and on the waterfront. He had been dissuaded from pursuing a career as an artist, not because his teachers thought he lacked talent, but because, as they put it, "a Black can't make it in the art world." I could understand the depths of his prejudice and his immediate inclination to be suspicious, which is not uncommon among African-American men of his generation. But in this situation, I knew he was wrong.

We sought a second opinion from an oncologist at Cedars-Sinai Hospital, who happened to be Black, but he confirmed the initial diagnosis. The choice of treatments was either an operation or a series of injections, which would mean traveling from Bend to Los Angeles every other week. After much discussion, Walt elected surgery. A few weeks later, we sat in a sterile, sparsely furnished office as two doctors stood behind a large desk and told us, "This surgery will affect your sex life."

The look in Walter's eyes was sheer fire. I feared he was thinking, *Here's another White man, telling me I can't perform,* and rather than risk an explosion, I immediately replied, "Well, Doctor, if that's what it takes, then that's what it takes. Walter and I have been blessed to have had the life and the love we've had." As we left the office, I placed my hand in Walt's and told him, "I have enough beautiful memories to last a lifetime."

That morning was the first time I saw tears come to Walt's eyes since he had been diagnosed, and in the weeks that followed, I repeatedly reassured him that our love could only grow stronger as we met this challenge together.

Walter had surgery in November of 1992. After six weeks of post-op care in Los Angeles, we returned to Bend. It was a few days before Christmas, in the midst of one of the worst Oregon winters in ten years. God knows how the two of us — me with a bad back, Walt just out of surgery — made our way through the high drifts of snow. We were barely settled in when the phone rang.

"Oh good — you're home." It was Drinda Bell, our next-door neighbor. She and her husband and their two children adored Walt and me, especially Walt. They couldn't do enough for us when he got sick. Drinda had mentioned on several occasions that it would be "nice" for Walt to have a dog to go hunting with. Each time she brought it up, I said firmly, "No, I can't take care of a dog."

Hearing Drinda's voice, I knew she hadn't listened.

A few minutes later, we stepped out our back door to see a small black bundle of energy romping in the snow. It was a black Labrador retriever, no more than ten weeks old, with a red bow around its neck. Walt bent down slowly and scooped that wriggling ball of fur into his massive arms. "Why, you're just as sweet as sugar," he cooed. And that's who she became — Walt's beloved Sugar.

I watched Walt get stronger and take walks with Sugar, and she inched her way into my heart as well. Despite occasional setbacks, Walt always tried to keep up a brave front, and his spirits were remarkably good. We were finally able to revel in the everyday pleasure of each other's company and to do what most couples take for granted: go to the movies, see friends, enjoy concerts. Never the outdoor type, I began to appreciate nature with Walt. I particularly enjoyed our spontaneous weekend getaways when we a rented a camper and slept under the stars. He even talked me into going on fishing trips. It was the first time in my life I felt truly free. I allowed myself to be sad and silly with Walt. But I could never put his condition completely out of my mind.

The first Mother's Day after his surgery, Walt was very weak but insisted on driving into town.

"What for?" I asked, with more than a hint of alarm.

"I have to go," he answered. "Now, don't baby me."

He was gone for quite a while, and I kept looking out the window. Finally his car reentered our circular driveway, and I watched him walk toward the door. In his hand were two bouquets of red roses. My heart melted. Suddenly, he stumbled on one of the two front steps. I wanted to run out and help, but I let him be. I didn't want to douse his pride. He walked into the kitchen and handed me the roses. "One bouquet," he said sweetly, "just wasn't large enough for you." That was one of the last times I remember his driving a car.

Throughout the period of coming to terms with Walt's illness, I never questioned God, the way I had after Medgar's death, for I had grown spiritually by then. Rather than being angry at God, I expressed my thanks to him for allowing Walter to come into my life, for granting me such a blessing. Walt and I had often prayed together, and his prayer was always the same: "God, not mine, but your will be done."

Because of my history with Medgar, Walt and I had had many discussions about death and dying. He had always told me, "We all must die sometime." Now as he faced his own mortality, Walt was at peace — with himself, his beliefs, with the life he had lived, and with God. That made it easier for him and for me, if indeed facing death can ever be easy.

He exercised regularly and even managed to go hunting with Sugar. We changed our diet too, switching from fatty foods to more healthful fare, but there came a time when nothing I prepared for him tasted right — it was all too sweet, too salty, too sour, metallic. Still, he never complained. "I'm going to beat this thing," he told me regularly. ⸙

Nursing Walt through his illness inevitably brought up bittersweet memories of others who had died. How odd it is to use the word "lost" as a euphemism for death, for we never lose those we cherish — they live on in our memories, and we carry them in our hearts. But when a loved one slips away gradually, images of his or her last days can also be painful to recall.

I remember how Aunt Myrlie suffered through my grandmother's decline. They still lived in the house at 1411 Farmer Street in Vicksburg, Mama then in her eighties, and Auntie in her sixties. In every long-distance conversation we had, my aunt agonized over the idea of putting her mother into a nursing home, even though Mama was becoming increasingly abusive. Among other things, Mama, who had been well-groomed her whole life and who definitely believed cleanliness was next to godliness, suddenly stopped wanting to take baths. Whenever Auntie tried to urge her into the tub, Mama inevitably shouted at her, "I'm self-cleaning. I don't need baths!"

One Saturday, Auntie's call from Vicksburg had a particularly desperate tone. Through her tears she told me that she had drawn a bath for Mama, but as she tried to get her into the tub, my grandmother hit her. Not long after that, Aunt Myrlie decided that Mama had become too much for her to handle. I always felt bad that I was so far away, unable to be there, unable to offer her practical advice. It's easy enough to suggest options to someone dealing with an older person, but unless you've done it yourself, you have no idea of the heartache, the energy drain, the feelings of helplessness.

I experienced those very feelings myself when Auntie was in her early eighties. Like Mama, Aunt Myrlie had been a fastidious, proud, and fiercely independent woman all her life. Like Mama, she began to deteriorate in small ways — her eyesight dimmed, her memory was unreliable. On one of my many visits to Vicksburg, I suggested that Auntie allow me to take over her bookkeeping. She agreed at first, but as we were getting ready to go to the bank to transfer power of attorney to me, she put down her purse and said, "I don't know if I should let you have control of this now. I can handle it for a while longer."

Every time I left Vicksburg, it was with a heavy heart. Just as Auntie had reluctantly placed Mama in the Shady Grove Nursing Home, I would soon have to make the same decision for her. In the meantime, I hired a string of home aides to live with her. She approved each one, but few lasted longer than a week.

Things went on in this unsettled way until one morning when I picked up the phone. "Baby, come home," I heard Auntie's voice say. "I need your help. I can't handle things anymore."

Never before had she asked for anything, this strong woman who had cared for us, who had managed Mama's and my finances. She had been there for me from the moment I was born. I flew out on the very next flight.

That night I settled into the front bedroom, which had always been Auntie's. She now occupied the room where I had slept with Mama until I was in high school. I had fallen into a fitful sleep when I became aware of another person's presence in the room. Keeping perfectly still, I opened my eyes and, in the dim light from the far end of the hallway, I could make out a figure standing in the doorway — a figure that was holding a gun. When my eyes adjusted to the light, I realized it was my aunt.

"Auntie," I said in a soft and consoling voice, "are you okay?"

She reached over and flipped on the light. "Who are you?" she demanded harshly. "Why are you in my bed, in my house?"

Say something that she can identify with, and hurry, I thought. "Auntie, I'm your baby — I'm Baby Sister."

"No you aren't," she said suspiciously.

As casually as I could, I reassured her. "Of course I am. I just came from Jackson to see you. Your other babies, Darrell, Reena, and Van, are waiting for me to come home. It's late and it's a long drive to Jackson." She relaxed and let her arm drop by her side. I eased out of bed, walked slowly to where she stood, and took the gun from her hand. I hugged her for as long as she would allow me. The situation had gone beyond my deepest fear and beyond anything I could control.

"Come help me pack my clothes," I said. "I must go to the children." When Auntie went back to her bed, I hid the gun in the closet behind some boxes. Shaken to the point that my knees were weak, I dressed as quickly as possible.

I kissed Auntie as I left. "See you tomorrow. Remember we are going to visit the nursing home."

"Okay, Baby," she replied. "Drive carefully and kiss the children for me."

I had lied to her, of course. No babies were waiting for me in Jackson; my children were grown by then, and we all lived on the West Coast. Tears blinded me as I turned onto Route 80 and drove toward the local Holiday Inn. Alone in my room, my body shook with gut-wrenching cries. I knew what I must do.

I anguished over Auntie even after she was safely ensconced in Shady Grove. I called her regularly and flew in to see her at least every other month, but it was never enough for either of us. She felt abandoned, and I felt guilty. She knew she was losing her faculties and couldn't do anything about it, and that hurt her badly. I considered moving her out west, so that at least she could be closer to the children and me, but doctors warned that it might hasten the end if I moved her to unfamiliar surroundings. She lived another three years, dying in 1993 at age eighty-six.

Moving aged relatives into a nursing home had, and for some still has, a negative connotation. Although it's more common nowadays, it's still a painful decision. With my generation and older, you simply didn't do it. Mama had cared for her grandmother — my beloved Grandma Martha Hoover — but times were different then. We lived in a close-knit community, and our neighbors dropped by with groceries, cooked meals, did errands, and physically helped care for the older person.

Currently, one American family in four takes care of an elderly relative, and with the growing legions of the "old-old" (as sociologists call those age eighty-five and up), it's likely that more and more people will have to face this problem in the future. The practice of caring for one's own remains particularly strong among African-Americans in the South, where tradition dies hard. Blacks, however, also have statistically higher rates of poverty and suffer more than Whites from health problems such as diabetes, hypertension, and asthma, and therefore are more likely to need daily care. Some gerontologists who study these trends fear that coming generations will no longer be able to take on the caregiving role, because adult children increasingly live far away from aging parents and other members of the extended family. Even when they do live nearby, as Walt did when he cared for his aging mother, the time, energy, stress, and, sometimes, lost wages can take a serious toll on the caregiver. In fact, according to one study, nearly half of all family caregivers experience severe, prolonged depression; two-thirds feel frustrated on a regular basis; and two out of five find the role reversal "debilitating."

I certainly don't want to burden my own children — no parent does. My belief is that one can avert such problems by planning well in advance. Too many adult children go into denial about their parents' aging; they want to imagine them always in their prime. I want my family to be realistic and have told them, "Supermom needs to coordinate plans with you for whatever role changes we have to face." I have resumed our family conferences, just as we had when my children were young. It's important to express my needs, wishes, and expectations to them now, because there may come a time when, due to mental or physical impairment, I can't address these issues cogently.

Thinking about Mama and Auntie, and seeing Walt's decline, made me appreciate the swift passage of time — and my own mortality. It's hard for a parent to trade places and to look to the younger generation for support, but at least my children have managed to maintain a sense of humor about it all. Whenever I complain about the aging process, one of them invariably comes back with, "But you haven't reached the stage where you're self-cleaning, Mom, have you?" It's said in jest, but we all know it's no laughing matter. ⁊

When Walt's health started failing, and it was clear that no medical intervention could stop the progression of his cancer, my children, who had grown to love Walt as a father, became doubly concerned for my future. Walt had taken care of me; he was my companion. Understandably, my children worried not only about my handling Walt's illness but also about how I would cope with the eventual loss of this dear man who had come to mean so much to all of us.

Walt and I made a few last plane trips together in 1994 before he became too weak to travel. He was at my side when I received an honorary degree from Columbia College in Chicago. We went to Three Rivers, Michigan, to visit my ailing aunt Frances, M'dear's half-sister.

My heart broke as my once strong, invincible Walt carried our suit-cases up the stairs; watching him, I knew he was seriously out of breath and in pain. And in June, Reena, Walt, and I went to the White House, to receive from President Clinton a signed document naming a new federal building in Jackson, Mississippi, the Medgar Wiley Evers Post Office. I observed to the president that it was almost thirty-one years to the day that his idol, President Kennedy, had extended condolences to my family in the very same room, and presented my children with *PT-109* pens and tie clips.

The next day, as we were dressing to go to Arlington National Cemetery, where we planned to visit Medgar's grave, Walt said, "You can't go empty-handed. Order a floral wreath, and we'll take it with us." The photo Reena took of Walt and me standing by Medgar's tombstone is a vivid reminder of that day and, more so, a tribute to Walter's generosity.

Walt took a turn for the worse after that trip. The spring in his step disappeared, and he began losing his balance. The cancer, we learned, had spread to his bones. We said good-bye in small ways every day, but I never wanted him to see how upset I was by his deteri-orating condition, so I'd tell him, "Honey, I'm going to do some work downstairs. If you need me, just push the intercom button." Once there, I'd play a George Benson CD — he was one of our favorites — and turn the stereo up just loud enough to muffle my sobs. Afterward, I'd wash my face, go back upstairs, and greet him with a cheery, "Hi, sweetheart."

Walt finally had to be hospitalized, because he was hemorrhag-ing. The night after he was admitted, the doctor said solemnly, "He may not last the night." Hearing that, Walt, who had been slipping in and out of consciousness, opened his eyes wide for a moment and then closed them, as if to contradict that pessimistic assessment. Acknowledging his patient's protest, the doctor looked at me and said conclusively, "Well, he certainly won't last beyond the week." Walter opened his eyes again. He was seriously ill, of course, but I could still discern the defiance in his eyes, which I'd seen so many times before.

"You can take him home," the doctor said after he'd finished examining Walt. "But call the relatives — he doesn't have long."

By the next afternoon, he was in our bed at home. His daughter Donetta — Nett — was first to arrive. Within days, the house was filled with our children, grandchildren, cousins, and friends. I have never felt such an outpouring; it was almost as though you could reach out and touch the collective strength of their love and prayers. On his fourth day home, to everyone's surprise, Walt got out of bed and walked into the living room on his own. Clearly, he was a bit high from his medication, but he was my Walt — tough, stubborn, and determined, as he put it, "to enjoy my family and friends."

When it was just the two of us again, the house grew still and somber. Walt's doctor had made arrangements with the Bend Hospice to have a nurse come once or twice a week, to monitor Walter's condition and to dispense the medicine necessary to keep him comfortable. The hospice coordinator assured us that the staff would always be available for consultation or emergencies, which was a great comfort to me. Even in the face of these preparations, though, Walt wasn't giving an inch. In fact, when his assigned hospice partner tried to speak comfortingly of the reality facing Walt ("You're dying"), my dear tough husband, who days before had been at the very brink of death, looked him straight in the eye and said sharply, "You don't know when *you're* going to go either, do you?"

After that crisis, sweet Walt, a man who had been given only a week to live, hung on for another six months. In accordance with his wishes, I had at last agreed to accept the NAACP nomination, and I firmly believe that he was determined to live long enough to be able to see me keep my promise: to run and win. During the months leading up to my officially announcing my candidacy, I reluctantly fielded reporters' calls and conducted a bit of necessary politicking from home. But most of the time, I was both physically preoccupied with Walt's care and distraught over his failing condition. The hospice had left me a chart indicating which medications were to be given on which days. Often, I'd be in the middle of ministering to Walt, giving him oral medication or reapplying his morphine patch, which had to be changed every few days, and the phone would ring. I finally had to engage an answering service. I cherished every minute I spent with Walt, and out of my deep love for him, I found the energy and resolve to keep going. I never wavered; I knew he'd have done the same for me.

I occasionally asked the hospice to send someone so that I could get away to do errands, but for the most part, I chose to be his caretaker and his protector. When he wanted to walk, he slowly positioned himself on the edge of the bed, then stubbornly stood alone. He placed his hands on my shoulders only for balance. Everyone warned me that I might not be able to support his six-foot-four frame, but I was certain I could. In any case, with God's help, I found the strength.

Once when I was helping Walt in the shower, he gasped, "Honey, I don't think I can make it. I think I'm going to pass out."

I tried not to panic. "Hold on, baby," I told him, opening the shower door. The water was still running, and we were both dripping wet. The bed was only fifteen feet away, but it might as well have been fifteen miles. As we made our way toward it, I kept urging him, "Stay with me, honey. It's going to be okay. It's going to be okay." With each step, I could feel his strength ebbing and his body sagging, but luckily his knees never caved in. All I could do was pray: *God, please help me get him to that bed. I can't let him fall.*

After that frightening experience, Walt never got out of bed again, and my duties as caretaker expanded to include giving him sponge baths. On one occasion, as I lifted one of his legs, I noticed he had a particularly pained expression on his face, and I worried that I had hurt him. "What is it, honey?" I asked, carefully lowering his leg.

He looked at me with a heart-rending show of fear and pride and said softly, "I never thought it would come to this."

I — who also have trouble asking for help — knew just what he meant. I tried to make light of his embarrassment. "Hey," I said playfully, "don't you remember what we always promised each other?"

"Whichever one had to take care of the other would do it gladly," he said somberly. "Yes, I remember. But I don't want to put this burden on you."

I looked at Walt, who had opened my heart again, who had been my husband for eighteen years, and I said, "Let me make something perfectly clear. Given the man that you are and all that you have done for me, for my children, and for others, being able to take care of you is a privilege. Don't ever forget that."

We cried in each other's arms then, and we would cry many times more in the weeks that followed. We finally stopped trying to pretend it didn't hurt. A few weeks before he died, in one of our many talks, I told him that he was "the love of my life." His eyes opened wide, and a huge smile danced on his face. "Thank you," he said with renewed strength in his voice. He never looked happier.

In his final days, I played music that Walt loved — Tramaine Hawkins's versions of "Amazing Grace," "I Found the Answer," and "It's Never Too Late." In a sense, we conducted a daily service, praying together, crying together, laughing, reminiscing. One day he said to me, "I am tired, so tired. I'm ready to go home." His words clearly cost him every bit of energy he had left, but then he added, "I just don't want to leave you."

I held my tears and lay my head on his shoulder. "I don't want you to leave me either. I don't know what I'll do without you."

"You'll be okay, baby," he reassured. "You'll make it just fine."

"Oh, my love, I know I can make it alone, but my heart will be empty without you," I said, wishing that a miracle would reverse the course of his disease. "But if you're ready, I'm ready. I love you too much to see you suffer. You can go whenever you want." ~

In February of 1995, as I prepared to attend the NAACP's annual meeting, Walter was still holding on. He was, of course, too sick to join me, so his brother, George, and his sister-in-law, Robbie, came to Bend to be with him. When it was time for me to leave, I went into our bedroom and sat next to him on the bed. He had lost a great deal of weight, his robust complexion had turned ashen, and the sharp lines in his handsome face now sagged. His frailty sent shivers of pain through my heart. I looked at Walt, and he at me. There were no words at first, but each knew what the other was thinking. *These might be our last moments together.* We embraced for a long, long time and finally spoke of how much we loved each other. I didn't want to leave him, but I also wanted to keep the promise I made to him: to win the election.

When I got to the bedroom door, I turned around and said sternly, "Don't you go anywhere while I'm gone. Don't you *dare* go while I'm gone."

And in a weak voice he answered, "I'll be here." I thought, *He's always kept his promises,* but I feared that this one was out of his control.

Two days later, after the results were in, I rushed to the phone. Robbie, who answered, told me Walter had already heard the good news. She said he grinned when he heard the details of my one-vote victory, let out a shout, and raised his fist in the air. Then he began fading.

"I've got to talk to him," I told her. She handed Walt the phone. "Honey, I won," I shouted into the receiver, hoping my exuberance would somehow boost his energy level. "And now I'm coming home to you."

"No, you stay there," he said in so feeble a voice that my heart was crushed. "You need to meet with those people. You need to reassure the board and your staff that everything is going to be different now."

"No, Walt, I'm coming home," I insisted. "You wait for me."

There was only silence on the other end. Terrified that he had passed out, I called, "Walt! Honey! Are you there?" *Oh God, let him still be there.* I would not forgive myself if I was not by his side when he took his last breath.

I called out to him again, and this time he answered. "I'm here. I just had to compose myself. I'm proud of you. I love you." That was the last conversation we had.

The flight back to Bend, which required two intermediate connections, was the longest in my life. When I finally arrived, George met me at the airport and drove me home. I went directly to our bedroom. Walt was in the throes of heavy, labored breathing, which I recognized as "the death rattle" my grandmother had talked about when I was a child. I had never been so close to Death before.

I sat on the bed hugging and kissing Walt, telling him, "I'm here, honey, I'm here." At one point, he opened his eyes. "I'm here with you," I repeated. His lips moved, but soundlessly. "It's okay. Don't try to speak." I stretched out next to him and stroked his head, and began softly singing to him. At one point, I drifted off to sleep, and when I awoke I became aware that his breathing was noticeably quieter. At first I thought, *Good, he's doing a little better.* But then I realized he was slipping away. I held him until, little by little, his breathing became shallower and shallower, and he finally let go.

The hospice workers arrived and shortly after them the mortician. They put Walt's body on a gurney, and I followed close behind as they wheeled him out the door and into the frigid Oregon air. When the van pulled away, carrying my Walt, I fell to my knees on the driveway, let out an agonized wail, and collapsed into the gravel.

I had suffered terribly when Medgar was killed, and long afterward I remembered the grief and anger and hatred. But perhaps because it happened so many years earlier, or perhaps because I wasn't with Medgar when he took his last breath, I didn't remember the sheer *physical* pain. With Walt gone, it felt as though a beast with huge claws had ripped out the center of my chest. My friend, my lover, my dream, my hopes, my shelter . . . my life — all were taken from me at once.

In the days that followed I went numb. One of the few times I wept openly was when I read our friend Jerry Mitchell's stirring tribute in the *Clarion-Ledger*, which began, "When Walter Williams walked Wednesday into the shadow of death, he never trembled." Jerry, who greatly admired Walt's integrity and recognized the depths of his quiet strength, went on to note, "Walter's name will never be listed in textbooks, be heard in glowing references on C-SPAN, or be repeated on the lips of scholarly historians. Yet, he displayed the attributes that this society sorely needs to embrace."

We buried Walt at Forest Lawn Cemetery in Los Angeles. Tom Bradley, his old friend, spoke of their youth, Jesse Jackson delivered the eulogy, and more than nine hundred people came to pay their respects. In the tribute I wrote for the memorial booklet, I recalled, "It was you, with the help of God, that kept me on the right path — both in my fight for justice in Mississippi and now in my journey forward to restore a great NAACP. I can still hear your voice saying, 'Ya gotta do what ya gotta do.'" My last remark, "You will be missed, Walter," was an understatement.

I started running from the pain and rarely stopped. A day later I was on a plane to New York, on my way to the Ford Foundation to raise money for the NAACP. Much as I had done after Medgar died, I kept myself busy — working, traveling, studying. As long as I kept moving, I didn't have to feel the loss. So I flew from one city to another, one NAACP branch to another, one hotel to another, getting on and off planes, putting out fires, and falling into bed at night exhausted. Admittedly, there were times when I found myself sitting on the floor in the dark, holding my knees to my chest and rocking back and forth. I would think about Walt and heave little dry sobs, but I usually could turn off my grief by remembering some chore undone, some phone call I had to make. I prayed for strength and guidance, but my primary coping strategy was to stay occupied.

One day, though, the emotions finally poured out. I had dropped off Sugar at the kennel and was driving home to do some last-minute packing. Suddenly, the tears just started to flow, and all the way home I screamed and cried. I couldn't stop. I could barely see; I don't know how I made it home, and when I finally did, I sat there in my driveway and dissolved. "God, God, not why . . . but why *now?* Couldn't he have lasted a little longer?" In my mind, I heard the answer: *You didn't want him to suffer. You said you'd let him go.*

When someone so dear, so vital, is gone, life goes on, but nothing is ever the same. I walked with Sugar, the way Walt and I had, and I sat on the deck he loved and looked at the mountains, which had always soothed his soul. But I was shrouded in emptiness and despair. "Where are you?" I'd often ask, glancing toward the heavens. Sometimes, wishing to be reunited with my beloved, I hoped my own end would hasten. I had but one enduring consolation: Walt had always said that he wanted to die at home with me next to him. We had both kept our last promises to each other. ⚕

Fluorescent lighting overhead, concourse A or B, walkways, gateways, snack bars, shops, backlit arrival and departure boards. I am at an airport once again, an environment so familiar I sometimes forget my destination. But today I know quite well where I'm going, and I am overwhelmed with misgivings. Only once before — in 1965, when the entire country seemed engulfed by the flames of civil unrest — did I resist a visit to my native state. Then, I feared what would greet me, but in the years since, Jackson has always provided a well of strength, encouragement, and love from family and friends. But there is more to my reluctance now than the fact that many of the people I loved are no longer there.

Myrlie, I ask myself, *could your hesitation be related to the fact that the third trial is over and Medgar's assassin is awaiting a decision from the Mississippi Supreme Court on his appeal to have the guilty verdict overturned?* Although Beckwith's conviction attests to the changes in Mississippi since Medgar's murder, there are still a few old dinosaurs — former members of the Citizens' Council — sitting on the state supreme court. I wonder if the justice system really has changed enough to put an end to the case once and for all.

Oh ye of little faith, trust in me, a spiritual voice inside me intones softly.

Debarking in Jackson, I am recognized by a redcap in the baggage claim area. "Welcome back, Mrs. Evers," says the kind, elderly Black man. "Let me take those for you," he offers, whisking my bags onto his cart.

I immediately hide my troubled, pensive look and in its place put on my public face. "Oh, thank you." I beam.

"It's so nice to see you again," he says. "Will you be with us for long?"

I make small talk until we reach the exit, and say to myself, *No matter how you feel, Myrlie, this is home.* The purpose of this trip is book research, to revisit the Mississippi of my youth, the Mississippi of my first marriage. Although I've flown into Jackson, I will travel by car beyond the boundaries of Hinds County, through the heart of the Mississippi Delta. I set out on the long drive with two friends, both journalists, one born in the South, the other a Yankee here to see the sights. Our journey northward begins on Route 49, a steep, winding highway that intersects a dozen sleepy Delta towns — dirt streets and dirt poor. "When you drive through the Delta," the southern journalist observes as we pass another row of shacks along the roadside, "you really feel like you're stepping back into the past."

I prefer Mississippi in the springtime and summer, when the stately cypress trees lining the road are green and lush, the fields bursting with life. But the landscape now is typical of late fall, red and gold leaves fluttering in the breeze, pine cones scattered underfoot. I can spot only a few clumps of raw cotton in the fields, brown, mowed down, and nearly bare after a summer's picking. It was in fields like these that Medgar loved to hunt squirrels and rabbits. We pass an elderly man selling turnip greens from the back of his truck, a familiar sight when I was a child growing up in Vicksburg. In many places, the ground is covered with kudzu, a vine that winds itself around and up to the top of every bush and tree in its path and eventually chokes all that it touches. As we drive near our first destination, I feel as if the kudzu is squeezing a primal scream from my soul.

Yazoo City is where my mother, Mildred — M'dear — and my stepfather, Lee, once lived. I spent many summers here, playing with Lee's son, Lee, Jr., who was a year older than I. On Sundays, we accompanied Lee's father, a minister, to neighboring towns whose names still make me smile — It, So-So, D'Lo, and Midnight. At the center of Yazoo stands the Confederate monument; I've seen similar ones in every town square in every county I've ever visited in Mississippi. I look for the dry cleaner's where my mother worked. And I recognize the neighborhood where Lee and M'dear once were walking when two White men got out of a car and tried to persuade M'dear to come home with them. I gratefully remember that Lee had the presence of mind to tell her to run to the nearest house and that he stood up to those men, but it makes me sad that my mother was vulnerable to such insults.

From Route 49 we cut across Route 62 and stop at a restaurant in Indianola for lunch. Even in 1997, being the only Black face in a roomful of White faces makes me uneasy. Especially here in the Delta, my instinct is to watch my back. After lunch, we continue north on Route 61, the road I drove so many times from Mound Bayou to Vicksburg. I remember the torrential rains, the claps of thunder so loud I could feel my car shake. And the lightning — there's something ominous about lightning in the Delta, where everything is so wide open you always feel like an easy target. Medgar logged thousands of miles along this north-south road and the back roads that intersect it, always being followed or believing he was.

Finally, an old weather-worn sign along the highway greets us. "Welcome to Mound Bayou, the oldest US all-Black city, incorporated in 1898." Forty-six years ago, Medgar and I began our married life and had our first two children here. Now I search for vestiges of the familiar, anything that will jog my limited memory. Although the streets are finally paved — no more stifling dust in summer or gumbo mud from winter rains — the town is for the most part unchanged. The movie theater that ran three-year-old films is not here, nor the magazine shop, with its equally out-of-date selection. Gone, too, is the building that housed the once proud Magnolia Mutual Life Insurance Company, where Medgar and I had worked. But apart from a school and a few new homes, little effort has been made to improve Mound Bayou's standard of living.

My heart sinks. Such a proud beginning for a town, and such scant advancement over nearly half a century. Perhaps I am making too swift a judgment. Perhaps I should talk to the city officials for a briefing on the progress that has been made. Perhaps I will, on another visit.

This is all I can absorb for one day. Driving back to Jackson, I sit silently with my memories, memories of all that no longer exists. Then, as if God were trying to remind me as well of all that has been gained, I begin to recall faces from my past — dearly departed souls whose spirits are lasting monuments to courage and resilience. There is Emmett Till, whose young life was brutally taken because he spoke to a White woman, and whose death Medgar investigated; it was news of that fourteen-year-old boy's murder in 1955 that first convinced many reluctant activists that it was, indeed, time to fight for a fair justice system. There are the nameless sharecroppers of Sunflower County, heart of the Delta, poor but proud and determined people, who withstood threats to life and property so that they might vote. There is the Reverend George Lee from Belzoni, killed because of his successful, though limited, voting rights efforts and, a few months after him, Lamar Smith, shot in broad daylight because he dared to register. There is Amzie Moore, one of Medgar's staunchest supporters, who lived in Cleveland and helped devise a coded system of communication for the few, brave freedom fighters in our underground. There is Aaron Henry, NAACP State Conference president, whose Fourth Street Drug Store in Clarksdale was a refuge from police brutality or Klan vengeance — sometimes one and the same in Mississippi — a way station where frightened souls hid before escaping in the dark of night across the state line into Tennessee, often in the trunk of someone's car. And there is the indomitable Fannie Lou Hamer. Though brutally beaten and several times jailed, she remained defiant, announcing for all the world to hear, "I'm sick and tired of being sick and tired [of this]. I *will* have the freedom to vote and run for office."

What a gathering of greatness! These valiant souls were the lifeblood of the Mississippi Delta, and feeling their presence makes the trip back to Jackson much easier. The kudzu begins to lose its hold. ⯈

I have avoided returning home for many years, because there is no one left to return to. Mama, Auntie, Big Mama Alice, M'dear, and Daddy are all gone, and many family friends have passed on as well. My high school classmates have moved to other locations. But Vicksburg is where my second day must take me. Now a mecca for gamblers, the city's waterfront is dotted with opulent resorts. Some of the downtown area looks the same, but the Valley is boarded up, Woolworth's and the A&P are gone; in their place are gourmet food stores and specialty shops.

The tour becomes a montage of scenes from early in my life, those formative years that helped determine my path. At sixty-five, I have become the woman I was meant to be; but I am also still growing, a work in progress. The playback is in slow motion, each stop a freeze-frame of a moment in the past. Driving along old Route 80, also known as Clay Street, we pause at Mount Heroden Baptist Church, my second home as a child and in whose sanctuary I married Medgar. We continue along Clay Street and turn right on Cherry Street. McIntyre Junior High School is dilapidated and scarred from neglect. We pass by Magnolia (now Bowman) High, drive through the "wealthy" neighborhood where Big Mama worked, and up the hill to Magnolia Street. All that remains of Mama's home on the hill is the hill itself. All traces of the first ten years of my life — gone.

As we drive along Farmer Street toward Auntie's house, I remember myself roller-skating backward down South Street, with its steep, block-long concrete sidewalk. I'm gaining momentum, speeding faster and faster, avoiding the familiar bumps until reaching safety at the bottom of the hill — gliding smoothly, deftly, and finally steering myself onto a grassy area. An even greater thrill was riding my bicycle down that hill, feet on the handlebars, arms outstretched as though flying. What freedom that was!

Each stop brings pangs of longing and poignant reminders of how much time has passed. My young friends and I felt so invincible. We dared to plot against the nasty White boys of the courthouse gang. We dared to have dreams. We saw challenges and met them. *Am I still up to a challenge?* I wonder.

I notice that many of the once stately homes and mansions are shabby and in disrepair. But nothing prepares me for the sight of my aunt's home at 1411 Farmer Street. I cannot, will not, get out of the car. The house that Auntie had so lovingly kept in pristine condition until she had to move to the nursing home is a shambles, and weeds have overgrown her magnificent gardens. The pride, the grace — gone. I am paralyzed, remembering the beautiful roses, gardenias, snapdragons, irises, and begonias that brought so much joy to us and to neighbors who purchased floral arrangements from Aunt Myrlie. I recall the blue ribbons she won for her dried flower exhibits at the state fair — in the Negro section, of course — the buds carefully selected and placed in ornate gold frames.

As one of my companions peers into the crumbling structure, a shudder rises from the depths of me. Her curiosity is an invasion of my privacy. I feel as though I've been caught naked with all of my physical imperfections on view. As I sit in the car, the frozen moment thaws into sadness, a sorrow that is an eloquent explanation of my reluctance to return home. Living brings about change, and change is not always pleasant or reassuring. ☙

Back in Jackson, I make the rounds: I lunch with Ed Peters and Bobby DeLaughter, and we discuss Beckwith's upcoming appeal. I see Sheriff Malcolm McMillan, whose deputies protected me during the trial; at his request, I visit a program at the penitentiary for young offenders. I spend time with Jerry Mitchell, and stop in at the *Clarion-Ledger,* where staffers greet me warmly. We drive down Medgar Evers Boulevard, past the magnificent bronze statue of Medgar, noting the library and post office dedicated in his name. Medgar would be amazed. So much of what he worked for has become a reality. Blacks now hold high political office at the national level and locally — both Vicksburg and Jackson have African-American mayors. Blacks are on the police force and in other government positions in Jackson. They occupy top management positions and own their own companies as well. And they live in neighborhoods once reserved for Whites. As I drive through one upscale enclave, in fact, I am taken aback by the splendor. Guynes Street, once *the* place for African-American families, is comfortable but modest by comparison.

The Jackson itinerary isn't as traumatic as the Delta or Vicksburg. I've returned three times a year since the trial in 1994 and many times before that. But this visit seems designed to evoke memories, images, as well as thoughts of my future. I think about the many times Walt and I toyed with the idea of moving here. He loved Mississippi, felt a strong spiritual connection to it. And, indeed, everywhere I go in Jackson, people extend a warm greeting. It *is* home. There would always be work for me here, programs to be developed and implemented. I could live in a wonderful neighborhood in a grand home. But is that what I want? I don't need a big house now; I'm alone. And what about my children and grandchildren, whose homes are two thousand miles from Jackson?

My good friends Jean Wells and Johnnie Pearl Young still live on Guynes Street, renamed Margaret Walker Alexander Street after the poet, who also has remained in her home there after these many years; Nan Evers, back from Chicago and long divorced from Charles, is a few blocks away. These women knew me *when.* Jean recently buried her husband, Houston, the man who drove Medgar to the hospital the night he was murdered; he had been bedridden for twenty-seven years. We talk about the profound pain of nursing one's husband and losing him. As we talk, Johnnie's own spouse, Thomas, lies dying in a dark bedroom a few footsteps away.

Seeing these women reminds me of who I was; looking at their lives makes me question what will become of me. All of us are at that stage of life when one contemplates the big questions: What is the rest of my life going to be like? What's going to happen when I can't run the way I've been running? I am so much my grandmother's granddaughter, my aunt's niece — women who did it all on their own, took care of everyone else, and then ferociously fought their decline. In the end, both had such a difficult time. Although I love Bend, Oregon — Walt's and my place — I wonder if I will have to uproot myself again and move back to California to be near Darrell, Reena, and Van. Will one of them have to take care of me, the way Jean and I nursed Houston and Walt, the way Johnnie Pearl must now minister to her critically ill husband?

Five days in Mississippi leaves me feeling unmoored. My traveling companions try to get me to talk, but my emotions are too private, too sad, too fearful. Moreover, my ruminations about the future are clouded by concerns for the present. Answers elude me, so I pray. I turn to the one source of sustenance that has been with me my entire life — my Provider, my God. I know he didn't bring me this far to abandon me.

STARTING OVER ... AGAIN

With my family in Bend, Christmas 1996. In the first row, Keanan and
Nicole. In the second, Cambi and Reena. In the back, Van, Daniel, I,
and Darrell. And in front, my Sugar.

I want to be an outrageous old woman
who never gets called an old lady.
I want to get leaner and meaner,
sharp-edged and earth-colored,
till I fade away from pure joy.

Anonymous

I think you need to lay down the struggling part of your life and just *be,"* says my good friend Maureen. We sit together in her office, I pondering sixty-five and discussing my options, she listening intently. Finally, she offers a bit of advice about choice-making.

"I would sit down and make a list of the places in the world I'd like to see. But now is also a time when you truly can enjoy your daily existence. So think of the simple pleasures that make you happy, too. In the professional arena, move into work that brings out the artistic and creative part of you — music, writing." This book is a positive start, she says, as are my appearances as a narrator with the Oregon Symphony.

"You could be anything you want to be, Myrlie," she continues, "anything from continuing to be a mentor to young people to being active on a national level, but in jobs that are not so arduous." Then she looks at me with that generous smile of hers. "And one other thing, Myrlie: Don't let a day go by without having fun."

How right she is. Only a few months earlier, I was stunned by news that once again reminded me of how short and fragile life can be and how important it is, when pondering the future, to put my loved ones at the top of the list.

In June of 1997, still caught up in the excitement of Van's wedding the previous weekend, I sat in Reena's living room, enjoying some rare downtime with my granddaughters, Cambi and Nicole, who relished watching their mother squirm as I reminisced about life in Claremont when she and their uncles were young. As we all laughed, the phone rang, and Reena told me it was my sister-friend Coretta King, who tearfully related that our dear friend Betty Shabazz lay in an intensive care unit in New York City, fighting for her life. A fire, allegedly set by Betty's grandson, had blazed through her apartment, leaving her with third-degree burns over 80 percent of her body.

"What does God have in mind?" I asked Coretta. "What lesson are we supposed to take from *this?*" In the wake of Betty's tragedy, we were hard-pressed to find an answer.

The three of us had planned to meet at a spa in Florida the following week — a same-time-next-year ritual of connection, girl talk, and rare self-indulgence we'd found reassuring in the past. Although we'd discuss work and chat some about our marriages — I being the only one who remarried — mostly we talked about our children. Our thirteen sons and daughters are, as Reena puts it, "members of a club no one would choose to join." United by accidents of birth and the misfortunes of death, they have grown up plagued by visibility and violence.

Although common experiences have shaped my children, each is a unique individual who has traveled his or her own road — not mine, not their father's. Reluctant to forever be "the children of" or to seek the limelight, they nevertheless share my desire to keep Medgar's memory alive and to support the cause of civil rights, and each has dealt with that struggle in a different way.

Darrell, who now owns a computer firm, in the past has found expression through his artwork. Among an early series of conceptual miniatures, for example, is one entitled *Brillo*, which displays a range of African-American hair types, from permed straight to ultrakinky — his answer to Claremont playmates who asked to touch his hair. Reena, who has worked in fashion and in the airline industry, now gives her three children precedence over the corporate climb. She prefers grass-roots activism to involvement with large national organizations, and has put energy into community groups such as the Claremont Task Force on Race Relations. Among other victories, she fought to get more books about African-Americans into the local library. And Van acknowledges that his choice of career — photography — puts *him* in control. Instead of being the eternal subject, he's behind the camera, literally calling the shots. He also has found quiet ways to "work toward the cause." For the NAACP's voter empowerment campaign, he and his friend Derrick Shields, a Disney artist, created a striking poster — a raised black fist, with two fingers forming a victory sign. Its slogan reads, "You say you want power? Vote." I presented a copy of the poster to President Clinton, which he had framed and hung in the entrance level of the White House.

As different as they are, my three children agree on one point. They want me there for them, and they want me to know their children. A grandmother on the road misses a lot of important moments. Of course, I want to be there for all of them, too — Reena's three children and grandchild, Darrell's son, and the children Van will have one day. They are "the grandchildren of," and I want them to understand what their grandfather died for and what I have worked for.

Sadly, my children's children haven't had much time with their grandmother. Other than holidays and birthdays, I rarely see Darrell's son, Keanan, who lives with his mother in Northern California. Reena's children usually get only a glimpse of me on my quick in-and-out visits to Claremont: "Kiss-kiss, my darlings. How's school? Do you need anything — I'll get it for you. Grandma loves you!" And then I'm gone. Nicole, Reena's youngest, once loved it when I read to her. Somehow, without my noticing it, though, she has turned ten, and now reads to me with great enthusiasm. Just as I missed Reena's children's growing up, I am missing the milestones of her grandchild — her son Daniel's boy, Daniel Michael, whom we all call Bubba — my great-grandson.

During one of my fly-by visits, Reena's older daughter, Cambi, was unusually quiet; she seemed to be studying me. Finally she asked, "Grandmama, when are you going to slow down? Are you ever going to stop and have time for us?"

I was stunned. "Of course, darling," I replied, almost ashamed that she felt she had to ask such a question. I kissed her forehead and hugged her slim fifteen-year-old body.

"Well, I hope so," she said, looking me straight in the eye. "Because if you don't do that soon, I won't be here."

"What do you mean?"

"I'll be gone. I'll be in college," she explained, "and then *I* won't have time to see *you.*"

Keanan, now thirteen, expressed similar sentiments in a recent phone conversation. "Grandmother Myrlie, am I ever going to see you again? You're always so busy. You're always gone."

Oh, the guilt and, God help me, the regret. I apologized for my absence, and I meant it with all my heart. "Grandmother will be slowing down soon. I promise."

"I hope so. I'd like to go some of those places with you and watch what you do," he said. "I can learn from it." And indeed he could. His is the generation that will continue our work. He and his contemporaries are the ones who have had the advantages, as well as the insight and intelligence to see that we are far from done. The responsibility did not end with Medgar Evers, and it does not end with Myrlie Evers-Williams. My children, my grandchildren, and others' children and grandchildren need to be inspired by us and our history. They will carry us forth. ℀

There comes a time in one's life — actually, there come many times — when the signs appear fast and furiously and, eventually, the message is clear. I call it DT — decision time. A young woman I met in my travels had another good term for it — a "when day." She explained: "My mom always said that God gave us good days, bad days, and when days. In the midst of a struggle, I have always prayed daily for him to tell me if this was my 'when day' — the time for me to make a decision and move forward." I thank her for allowing me to share that bit of family wisdom.

Shortly after the trip to Mississippi, I realized that I must be getting close to having a when day. The evidence had been accumulating, and I'd grown more weary by the day. It was time for me to step down from my position as chairman of the NAACP. My children repeatedly expressed concern about my health; they knew that the traveling and breakneck schedule were taking a toll. Caring friends wondered, "What are you trying to prove, Myrlie?" That was a question I was asking myself as well.

The day after I was elected chairman, a reporter had asked, "What timetable have you set for yourself to clean house?"

"It's difficult to say," I had responded honestly, explaining that one person alone could not accomplish the tasks at hand. "It will take time and team effort," I said, concluding on a lighthearted note: "But I certainly don't intend to be chairman for life — two years at most."

Now, almost three years later, the words "not for life" echoed in my mind. Reviewing the accomplishments of my administration, I was filled with pride. The organization was back on track, solvent and growing stronger by the day, and ready to embark on its objectives for the next century. It was time for me to pass the torch. Most institutions have to experience periodic, orderly changes of command. I was certain that a board member of quality would step forward to take my place. New blood would be good for the NAACP, and a change of scene would be good for me.

President/CEO Mfume and I had discussed for several months the possibility of my making such a decision. I had tabled the matter long enough, I realized. For several days, I worked at composing a letter to members of the board of directors, measuring my words, anticipating the impact.

"Much thought and prayer has led me to this decision," I wrote, quoting the Book of Ecclesiastes: "To every thing there is a season, and a time to every purpose under heaven." I went on to say that I appreciated the board members' confidence in my leadership and that I recognized we could never have accomplished such a "miraculous turnaround" had it not been for the joint efforts of everyone involved. I had kept my promises, I reminded them, and I would continue to serve on the board of directors and to assist the NAACP in meeting its goals. I concluded the letter by saying: "You are my family and have been for more than 45 years. May God bless you always."

I called Mfume to tell him of my decision, informing him that I would FedEx my letter to the board members on February 9, 1998, and issue a press release the following day. In the next few days, there was an outpouring of phone calls, letters, and telegrams, many from surprised and disappointed supporters, beseeching me to reconsider. But my decision was final. I left the position knowing that whoever took over as chairman would be free to focus on the implementation of programs and long-range plans, without getting bogged down in internal discord and financial problems. "The cleanup woman," as some called me, had done her job.

A few weeks later, at the association's annual meeting, I made my final speech as chairman of the board and was overwhelmed by the response. During the open-mike portion of the program, an impressive woman with the booming voice of an evangelical preacher stepped up. "Thank you, Madam Chairman. You have been an inspiration to me." At that moment, I knew that I no longer needed a podium, I no longer needed an office. I would always make my voice heard; I would always work in the service of human good.

Julian Bond, whom Mfume and I were convinced would make an excellent chairman, easily won the election — twenty-nine board members voted for him, while the remaining twenty-four votes were split among his five rivals. I was pleased to see Julian, an old friend and fellow civil rights activist from the 1960s, take over the reins; he has a similar vision for the organization, a dedication to integration and inclusion. He assured the press that he wanted the NAACP's voice to be heard "wherever race is discussed." He acknowledged, too, that being chairman was "a daunting responsibility," and then graciously added, "Although Myrlie Evers-Williams has tiny feet, there will be big shoes to fill."

In the weeks that followed, I heard good news on the legal front as well. Bobby DeLaughter called to tell me that the Mississippi Supreme Court had denied Beckwith's appeal. His call caught me just as I was returning from a visit to Forest Lawn, where I laid flowers at Walt's grave. DeLaughter offered to send me a copy of the decision. Despite the legalese, the last line of the ruling later brought tears of relief to my eyes: "Conviction of murder and sentence of life in the custody of the Mississippi Department of Corrections affirmed." I prayed to God almost daily that that chapter, finally written, would never be revised. Those prayers were answered in October 1998, when the U.S. Supreme Court refused to hear Beckwith's appeal.

In the meantime came word that U. S. District Court judge William Barbour had ruled that the long-sealed files of the Sovereignty Commission were to be opened to the public on March 17, 1998 — coincidentally, my sixty-fifth birthday. The Sovereignty Commission, the state of Mississippi's de facto spy agency, had kept a watch on Medgar as well as other civil rights activists, and had aided in Beckwith's defense and in the cover-up of countless other crimes. When it was disbanded in 1977, the legislature had ordered the files to be sealed for fifty years. Almost immediately, the American Civil Liberties Union sued to open the records, but one legal roadblock after another had stood in the way. Jerry Mitchell's discovery of the commission's role in Beckwith's trial certainly accelerated the campaign to open the files; and I along with other activists had kept the pressure on.

The first day the files were open to the public, people lined up for hours, hoping to gain evidence or to simply learn more about how their family histories were influenced by the commission's covert activities. In all, there are some 124,000 pages in the files, information on 60,000 Mississippians, who, in the eyes of commission members, threatened segregation and therefore were a danger to the state. I secured Medgar's and my files — records which totaled well over fifteen hundred pages.

As the Beckwith guilty verdict set a legal precedent for trying other unfinished civil rights cases, the opening of these files also may lead to new court victories. At this writing, in fact, at least one other long-standing case is now closed. A Mississippi jury recently found Sam Bowers, Imperial Wizard of the White Knights of the Ku Klux Klan (in Mississippi), guilty of ordering the 1966 murder of civil rights activist Vernon Dahmer, a merchant who had used his Hattiesburg store to collect poll taxes and help Negroes register to vote. Although three Klansmen were tried and given life sentences for detonating the fatal firebomb that destroyed Dahmer's store and home, and a fourth pleaded guilty and testified that Bowers had masterminded the crime, Bowers had been set free after two mistrials. New information gleaned from the commission's files finally convinced a jury to set the case right. It is my hope that in the near future other miscarriages of justice will be corrected as well.

By far one of the proudest moments of my life occurred in July, at the NAACP's 1998 annual conference in Atlanta, Georgia, when my dear sister Coretta Scott King presented me with the Spingarn Medal, as Reena and her three children stood by my side. I was the eighty-third recipient of this prestigious award, named after the organization's chairman in 1914 and bestowed each year on an African-American "who shall have made the highest achievement in any honorable field of endeavor during the preceding year or years." I was deeply moved to be placed in the company of past winners such as W.E.B. DuBois, George Washington Carver, Martin Luther King, Jr., Maya Angelou, Bill Cosby, Leontyne Price, Colin Powell, and, of course, my own dear Medgar, who was awarded the medal posthumously in 1964. Even more important, the award signified recognition of what *I* had done — not because I was "the widow of."

I gratefully accepted the award before the audience of some 1,700 members and shared the glory of the moment by asking the board of directors to stand and be recognized for their accomplishments. We had come together at last. I am thankful for the three years and all that came with them — frustrations and relief, anger and joy. The experience lifted me to another level in my life, once again enabling me to spread my wings and fly. That evening included a performance by Patti LaBelle, whose trademark song, "A New Attitude," brought the audience to its feet. The words had special significance to me as well as to the organization, and when Ms. LaBelle sang that final note, I sat down and said with praise and deep satisfaction, "Amen! Amen!" *~

Freed from the daily demands of the NAACP, I have turned my full attention to the Medgar Evers Institute. The institute, I hope, will continue to pursue the goals Medgar worked and died for: to improve racial and ethnic relations in America and to promote leadership programs for youth. I continue to be moved by the people I meet who once worked with Medgar, or at least knew of him or were inspired by him, and who have carried the message. I believe the future of this country lies in our ability to work together as one people to create a truly just society. Just as Medgar wanted to see the early civil rights organizations cooperate rather than compete, the institute will support and collaborate with other organizations and institutions working toward similar goals. We have already sponsored two seminars on race in America (in June and December of 1997); among the prominent participants at these multiracial, multiethnic gatherings were Christopher Edley, professor at Harvard University Law School, and Linda Chavis-Thompson, executive vice president of the AFL-CIO, both of whom are also members of President Clinton's Advisory Council on Race.

My newfound freedom also has had an unanticipated effect: I have begun to feel just how tired I am. My doctor has warned me, yet again, that I must slow down. My blood pressure is dangerously high. I'm fortunate, though; this is a treatable condition, not a terminal disease. The choice is mine.

It is a great gift of maturity to come to realize that age is only a number and that we can go through these years with grace and wisdom . . . if only we care for our bodies and our minds. I suspect that Walt is winking from on high, realizing that I'm now going through the unavoidable vagaries of aging that he experienced but was too proud to talk about. Every morning, he'd get out of bed, stand straight and tall, and then lift his arms overhead. And I would think, *Look at this vain man, flexing his muscles for me.* I realize now he was just stiff. He also wore sunglasses when he drove at night, and I'd say, "What're you — Mr. Cool?"

"Maybe so," he'd answer with a sly grin. "That's for you to find out someday!"

Well, Walt Baby, I have. I know now that wearing dark glasses cuts down on the glare, and I can see better with them at night. And now I do *my* stretches in the morning to keep my body limber, and get on an exercise bike or treadmill to build up my endurance level.

I haven't stopped running completely, of course. But I've actually canceled some trips in recent months, stayed home, and made an effort to find precious moments of peace, even if only to take several five-minute walks each day with Sugar. Walking in nature is like a quiet meditation; seeing God's bounty — the mountains, trees, small animals scurrying by — makes me feel closer to him. And, of course, I pray morning and night, asking the good Lord to give me the strength and guidance to find my way. I have had enough trouble to last a lifetime. And if there's one thing I've learned, it's to expect surprise. Keeping myself in good physical and mental condition prepares me for whatever challenges lie ahead. My "new attitude" makes a difference not only in how I get through my day, but how I view the future. The way I look at it, I'm finally doing for me what I've spent years doing for others. ⋧

Flying into Oregon from Los Angeles, I see a familiar Pacific Northwest spectacle: snow. Not the kind we had in Mississippi, to be sure. But the sight reminds me of a photo that Medgar once took of our youngsters Darrell and Reena happily building a snowman. Nearby stands a teary two-year-old Van, afraid of his first snowfall. A second photo in our album is a scene almost identical to the first, except that Reena is in a hands-on-hips pose, looking sassy and bad as she can be, fire in her eyes. That was the first of many times she asked, "Mommy, what do you want to be when you grow up?"

I smile at the memory, and as the plane makes its descent, and the trees and rivers form an abstract painting on the white snow, I whisper to myself, "I'm going to find out again, Sunshine. I'm going to find out again."

ACKNOWLEDGMENTS

No flight is singular in its journey, and mine would not have been possible without the propelling force of those who provided spiritual, physical, and emotional support along the way to my becoming the woman I was meant to be:

My children, Van, Reena, Darrell — my eternal support system, whose love and encouragement have remained steady throughout all of our challenges; my grandchildren, my motivators — Daniel, Cambi, Nicole, Keanan; Jan Harris-Temple, for her brilliant, creative insight and collaboration; journalist Jerry Mitchell, for his unrelenting investigative reporting and friendship; attorney Bobby DeLaughter, who stayed the course until the scales of justice were balanced; Mildred Roxborough, the uncompromising NAACP historian whose guidance over the years has been invaluable; Dr. Mark Peters, Dr. Steven Greer, and Dr. Robert C. Mathews, for keeping the body and sight intact; Murry Sidlin, resident conductor, Oregon Symphony Orchestra, who reopened the door to my dormant musical skills; Alan Walker, my lecture agent, for jump-starting this book; Richard Kot, the best editor ever, who guided me through this book journey; Eileen Cope, my agent at Barbara Lowenstein Associates, and inspiration to reach young adult women; Melinda Blau, my cowriter, for her unique ability to restructure entire paragraphs into one sentence, and for getting the job done — regardless of the hour, day or night; and other family members and friends, whose prayers have sustained my being.

And, praise to my God, who continues to be patient — I stretch my arms to thee.

— *Myrlie Evers-Williams*
Bend, Oregon

It has been an honor and an awe-inspiring experience to work with Myrlie Evers-Williams, and to walk with her in her many worlds. From the day our eyes first met in an office on West Twenty-Seventh Street in New York City, I knew Myrlie was a force to be reckoned with. In the months to come I was to earn her trust, plumb the depths of her psyche, share tears, laughter, and home-cooked meals, and on occasion even incur her wrath. I am grateful for all of it and for the relationship we developed along the way.

I want to thank the Evers children, Darrell, Reena, and Van, for their time and trust; it's easy to understand why Myrlie calls them her "most outstanding achievement." Fiercely protective of their mother and understandably suspicious of the press, all three welcomed me warmly and allowed me to peek into their lives; in Reena's case, this included meeting her three delightful children, Danny, Cambi, and Nicole.

Friends and colleagues of Myrlie's also provided stories, insights, and bits of wisdom that have found their way into these pages: Margaret Walker Alexander, Drinda Bell, Margaret Cook, Bobby DeLaughter, Nan Evers, Steve Giovanisci, Bert Hammond, Polly Hinton, Jean Wells, Norma Johnson, Maureen Kindel, Barbara Krumwiede, Art McClure, Malcolm McMillan, Skip Meury, Ed Peters, Brenda Ross, Alan Walker, Johnnie Pearl Young.

Special thanks goes to Jerry Mitchell of the *Clarion-Ledger*, who escorted us through the Delta, provided insightful commentary about Mississippi, and generously shared his observations and memories of Myrlie. Other bits and pieces of history were supplied by Ed Bryson, Dennis Smith, and Lucille Anderson of WLBT in Jackson; M. Dion Thompson and Mary Corey of the *Baltimore Sun*; Pam Jones of Castle Rock Entertainment. Bill Novak, master of this genre, helped me understand the process; and Mary Walker Green shared precious family wisdom.

This book could never have happened without the people behind the scenes. My agents, Eileen Cope and Barbara Lowenstein, had the foresight to know that Myrlie and I would click and the perseverance to see the project through. Rick Kot, my astute and charming editor and now also my friend, is one of a dying breed who actually line-edits. The rest of the team at Little, Brown earned my gratitude as well, especially Michael Liss and Liz Markovits, for keeping the process in motion and everyone informed, and Peggy Leith Anderson, for her crackerjack copyedit of the final manuscript. On my home turf, I am indebted to Debbie McMullen, who efficiently transcribed the tapes, and Helen Garfinkle, who via cyberspace offered cogent insights about the raw material.

I also appreciate family and friends who stood by in the face of my eternal preoccupation with this book: Barbara Biziou, Mark Blau, Caroline Collins, Jean Houston, Bertha Josephson, Margaret Kierstein, Ruth Kramer, Leah Kunkel, Henrietta Levner, Carla Messina, Leslea Newman, Sylvia Rubin, Pamela Serure, Sandra Sonn (and family), Ron Taffel, Cay Trigg, Dorothy Varon, Mary Vazquez, Lynn Werthamer, Reggie Weintraub, Jesse Zoernig. Special thanks to my indispensable wordsmith, who asks me not to list her name, and to Lorena Sol. Most of all and always, I appreciate the support of Jennifer and Jeremy Blau, who cheer me on and do me proud. Finally, I wish to remember my father, Julius Tantleff, who died as the seeds of this project were being sown and whose spirit I have felt with me ever since.

— *Melinda Blau*
Northampton, Massachusetts